Jehu
Prayers

<u>Dr. D. K. Olukoya</u>

THE JEHU PRAYERS
© 2012 DR. D. K. OLUKOYA
ISBN 978-061-582-845-9
December 2012

Published by

The Battle Cry Christian Ministries
322, Herbert Macaulay Way,
Yaba, Lagos.

I salute my wonderful wife, Pastor Shade,
for her invaluable support in the ministry.
I appreciate her unquantifiable support in the book
ministry as the cover designer, art editor and art advisor

All Scripture quotations are from the
King James version of the Bible.
Unless otherwise stated.

Cover page illustration by
Pastor (Mrs.) Shade Olukoya

INTRODUCTION
THE JEHU PRAYERS

There are prayers that the enemy cannot toy with. There are prayer points that will be too hot for the enemy to confront. When the mystery of Jehu prayers is at work, arrows that are sent by the enemy will go back to the sender and so much violence will be discharged that the enemy will regret ever trying to go into conflict with a member of the Jehu army.

In these last days, God has established an elite force called the Jehu army, made up of aggressive warriors who are not ready to take nonsense from the enemy. This divine force has constituted serious headache to the enemy. Its symbol is holy fury. Its trade mark is fire. Its mission is to totally disgrace and bury Enemy's army.

TRAINING FOR WARRIORS

Members of the Jehu army are men and women whose fingers are trained to fight, who are always ready to fight to finish and who are not ready to tolerate nonsense from the kingdom of darkness. They are men and women trained in a special way for serious areas of warfare.

God has surveyed the length and breadth of the arrows, attacks, hostilities and wicked problems which people would face in this end-time and come up with a solution, the raising up of The Jehu company or the Jehu army.

The prayer manual you hold in your hands is a priviledged document vomited by the Holy Spirit to make you a threat to the kingdom of darkness. With the Jehu prayers your story will change. Your Goliath will die, your Herod will be defeated and your stubborn pursuers will begin to pursue themselves.

The Jehu prayers will shake the earth and the kingdom of darkness. Wonderful changes will occur. Testimonies will fall upon testimonies. Victory will attract more victory. Power will change hands. Problems will fade away. Your Jericho walls will collapse. Your victory will be celebrated. You will dance your dance and sing your song.

THE FORCE OF THE BATTLE

From the archive of heaven God has favoured you with this secret document.

Every prayer point in the Jehu prayers has been charged with uncommon authority and power to force the enemy to surrender. With Jehu prayers in place, no one will remain a victim of satanic attacks and ugly embarrassments. No household will continue to suffer defeat as long as there is a copy of the Jehu Prayers in it. No community or nation will continue to experience satanic invasion as long as there is a member of the Jehu army there who is armed with this dangerous book. With the unprecedented victory which this book will introduce, this generation will never be the same.

I congratulate you for being one of the favoured ones who has been given the priviledge of arresting the tide of evil in your personal life, in your family, in your church, in your community as well as in your nation.

THE REASON

A lot of people are wondering about Jehu prayers. Why must we take warfare to such a high point? There are obvious answers. The precarious situation in the world and the dangerous trends in the lives of individuals call for a new strategy and a powerful force to dismantle the stronghold of darkness. In view of the high spate of satanic attacks, wicked manipulation of witchcraft agents coupled with terrible oppression being unleashed on many people, God has given us a strategy that will arrest, paralyse, destroy and completely route out every emissary of darkness and put an end to their activities.

THE NEED OF THE HOUR

Jehu prayers are the greatest need of the hour. They are strange warfare strategy for attacking the dark forces, especially the company of witches and wizards. It is crystal clear, therefore, that the concept of the Jehu company and the spiritual mechanism behind every Jehu prayer point will go very far in placing you on the mountain top of all-round victory.

God does not want any of His children to be a war casualty. He would not stand and watch the enemy defeat and disgrace you. By placing this prayer manual in your hands, He is enlisting you into the Jehu army. By His divine decree it is bye-bye to defeat. It is good bye to satanic disgrace and shame. You are now a seasoned warrior. You are now an overcomer. You have become a warrior whose sword cannot be touched. From this moment, every power that dares you shall be destroyed. You are no longer an ordinary person.

As a member of the Jehu army, your victory is guaranteed. You shall move from conquest to conquest. Your life shall be garnished with uncommon testimonies. As you join the Jehu company you must know that you can no longer live carelessly. You now belong to a dangerous group which the enemy dreads. Beloved, the Jehu company stands for a divine combat squad with the mission of operation wipe out.

MAN'S GREATEST ENEMY

The devil has used the dragnet of witchcraft to hold on to the world. The revival of satanism on the face of the earth is a sign of desperation for the forces of darkness which have opened their doors to train men in wickedness, politics, business, education, research, medicine and music have been penetrated by satan through witchcraft.

The enemy hates mankind and our progress with perfect hatred. This enemy supervises personal and national disasters. He has converted fertile lands to deserts. He has destroyed women with terrible destruction. He specialises in drinking blood and eating flesh. He has converted intelligent men to dullards and has destroyed and dismantled many profitable foundations. He controls many nations of the world.

THE ENEMY CALLED WITCHCRAFT

This enemy is known as witchcraft. Every nation has its own kind of witchcraft, but the witchcraft is the same.

Nahum 3:1-4 says: **"Woe to the bloody city! It is all full of lies and robbery; the prey departeth not; The noise of a whip, and the noise of the rattling of the wheels, and of the prancing horses, and of the jumping chariots. The horseman lifteth up both the bright sword and the glittering spear: and there is a multitude of slain, and a great number of carcases; and there is none end of their corpses; they stumble upon their corpses: Because of the multitude of the whoredoms of the wellfavoured harlot, the mistress of witchcrafts, that selleth nations through her whoredoms, and families through her witchcrafts."**

Exodus 22:18: "Thou shalt not suffer a witch to live."
Luke 10:19: "Behold, I give unto you power to tread on serpents and

scorpions, and over all the power of the enemy: and nothing shall by any means hurt you."

What is witchcraft? It is:
a.   Conference of evil spirits.
b.   Using satanic power to subdue people.
c.   Using satanic weapons.
d.   Summoning evil powers.
e.   Counterfeit spiritual authority.
f.   Accessing wicked powers from the earth and the heaven.
g.   The practice of magic, sorcery and wizardry.

The Jehu Prayers
God hates witchcraft with perfect hatred and issues physical and spiritual death sentences upon it.

The devil has repackaged witchcraft to suit the taste of the modern world. Many people are under bondage now, not knowing how to escape. They have been captured, not knowing the way out.

Symptoms of witchcraft oppression
1.   Untimely death
2.   Constant failure
3.   Marital failure
4.   Fighting to get anything done
5.   Chain problems
6.   Buried talents
7.   Devourers
8.   Spiritual stagnancy
9.   Witchcraft dreams
10.   Experiencing almost there
11.   Prayer paralysis
12.   Strange accidents
13.   Dead organs
14.   Vagabond anointing
15.   Spiritual blindness
16.   Mark of hatred

WEAPONS OF WARFARE

7.   Violent aggression
8.   Planning courageously
9.   Holy zeal
10.   Precise obedience
11.   Hatred of evil
12.   Anointing to subdue and eliminate every power of darkness

To destroy the destroyer seven things are needed

1.   Complete repentance
2.   Holy anger
3.   Holy violence
4.   Holy crying
5.   Holy madness
6.   Violent faith
7.   Violent praises

THE DAY OF POWER

These are the days of the manifestation of the power and the spirit of Jehu. Warfare has started. The Jehu company has been anointed. Now, it is time to smite the enemy. The elite strike force has been established.

2 Kings 9:6-8 says: "And he arose, and went into the house; and he poured the oil on his head, and said unto him, Thus saith the LORD God of Israel, I have anointed thee king over the people of the LORD, even over Israel. And thou shalt smite the house of Ahab thy master, that I may avenge the blood of my servants the prophets, and the blood of all the servants of the LORD, at the hand of Jezebel. For the whole house of Ahab shall perish: and I will cut off from Ahab him that pisseth against the wall, and him that is shut up and left in Israel: When you begin to make use of the prayer points in this book, Jezebel shall be arrested and disgraced. The prayer points must be said with holy aggression and divine fury. "

2 Kings 9:20 says: "And the watchman told, saying, He came even unto them, and cometh not again: and the driving is like the driving of Jehu the son of Nimshi; for he driveth furiously."

SPIRITUAL MADNESS

A good measure of madness is allowed. The devil does not understand the language of gentleness. The only language he understands is the language of aggression.

What happens when the aggression is in full force? The answer is in 2 Kings 9:31-37 which says: **And as Jehu entered in at the gate, she said, Had Zimri peace, who slew his master? And he lifted up his face to the window, and said, Who is on my side? who? And there looked out to him two or three eunuchs. And he said, Throw her down. So they threw her down: and some of her blood was sprinkled on the wall, and on the horses: and he trode her under foot. And when he was come in, he did eat and drink, and said, Go, see now this cursed woman, and bury her: for she is a king's daughter. And they went to bury her: but they found no more of her than the skull, and the feet, and the palms of her hands. Wherefore they came again, and told him. And he said, This is the word of the LORD, which he spake by his servant Elijah the Tishbite, saying, In the portion of Jezreel shall dogs eat the flesh of Jezebel: And the carcase of Jezebel shall be as dung upon the face of the field in the portion of Jezreel; so that they shall not say, This is Jezebel.**

Beloved, we are living in an era of the greatest war which the world has ever witnessed. What we have read so far are details of what happened when operation Jehu was carried out. As we begin to carry out our own operation by making use of this prayer manual, we should expect great things to happen. The truth is that God is set to do more than He ever did in the time of Jehu

CONTENTS

SECTION TWO

OBTAINING YOUR PORTION

SECTION THREE

WINNING THE MARRIAGE BATTLE

SECTION FOUR

JEHU PRAYERS; BREAKING THE CHAINS

SECTION FIVE

WINNING FOUNDATIONAL WARS

SECTION SIX

VITAMINS FOR EXPLOSIVE MANIFESTATION

WEAPONS OF WARFARE

You must use the weapon of violence
morning, noon, and night. You must declare
violent war against seen and unseen
enemies. If the enemy is making use of
bombs, you should not make use of cutlass
and arrows. You must meet the enemy fire
for fire and violence for violence.

WEAPONS of WARFARE

Chapter 1

VIOLENCE BY FIRE (1)

You need these prayer points to defeat satanic attacks. Violence of fire is your sure weapon for unchallengeable victory. You need these prayer points when you want to face the enemy and declare enough is enough. This is a battle that will give you the head of Goliath as a trophy.

Chapter 2

VIOLENCE BY FIRE (2)

You need to declare violence by fire warfare when you discover that the network of dark power is passing you like a baton from hand to hand. These prayer points must take you to the heights of warfare where you will be empowered to cry unto God and your enemies will be frightened and turn back.

Chapter 3

KILLING THE DRAGON

Prayers for killing the dragon are uncommon prayers. Mercy must be forgotten when it comes to dragon killing prayers. The prayers must be said swiftly, mercilessly, violently and with fire. Once you kill the dragon, elementary powers will give way.

Chapter 4.

LET ME BE WISER THAN MY ENEMIES

Victory begins when your wisdom surpasses the enemy's wisdom. You are at a vantage point when you are wiser than your enemies. When you pray until greater wisdom is bestowed upon you, the strategy of the enemy will be rendered null and void.

Chapter 5.

ENOUGH IS ENOUGH

To obtain unchallengeable victory you must pursue and overtake your enemy. This kind of battle is offensive rather than defensive. Instead of being pursued by your enemies you must stand your ground and pursue them. Enough is enough prayers are meant for men and women who can no longer tolerate what the enemy is doing. They are prayers for those who have had enough and are no longer ready to give any room for the enemy to operate.

Chapter 6.

CRUSHING WICKEDNESS

- The rule of the thumb, therefore, is crush wickedness before it crushes you. If God would only open your eyes to behold the agenda of wicked wasting powers, you will decide to do everything that lies within your power to crush the totality of their agenda.

Chapter 7.

POWER AGAINST BATTLE EXTENDERS

This prayer programme will alter the course of your journey and change your destiny for good. You need these prayer points if you have discovered that you are aiming at the wrong destination. This is a do or die battle. It is a battle you must fight and win.

Chapter 8.

BREAKING THE DARK MYSTERY OVER YOUR LIFE

When battles are prolonged, weariness will capture the heart of the victims. You must deal decisively with any power that has vowed that your battle will not cease. There is always a sinister motive behind the extension of any battle by the devil. It is your responsibility to squash any attempt at extending your battles.

Chapter 9.

DEALING WITH SATANIC ROBBERS

If you want to enjoy your life and fulfill your destiny, you must locate satanic robbers and barricade your spiritual properties with the fire of the Holy Ghost. You must not suffer any satanic robber to leave. The thief must be located, caught, punished and forced to vomit what he has eaten and restore what he has stolen. This is your season of recovery.

Chapter 10.

DEALING WITH ABORTION OF OPPORTUNITIES

This prayer programme is meant for those who have discovered that good opportunities slip through their hands. If you have discovered that you are constantly missing good opportunities or when there are stumbling blocks between you and your opportunity, the prayer points will change your situation.

Chapter 11.

BINDING THE STRONGMAN

Fighting against the strongman is no child's play. When any battle gets to the level of the strongman the warrior has a serious battle in his hands. The conditions of several people have proved stubborn simply because a strongman is in charge. The weapon needed to fight the strongman is a serious one. When the enemy has taken your case to the table of the strongman, you must be prepared to fight until the strongman is defeated and victory is yours.

Chapter 12.

KILLING GLORY KILLERS

You need these prayer points if you discover that some powers are attacking your glory. You must pray fervently if discover that demonic agents are gradually turning your glory to shame.

Chapter 13.

SILENCING ENEMIES OF MY NEW SONGS

You must locate every enemy of your new song and command them to be busy with useless assignments. You need to pray that whatever will sentence you to mourning, murmuring and complaining should be consumed by the fire of the Holy Ghost.

Chapter 14.

BURY YOUR HAMAN

Wicked powers must not be spared. You need to bury your Haman. Haman must be located, paralysed and forced to do repeated summersaults until confirmed dead. You must destroy Haman before he destroys you. You need these prayer points if your destiny is colourful.... The destiny of several people are attached to your destiny.

Chapter 15.

PULLING DOWN STRONGHOLDS

Prayers for pulling down strongholds are uncommon prayers that must be handled with the highest degree of fervency possible. Strongholds of darkness are responsible for knotty problems people go through day in day out. You need these prayer points when any season of your life is characterised by tragedies, terrible mishaps and problems sponsored by the kingdom of darkness. You need them who your destiny is floating on the ocean of life.

Chapter 16.

WHERE IS THE LORD GOD OF ELIJAH?

You need to invoke the power of the Lord God of Elijah when you are sick and tired of the evil onslaughts of the kingdom of darkness. This prayer programme is needed by men and women who want God to appear suddenly and intervene in their situations. It is a powerful battle cry for those who have an eye on winning victory at all cost.

CHAPTER ONE

VIOLENCE
BY FIRE

1

VIOLENCE
BY FIRE

1

IFE IS A BATTLE. The truth is that there is no rest on this side of eternity. The end of one battle signals the beginning of another. As long as satanic soldiers do not go on holidays, God's children should be on the battle field at all times. Hence, a song writer says: Christians seek not yet repose. Hear thy guardian angel say, thou art in the midst of foes. Watch and pray."

You must use the weapon of violence morning, noon, and night. You must declare violent war against seen and unseen enemies. If the enemy is making use of bombs, you should not make use of cutlass and arrows. You must meet the enemy fire for fire and violence for violence.

Isaiah 9:5 says:

> For every battle of the warrior is with confused noise, and garments rolled in blood; but this shall be with burning and fuel of fire.

This passage describes aggressive warfare which the enemy cannot withstand. To say this prayer effectively take the following steps:

1. Identify the hiding place of the enemy.
2. Target the weapon of warfare used by the enemy.
3. Attack the enemy with superior weapons.
4. Keep bombarding the enemy.
5. Pull down satanic strongholds.
6. Command the powers that are trying to lead you into captivity to go into captivity.
7. Fight the good fight of faith.
8. Locate the enemy's weak point.
9. Raise the name of Jesus as your banner of victory.
10. When the enemy comes up with any form of fake revival, resist him unto blood and strive for victory.

 PRAYER POINTS

1. Stubborn pursuers.
2. Household wickedness.
3. Powers of the night.
4. Forest demons.
5. Witchcraft manipulation.
6. The power of the empties.
7. Powers that bite without ruminant.
8. Satanic fetish priests.
9. Night caterers.
10. Dream manipulators.
11. The spirit of Herod.
12. The spirit of Nebuchadnezzar.
13. The spirit of Balaam.
14. Unrepentant Pharaoh.

15. Territorial powers.
16. The powers that will not let you go.
17. Battles that are raised against you by a network of dark forces.

 Violence of fire is your sure weapon for unchallengeable victory. You need these prayer points when you want to face the enemy and declare enough is enough. This is a battle that will give you the head of Goliath as a trophy.

PRAYER POINTS

These prayers are to be prayed **aggressively** between the hours of **midnight** and **1.00am** for **three** days.

Confession: Psalm 56:9: *When I cry unto thee, then shall mine enemies turn back: this I know; for God is for me.*

1. Let the teeth of the enemy over my life break, in the name of Jesus.
2. I render every aggressive altar impotent, in the name of Jesus.
3. Let the covenant with the earth against my life be broken, in the name of Jesus.
4. Every evil altar erected against me, be disgraced, in the name of Jesus.
5. Let every covenant with the sun against my life be broken, in the name of Jesus.
6. Anything done against my life under demonic anointing, be nullified, in the name of Jesus.
7. Let every covenant with the moon against my life be broken, in the name of Jesus.
8. I curse every local altar fashioned against me, in the name of Jesus.

9. Let every covenant with the stars against my life be broken, in the name of Jesus.

10. Let the hammer of the Almighty God smash every evil altar erected against me, in the name of Jesus.

11. Every bird of darkness working against my progress, fall down and die, in Jesus' name.

12. O Lord, send Your fire to destroy every evil altar fashioned against me, in the name of Jesus.

13. I arrest every evil bird fashioned against my breakthroughs, in the name of Jesus.

14. Every evil priest ministering against me at the evil altar, receive the sword of God, in the name of Jesus.

15. Every bird of darkness on assignment against my destiny, be roasted, in the name of Jesus.

16. Let the thunder of God smite every evil priest working against me on the evil altar and burn them to ashes, in the name of Jesus.

17. I spray the blood of Jesus on the covens of witchcraft around me, in the name of Jesus.

18. Let every satanic priest ministering against me at evil altars fall down and die, in the name of Jesus.

19. Any power assigned to use me as sacrifice, die, in the name of Jesus.

20. Any hand that wants to retaliate or arrest me because of these prayers points I am praying, dry up and wither, in the name of Jesus.

21. Wicked altars set up against me, set your owners ablaze, in the name of Jesus.

22. Every stubborn evil altar priest, drink your own blood, in the name of Jesus.

23. I shall not be a candidate of the eaters of flesh and drinkers of blood, in Jesus' name.

24. I possess my possession stolen by the evil altar, in the name of Jesus.

25. Holy Ghost fire, barricade my life from the rage of satanic

birds, in the name of Jesus.

26. I withdraw my name from every evil altar, in the name of Jesus.

27. My destiny, reject every bewitchment fashioned against me by the birds of darkness, in the name of Jesus.

28. I withdraw my blessings from every evil altar, in the name of Jesus.

29. Any sickness assigned to overtake my life, die, in the name of Jesus.

30. I withdraw my breakthroughs from every evil altar, in the name of Jesus.

31. Strange words assigned to trap me, scatter, in the name of Jesus.

32. I withdraw my glory from every evil altar, in the name of Jesus.

33. Every evil pot raised to control my life, catch fire, in the name of Jesus.

34. I withdraw my prosperity from every evil altar, in the name of Jesus.

35. Everyone who has accepted witchcraft for my sake, be disgraced, in the name of Jesus.

36. I withdraw anything representing me from every evil altar, in the name of Jesus.

37. Every power crippling against me, fall down and die, in the name of Jesus.

38. Mention the organ that you know is not behaving the way it should and begin to say: "I withdraw you from every evil altar, in the name of Jesus." *Say this seven hot times.*

39. Any power programming evils against me, using evil birds, be dismantled, in Jesus' name.

40. Let the wind of the Holy Spirit bring every scattered bone together now, in the name of Jesus.

41. I fire back every arrow of evil birds, in the name of Jesus.

42. I use the blood of Jesus to reverse every poor record of the past about my life, in the name of Jesus.

43. Thou power of familiar spirits that peep and mutter, I arrest your power, in Jesus' name.
44. I refuse to accept satanic substitute for my destiny, in the name of Jesus.
45. I shall not be a spiritual casualty, in the name of Jesus.
46. I refuse to be caged by the enemy of good things, in the name of Jesus.
47. O Lord, take away my portions from casualty, in the name of Jesus.

Every destiny-paralysing power fashioned against my destiny, fall down and die, in the name of Jesus.

48. Let every internal coffin in my life receive the fire of God and be roasted now, in the name of Jesus.
49. My God, my life shall not be left with the wind, in the name of Jesus.
50. Every destiny-paralysing power fashioned against my destiny, fall down and die, in the name of Jesus.
51. The meanderings of the enemy will not prosper in my life, in the name of Jesus.
52. Every habitation of witchcraft birds that is fashioned against my life, be desolate, in the name of Jesus.
53. My life, jump out of every inherited witchcraft cage, in the name of Jesus.
54. Holy Ghost fire, barricade my habitation from the rage of satanic birds, in the name of Jesus.
55. Let the excesses of darkness be checked by fire, in the name of Jesus.
56. Imagination of darkness against me, backfire, in the name of Jesus.

57. Anything buried to bury me, bury your owner, in the name of Jesus.

58. Every power nominating me for domination or termination, die, in the name of Jesus.

59. Pharaoh of my life, run to the Red Sea and perish, in the name of Jesus.

60. Every strange imagination against me, I nullify you, in the name of Jesus.

61. Power to disgrace every bird of darkness, come upon me now, in the name of Jesus.

62. My life, become untouchable to every bird of darkness, in the name of Jesus.

63. All my virtues swallowed by satanic birds, be vomited, in the name of Jesus.

64. The altar of the Lord is here, let every satanic altar around me be scattered, in the name of Jesus.

65. Time, you shall not hurt my destiny, in the name of Jesus.

66. Any power affecting the testimony of the Lord in my life, fall down and die, in the name of Jesus.

67. Whether the world goes up or down, my harvest shall continue to prosper, in the name of Jesus.

DAY 2

Praise Worship

1. I break the law of death over my life, in the name of Jesus.

2. Every inherited evil limitation in any area of my life, depart now, in the name of Jesus.

3. Every monitoring bird of darkness fashioned against me, be disgraced, in the name of Jesus.

4. Every architect of spiritual coffins, I command you to fall down and die, in the name of Jesus.

5. I shall destroy every company of satanic birds fashioned against me, in the name of Jesus.

6. Every cloud of uncertainty, clear away now, in the name of Jesus.
7. Every witchcraft bird flying against my destiny shall fly no more, in Jesus' name.
8. I refuse to be converted to a living dead, in the name of Jesus.
9. Every covenant of death with this year, be broken, in the name of Jesus.
10. Let every evil laying on of hands and shaking of evil hands be nullified, in the name of Jesus.
11. I am invisible to aggressive elements, in the name of Jesus.

Every caged star, be released now, in the name of Jesus.

12. Every satanic consultation concerning my life, be nullified, in the name of Jesus.
13. My portion and water shall be secured, in the name of Jesus.
14. Every decision taken against my life by witchcraft spirits, be nullified, in the name of Jesus.
15. I destroy every magic in any house I have entered, in the name of Jesus.
16. I reject aborted victories in every area of my life, in the name of Jesus.
17. Every evil power that has established authority in my family, be dismantled, in the name of Jesus.
18. Every caged star, be released now, in the name of Jesus.
19. Wherever I go, satanic agents will not steal my portion, in the name of Jesus.
20. My imagination and dreams will not be used against me, in the name of Jesus.

21. Holy Ghost fire, burn away the memory of my life from the possession of every satanic bird, in the name of Jesus.

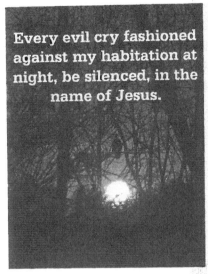

Every evil cry fashioned against my habitation at night, be silenced, in the name of Jesus.

22. O God, arise and visit with thunder and earthquake, all shrines assigned against me, in the name of Jesus.

23. Every evil cry fashioned against my habitation at night, be silenced, in the name of Jesus.

24. All satanic altars erected against my destiny, be overthrown by fire, in the name of Jesus.

25. O God, arise and let all my stubborn enemies scatter, in the name of Jesus.

26. O God, arise and set unquenchable fire upon every coven of darkness assigned against me, in Jesus' name.

27. Let the altars of the wicked assigned against me be dismantled, in the name of Jesus.

28. All images carved against my life, break into pieces after the order of dagon, in the name of Jesus.

29. O God, arise and let evil altars scatter, in the name of Jesus.

30. O God, arise and cause confusion in the camp of my enemies, in the name of Jesus.

31. I remove the portion of the serpent from my own life, in the name of Jesus.

32. I decree that my oppressors shall consult their powers in their confusion but there will be no response, in the name of Jesus.

33. I rebuke every evil linkage with my life with any evil, in the name of Jesus.

34. Holy Ghost fire, arise and stir up civil war in the camp of

my enemies, in the name of Jesus.

35. Thou power of the night fashioned against me, be disgraced, in the name of Jesus.

36. I command every satanic intermediary working against me to lose heart, in the name of Jesus.

37. Let the rod of the wrath of the Lord come upon every enemy of my ___, in the name of Jesus.

38. O God, arise and bring the plans of my oppressors to nothing, in the name of Jesus.

39. Let the angels of God invade them and lead them into darkness, in the name of Jesus.

40. My Father, set up a fierce king against my oppressors and let thim treat them with great torture, in the name of Jesus.

Holy Ghost fire, arise and stir up civil war in the camp of my enemies, in the name of Jesus.

41. Anything glorifying satan in my life, fall down and die, in the name of Jesus.

42. Let the power of God intimidate and frustrate all diviners assigned against me, in the name of Jesus.

43. I command the sword of the Lord to rise against all enemies surrounding my breakthroughs, in the name of Jesus.

44. O God, arise and wipe out the understanding of my stubborn pursuers, in the name of Jesus.

45. Every biting demon, be silenced, in the name of Jesus.

46. By the power in the blood of Jesus, let all soothsayers, witch doctors and enchanters arraigned against me be cut off, in the name of Jesus.

47. Let the oil lost in my life be returned, in the name of Jesus.

48. O God, pour out the spirit of dizziness upon all evil spiritual consultants speaking against me, in Jesus' name.

49. I pull down every throne of iniquity, in the name of Jesus.
50. Let these evil spiritual consultants stagger in all they do as a drunkard staggers in his vomit, in Jesus' name.
51. God will find rest in my life, in the name of Jesus.
52. Let the hand of the Lord turn against them day by day, in the name of Jesus.
53. Let their flesh and skin become old and let their bones be broken, in the name of Jesus.
54. Let them be compassed with gall and travail, in the name of Jesus.
55. Let the wall of challenges against my breakthrough break, in the name of Jesus.
56. My neck shall not be broken by territorial spirits, in the name of Jesus.
57. I release earthquake against my full-time enemies, in the name of Jesus.
58. Let God spit fire on the camp of my enemy today, in the name of Jesus.
59. My portion is not with the dead, in the name of Jesus.
60. Let angels of God hedge them about and block their paths, in the name of Jesus.
61. O Lord, make their chains heavy.
62. When they cry, shut out their cries, in the name of Jesus.
63. Every medicine poured on the ground to subdue my life, I destroy them by fire, in the name of Jesus.
64. I destroy the hand of any witchdoctor working against me, in the name of Jesus.
65. Any blood sacrifice against me, let the life in the blood be provoked to smite those that make the sacrifice, in the name of Jesus.
66. O life that has been allowed to die through rituals against me, arise and strangulate your killers, in the name of Jesus.
67. O Lord, make the paths of my enemies crooked, in the name of Jesus.

DAY 3

Praise Worship

1. O Lord, make the ways of my enemies to be hewed with sharp stones, in the name of Jesus.
2. O heavens, O earth, hear the word of the Lord: you must not execute the counsel of my enemies, in the name of Jesus.
3. Let the power of their own wickedness fall upon them, in the name of Jesus.
4. O God, pass through the camp of my enemies with affliction and drain their anointing of wickedness, in the name of Jesus.
5. I quench every anger energised through this land against me, in the name of Jesus.

> I de-programme and cancel all negative prophecies pronounced against me, in the name of Jesus.

6. Every power assigned to wreck my destiny, your end has come; die, in the name of Jesus.
7. I subjugate the power of witches, in the name of Jesus.
8. I de-programme and cancel all negative prophecies pronounced against me, in the name of Jesus.
9. Holy Ghost fire, challenge every stranger in my life, in the name of Jesus.
10. O Lord, guide me into the mysteries of my life.
11. O Lord, set Your watch afresh over my life, in the name of Jesus.
12. O Lord, give me the keys to unlock the hidden riches of secret places.

13. O Lord, turn them aside and pull them in pieces.

14. All ancient doors that have hindered the plan of God for my life, be unlocked by fire, in the name of Jesus.

15. O Lord, make their ways desolate.

16. I destroy every agreement made at covens and satanic centres against me, in the name of Jesus.

17. O Lord, fill them with bitterness and let them be drunken with wormwood.

18. Every secret code, evil register and archive of the enemy in my place of birth, be roasted, in the name of Jesus.

19. O Lord, hold back tomorrow from obstructing me, in the name of Jesus.

20. O God, arise and cast abominable filth upon witches and wizards and set them as gazing stock, in the name of Jesus.

21. O Lord, pour oil into my life and heal my roots, in the name of Jesus.

Let the covens of witchcraft become desolate, let there be no one to dwell in them, in the name of Jesus.

22. Let the tables of witches and wizards become snares unto them, in the name of Jesus.

23. Let heaven begin to defend me, in the name of Jesus.

24. Let the eyes of witches monitoring my life be darkened, in the name of Jesus.

25. O Lord, break their teeth with stones, in Jesus' name.

26. Let the covens of witchcraft become desolate, let there be no one to dwell in them, in the name of Jesus.

27. O Lord, cover them with ashes.

28. I command crashlanding of witches and wizards assigned against my breakthrough, in the name of Jesus.

29. O Lord, remove their souls from peace and let them forget prosperity, in the name of Jesus.
30. I command the sun to smite my oppressors in the day, and the moon and the stars to smite them at night, in the name of Jesus.
31. I command stubborn problems to wither, in the name of Jesus.
32. I command the stars in their courses to fight against my stubborn pursuers, in the name of Jesus.
33. Let my dread be upon the earth, in the name of Jesus.
34. O God, arise, roar and prevail over my enemies, in the name of Jesus.
35. Let the rivers inside of me come alive, in the name of Jesus.
36. Let the gathering of the wicked against me be harvested for judgement, in the name of Jesus.
37. O Lord, destroy the alignment of witches, in the name of Jesus.
38. Every stumbling block to God's prophetic agenda on my life, be rooted out, in the name of Jesus.
39. Every conglomeration of witches, be melted, in the name of Jesus.
40. All negative words that have been spoken against me by evil men, die, in the name of Jesus.
41. I loosen my life from every witchcraft poisoning, in the name of Jesus.
42. All evil records, evil marriage certificates and registers that are kept in satanic archives against me, be wiped off by the blood of Jesus.
43. I crush under my feet all the evil powers trying to imprison me, in the name of Jesus.
44. I programme divine health, divine favour, long life and spiritual advancement into my life by the power in the blood of Jesus, in Jesus' name.
45. Let the mouth of my enemies be put in the dust, in the name of Jesus.

46. I close down every spiritual ship carting away my benefits, in the name of Jesus.
47. Let there be civil war in the camp of the enemies of my _ _ _, in the name of Jesus.
48. O God, arise and lay waste all the operations of dark forces working against me, in the name of Jesus.
49. I destroy the poison in my life, in the name of Jesus.
50. Every power that has formed an evil cloud over my head, scatter, in the name of Jesus.
51. Every wall of partition between me and my breakthroughs, break, in the name of Jesus.
52. Every evil mystery over my life, be destroyed, in the name of Jesus.
53. I release panic upon my full-time enemies, in the name of Jesus.

Every wall of partition between me and my breakthroughs, break, in the name of Jesus.

54. Let stubborn confusion come upon the headquarters of my enemies, in the name of Jesus.
55. I loose confusion upon the plans of my enemies, in the name of Jesus.
56. Let the evil pressure behind my problems disappear now, in the name of Jesus.
57. Let the power that raised Jesus from the dead, break my yokes now, in the name of Jesus.
58. The life and spirit behind my reproach, break off, in the name of Jesus.
59. Everything that curses me onto death, die now, in the name of Jesus.

60. O Lord, give my enemies a cup of trembling to drink, in the name of Jesus.
61. O Lord, give my enemies a cup of confusion to drink, in the name of Jesus.
62. Every stronghold of darkness, receive acidic confusion, in the name of Jesus.
63. I loose panic and frustration on satanic orders issued against me, in the name of Jesus.
64. I command every evil power fighting against me to fight against and destroy one another, in Jesus' name.
65. I resist the threat of death in my dream, in the name of Jesus.
66. Every evil dream that other people have had about me, I cancel them in the astral world, in the name of Jesus.
67. I shall not be numbered amongst the wasted, in the name of Jesus.
68. Let this day be my open door, in the name of Jesus.

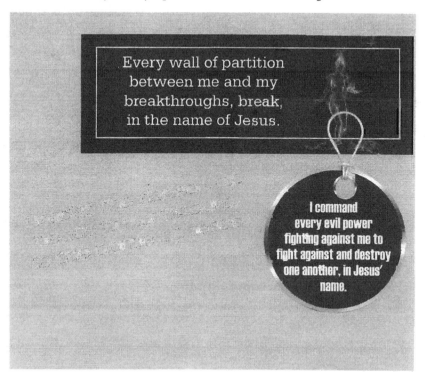

Every wall of partition between me and my breakthroughs, break, in the name of Jesus.

I command every evil power fighting against me to fight against and destroy one another, in Jesus' name.

CHAPTER TWO

VIOLENCE BY FIRE

2

Agents of darkness cannot be cajoled or appeased. The only way you can experience total victory over them is through violence and fire.

VIOLENCE
BY FIRE

2

ARFARE DEMANDS VIOLENCE. The fact that you are fighting against dark forces demands that you make use of the weapon of fire. Fire and violence go hand in hand. The Bible makes it crystal clear that right from the days of John the Baptist the kingdom of God suffereth violence and the violent taketh it by force. Agents of darkness cannot be cajoled or appeased. The only way you can experience total victory over them is through violence and fire.

You need this prayer programme:

1. When you discover that certain negative conditions have repeatedly occurred.
2. When you discover that evil powers have vowed to finish you.
3. To enable you to deal with stubborn ancestral powers.
4. To get rid of re-occurent problems.
5. To enable you to exterminate an array of deaf and dumb spirits who have vowed that they will never give up until they have achieved their goals.

6.   When you discover that the network of dark power are passing for you a baton from hand to hand.
7.   The prayer points will take you to the height of warfare where you will be empowered to cry unto God and your enemies will be frightened and turn back.

The prayers points below must be handled with the spirit of an aggressive warrior. Picture yourself on the battle front facing an array of wicked satanic solders. If you fail to attack them violently they may descend on you and attack you. Violence is the only language the enemy fears. When you combine violence with fire the devil trembles, evil spirits flee, and satanic burglars drop whatever they have stolen and flee.

The secret of victory is that when I cry, my enemies shall turn back!

Psalms 56:10 says:

> *In God will I praise his word: in the LORD will I praise his word.*

The prayer of violence by fire requires the following:

1.   Stubborn faith.
2.   Holy aggression.
3.   Be on the offensive rather than defensive.
4.   Let there be holy cry that is energised by fire.
5.   Have no mercy for the enemy.
6.   Request for angelic assistance.
7.   Keep the fire burning repeatedly.
8.   Make use of these prayer points with fasting.
9.   Make use of these prayer points at the mid-night hour.
10. Fight until the enemy is crushed and you earn the victors crown.

PRAYER SECTION

These prayers are to be prayed **aggressively** between the hours of **midnight** and **1.00 a.m.** for **three** days.

Confession: **Psalm 56:9:** *When I cry unto thee, then shall mine enemies turn back: this I know; for God is for me.*

Praise Worship

1. Let the teeth of the enemy over my life break, in the name of Jesus.
2. Let the covenant with the earth against my life be broken, in the name of Jesus.
3. Let every covenant with the sun against my life be broken, in the name of Jesus.
4. Let every covenant with the moon against my life be broken, in the name of Jesus.
5. Let every covenant with the stars against my life be broken, in the name of Jesus.
6. Every bird of darkness working against my progress, fall down and die, in Jesus' name.
7. I arrest every evil bird fashioned against my breakthroughs, in the name of Jesus.
8. Every bird of darkness on assignment against my destiny, be roasted, in the name of Jesus.
9. I spray the blood of Jesus on the covens of witchcraft around me, in the name of Jesus.
10. Any power assigned to use me as sacrifice, die, in the name of Jesus.
11. Wicked altars set up against me, set your owners ablaze, in the name of Jesus.
12. I shall not be a candidate of the eaters of flesh and drinkers of blood, in Jesus' name.

13. Holy Ghost fire, barricade my life from the rage of satanic birds, in the name of Jesus.
14. My destiny, reject every bewitchment fashioned against me by the birds of darkness, in the name of Jesus.
15. Any sickness assigned to overtake my life, die, in the name of Jesus.
16. Strange words assigned to trap me, scatter, in the name of Jesus.
17. Every evil pot raised to control my life, catch fire, in the name of Jesus.
18. Everyone who has accepted witchcraft for my sake, be disgraced, in the name of Jesus.
19. Every power crippling against me, fall down and die, in the name of Jesus.
20. Any power programming evils against me, using evil birds, be dismantled, in Jesus' name.
21. I fire back every arrow of evil birds, in the name of Jesus.
22. Thou power of familiar spirits that peep and mutter, I arrest your power, in Jesus' name.
23. I shall not be a spiritual casualty, in the name of Jesus.
24. O Lord, take away my portions from casualty, in the name of Jesus.
25. My God, my life shall not be left with the wind, in the name of Jesus.
26. The meanderings of the enemy will not prosper in my life, in the name of Jesus.
27. Every habitation of witchcraft birds fashioned against my life, be desolate, in the name of Jesus.
28. My life, jump out of every inherited witchcraft cage, in the name of Jesus.
29. Holy Ghost fire, barricade my habitation from the rage of satanic birds, in the name of Jesus.
30. Let the excesses of darkness be checked by fire, in the name of Jesus.
31. Imagination of darkness against me, backfire, in the name of Jesus.

32. Anything buried to bury me, bury your owner, in the name of Jesus.
33. Every power nominating me for domination or termination, die, in the name of Jesus.
34. Pharaoh of my life, run to the Red Sea and perish, in the name of Jesus.
35. Every strange imagination against me, I nullify you, in the name of Jesus.
36. Power to disgrace every bird of darkness, come upon me now, in the name of Jesus.
37. My life, become untouchable to every bird of darkness, in the name of Jesus.
38. All my virtues swallowed by satanic birds, be vomited, in the name of Jesus.
39. The altar of the Lord is here, let every satanic altar around me be scattered, in the name of Jesus.
40. Time, you shall not hurt my destiny, in the name of Jesus.
41. Any power affecting the testimony of the Lord in my life, fall down and die, in the name of Jesus.
42. Whether the world goes up or down, my harvest shall continue to prosper, in the name of Jesus.

DAY 2

1. I break the law of death over my life, in the name of Jesus.
2. Every monitoring bird of darkness fashioned against me, be disgraced, in the name of Jesus.
3. I shall destroy every company of satanic birds fashioned against me, in the name of Jesus.
4. Every witchcraft bird flying against my destiny shall fly no more, in Jesus' name.
5. Every covenant of death with this year, be broken, in the name of Jesus.
6. I am invisible to aggressive elements, in the name of Jesus.
7. My portion and water shall be secured, in the name of

Jesus.

8. I destroy every magic in any house I have entered, in the name of Jesus.

9. Every evil power that has established authority in my family, be dismantled, in the name of Jesus.

10. Wherever I go, satanic agents will not steal my portion, in the name of Jesus.

11. Holy Ghost fire, burn away the memory of my life from the possession of every satanic bird, in the name of Jesus.

12. Every evil cry fashioned against my habitation at night, be silenced, in the name of Jesus.

13. O God, arise and let all my stubborn enemies scatter, in the name of Jesus.

14. Let the altars of the wicked assigned against me be dismantled, in the name of Jesus.

15. O God, arise and let evil altars scatter, in the name of Jesus.

16. I remove the portion of the serpent from my own life, in the name of Jesus.

17. I rebuke every evil linkage with my life with any evil, in the name of Jesus.

18. Thou power of the night fashioned against me, be disgraced, in the name of Jesus.

19. Let the rod of the wrath of the Lord come upon every enemy of my father's house, in the name of Jesus.

20. Let the angels of God invade them and lead them into darkness, in the name of Jesus.

21. Anything glorifying satan in my life, fall down and die, in the name of Jesus.

22. I command the sword of the Lord to rise against all enemies surrounding my breakthroughs, in the name of Jesus.

23. Every biting demon, be silenced, in the name of Jesus.

24. Let the oil lost in my life be returned, in the name of Jesus.

25. I pull down every throne of iniquity, in the name of Jesus.

26. God will find rest in my life, in the name of Jesus.

27. Let the hand of the Lord turn against them day by day, in the

name of Jesus.

28. Let their flesh and skin become old and let their bones be broken, in the name of Jesus.

29. Let them be compassed with gall and travail, in the name of Jesus.

30. Let the wall of challenges against my breakthrough break, in the name of Jesus.

31. My neck shall not be broken by territorial spirits, in the name of Jesus.

32. I release earthquake against my full-time enemies, in the name of Jesus.

33. Let God spit fire on the camp of my enemy today, in the name of Jesus.

34. My portion is not with the dead, in the name of Jesus.

35. Let the angels of God hedge them about and block their paths, in the name of Jesus.

36. O Lord, make their chains heavy.

37. When they cry, shut out their cries, in the name of Jesus.

38. Every medicine poured on the ground to subdue my life, I destroy them by fire, in the name of Jesus.

39. I destroy the hand of any witchdoctor working against me, in the name of Jesus.

40. Any blood sacrifice against me, let the life in the blood be provoked to smite those em, in the name of Jesus.

41. O life that has been allowed to die through rituals against me, arise and strangulate your killers, in the name of Jesus.

42. O Lord, make their paths crooked.

DAY

PRAYER POINTS

Praise Worship

1. O Lord, make their ways to be hewed with sharp stones.

2. Let the power of their own wickedness fall upon them, in the name of Jesus.

3. I quench every anger energised through this land against me, in the name of Jesus.

4. I subjugate the power of witches, in the name of Jesus.

5. Holy Ghost fire, challenge every stranger in my life, in the name of Jesus.

6. O Lord, set Your watch afresh over my life, in the name of Jesus.

7. O Lord, turn them aside and pull them in pieces.

8. O Lord, make their ways desolate.

9. O Lord, fill them with bitterness and let them be drunken with wormwood.

10. O Lord, hold back tomorrow from obstructing me, in the name of Jesus.

11. O Lord, pour oil into my life and heal my roots, in the name of Jesus.

12. Let heaven begin to defend me, in the name of Jesus.

13. O Lord, break their teeth with stones, in Jesus' name.

14. O Lord, cover them with ashes, in Jesus' name.

15. O Lord, remove their souls from peace and let them forget prosperity, in Jesus' name.

16. I command stubborn problems to wither, in the name of Jesus.

17. Let my dread be upon the earth, in the name of Jesus.

18. Let the rivers inside of me come alive, in the name of Jesus.

19. O Lord, destroy the alignment of witches, in the name of Jesus.

20. Every conglomeration of witches, be melted, in the name of Jesus.

21. I loosen my life from every witchcraft poisoning, in the name of Jesus.

22. I crush under my feet all the evil powers trying to imprison me, in the name of Jesus.

23. Let their mouth be put in the dust, in the name of Jesus.

24. Let there be civil war in the camp of the enemies of my __ _, in the name of Jesus.
25. I destroy the poison in my life, in the name of Jesus.
26. Every power that has formed an evil cloud over my head, scatter, in the name of Jesus.
27. Every wall of partition between me and my breakthroughs, break, in the name of Jesus.
28. Every evil mystery over my life, be destroyed, in the name of Jesus.
29. I release panic upon my full-time enemies, in the name of Jesus.
30. Let stubborn confusion come upon the headquarters of my enemies, in the name of Jesus.
31. I loose confusion upon the plans of my enemies, in the name of Jesus.
32. Let the evil pressure behind my problems disappear now, in the name of Jesus.
33. Let the power that raised Jesus from the dead, break my yokes now, in the name of Jesus.
34. The life and spirit behind my reproach, break off, in the name of Jesus.
35. Everything that curses me onto death, die now, in the name of Jesus.
36. O Lord, give my enemies a cup of trembling to drink, in the name of Jesus.
37. O Lord, give my enemies a cup of confusion to drink, in the name of Jesus.
38. Every stronghold of darkness, receive acidic confusion, in the name of Jesus.
39. I loose panic and frustration on satanic orders issued against me, in the name of Jesus.
40. I command every evil power fighting against me to fight against and destroy one another, in Jesus' name.
41. I resist the threat of death in my dream, in the name of Jesus.

42. Every evil dream that other people have had about me, I cancel them in the astral world, in the name of Jesus.

43. I shall not be numbered amongst the wasted, in the name of Jesus.

44. Let this day be my open door, in the name of Jesus.

CHAPTER THREE

KILLING
THE DRAGON

KILLING THE DRAGON

THERE ARE WICKED POWERS to contend with One of the entities that must be disgraced and paralysed is the spiritual entity called the dragon. It is a sort of principality in the spiritual realm. These are generals in the satanic kingdom. They are symbols of uncommon wickedness. Those who fall prey to ferocious dragons may never live to tell the story. Therefore, warriors who want to tackle dragons must be well equipped and should not pray like gentlemen. A dragon is a spirit that has been empowered by the kingdom of darkness to swallow their victims alive.

Psalms 91:13 says:

> *Thou shalt tread upon the lion and adder: the young lion and the dragon shalt thou trample under feet.*

Revelation 12:11 says:

> *And they overcame him by the blood of the Lamb, and by the word of their testimony; and they loved not their lives unto the death.*

THE NATURE OF THE DRAGON

1. The dragon is a poisonous entity.
2. It is armed to the teeth.
3. It venom when injected into the system of a victim causes instant termination of life.
4. Many victims of the wicked have become casualties that are for the grave

Unless you attack the dragon, it will attack you. The battle against it is not for inexperienced soldiers. Its spirit must be attacked. Its power must be destroyed. Its strength must be weakened. The only antidote for dealing with wicked dragons is total destruction and death.

Every destiny-paralysing power fashioned against my destiny, fall down and die, in the name of Jesus.

Prayers for killing the dragon are uncommon prayers. Mercy must be forgotten when it comes to dragon killing prayers. The prayers must be said swiftly, mercilessly, violently and with fire. Once you kill the dragon, elementary powers will give way.

Killing the dragon can be likened to killing the captain of the satanic army. Of course, the moment you finish the dragon all the other powers will flee. These prayer points must be said persistently. Do not expect the dragon to give up after the initial blow. You need to rain blows upon blows on it before you will be able to finish its wicked mission. Never spare it; for even if you avoid it you will not be spared. The only secret of victory over the dragon is to fight your way to victory.

This prayer programme differs from other prayer programmes. You need to possess the spirit of the warrior, the faith of an overcomer, the aggressiveness of a soldier and the doggedness of a fighter. The battle may be tough. You may experience certain manifestations. Keep on fighting. You are not involved in this battle for the fun of it. Total victory must be your goal. Every dragon fighting against you must die. Every weapon fashioned against you must not prosper.

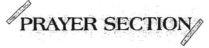

PRAYER SECTION

Confession:

Psalm 91:13: *Thou shalt tread upon the lion and adder: the young lion and the dragon shalt thou trample under feet.*

Isaiah 54:17: *No weapon that is formed against thee shall prosper; and every tongue that shall rise against thee in judgment thou shalt condemn. This is the heritage of the servants of the Lord, and their righteousness is of me, saith the Lord.*

Luke 10:19: *Behold, I give unto you power to tread on serpents and scorpions, and over all the power of the enemy: and nothing shall by any means hurt you.*

Revelation 12:11: *And they overcame him by the blood of the Lamb, and by the word of their testimony; and they loved not their lives unto the death.*

Job 5:12: *He disappointeth the devices of the crafty, so that their hands cannot perform their enterprise.*

Psalm 18:44-45: *As soon as they hear of me, they shall obey me: the strangers shall submit themselves unto me. The strangers shall fade away, and be afraid out of their close places.*

PRAYER POINTS

PRAISES

1. Witchcraft serpent fashioned against my blood, depart now and go back to your sender, in the name of Jesus.
2. Every agenda of the serpent for my destiny, scatter, in the name of Jesus.
3. Holy Ghost fire, penetrate my body, soul and spirit and destroy every plantation of the serpent, in the name of Jesus.
4. Every serpent of my father's house assigned against my destiny, loose your hold, in the name of Jesus.
5. My Father, arise and uproot from my system every plantation of the serpent, in the name of Jesus.
6. Serpents of my father's house, dragons of my father's house, die by fire, in the name of Jesus.
7. Holy Ghost, arise in the thunder of Your fire and destroy every plantation of darkness in my body, in the name of Jesus.
8. Serpents of darkness, get out and die, in the name of Jesus.
9. Every covenant tying me down with mobile serpents, catch fire, in the name of Jesus.
10. I cover everything within me, everything around me and everything over me now with the blood of Jesus.
11. Let demonic serpents be rendered venomless in every area of my life, in the name of Jesus.
12. Thou serpent of impossibility, die, in the name o Jesus.
13. Thou serpent and scorpion of affliction, die, in the name of Jesus.
14. Every serpent and scorpion anointed against my destiny, dry up and die, in the name of Jesus.
15. Let every serpentine spirit and poison depart from my tongue, in the name of Jesus.
16. I break every egg that the serpent has laid in every department of my life, in the name of Jesus.

17. Every serpentine and scorpion power militating against my life, be disgraced, in the name of Jesus.
18. O Lord, let all the serpents and scorpions assigned against me fight themselves, in the name of Jesus.
19. Every serpent sent to destroy me, return to your sender, in the name of Jesus.
20. My spiritual strength sapped by the serpent, receive divine touch of God and be released, in Jesus' name.
21. You serpent, loose your grip upon my spiritual strength, in the name of Jesus.
22. Every pollution done to my spiritual life and health by the serpent, be cleansed by the blood of Jesus.

Every destiny-paralysing power fashioned against my destiny, fall down and die, in the name of Jesus.

23. Every serpentine manipulation upon my health, be frustrated and rendered impotent, in the name of Jesus.
24. All you serpents, I command you to vomit my prosperity, health, marriage, finances and spiritual strength that you have swallowed, in the mighty name of our Lord Jesus Christ.
25. I tread upon all serpents and scorpions. They cannot harm me, in the name of Jesus.
26. Let the bullet from heaven kill every serpent of death, in the name of Jesus.
27. I cut every soul-tie with any serpentine spirit, in the name of Jesus.
28. I excise the poison and venom of the scorpions and serpents from my flesh, in Jesus' name.

29. I trample upon every serpent and scorpion monitoring the progress of my life, in the name of Jesus.
30. I cast all serpents of infirmity into the fire of judgement, in the name of Jesus.
31. I cut myself free from the hands of serpents and scorpions, in the name of Jesus.
32. I remove the portion of the serpent from my own life, in the name of Jesus.
33. Let every serpent-spirit unwind and depart, in Jesus' name.
34. Let the serpent of the Lord swallow the serpent of my Pharaoh, in the name of Jesus.
35. Let the serpent of the Lord bite every hidden enemy of my life, in the name of Jesus.
49. Every crocodile and serpentine spirit, I kill you by the hook of the Lord, in the name of Jesus.
36. Holy Ghost fire, kill every serpent and scorpion targeted against my Israel, in the name of Jesus.
37. As a child of the Lion of Judah, I chase out serpents from my life, in the name of Jesus.
38. Every serpent and scorpion of poverty, die, in the name of Jesus.
39. Every poison of serpents and scorpions, come out of me, in the name of Jesus.
40. Let every crooked serpent be destroyed, in the name of Jesus.
41. My life, reject every serpent and scorpion, in the name of Jesus.
42. O God, arise and grind foundational serpents to ashes, in Jesus' name.
43. Let the serpent of impossibility be dissolved by the fire of the God of Elijah, in the name of Jesus.
44. Every dreaming serpent, go back to your sender, in Jesus' name.
45. Every serpent and scorpion working against my destiny, dry up and die, in the name of Jesus.

46. Every dream-serpent, die, in the name of Jesus.
47. Every serpent in my foundation, die, in the name of Jesus.
48. Serpent of the Lord, bite every serpent in my family line, in the name of Jesus.
49. Every serpent in my foundation, die, in the name of Jesus.
50. Every scorpion in my foundation, die, in the name of Jesus.
51. You serpent, loose your grip upon my spiritual strength, in the name of Jesus.
52. Every serpentine manipulation of my health, be frustrated and be rendered impotent, in the name of Jesus.
53. Every serpent that has refused to let me go, Holy Ghost fire, dry it up, in the name of Jesus.
54. Every serpentine idol in my family, I break your link with my family, in the name of Jesus.

Every destiny-paralysing power fashioned against my destiny, fall down and die, in the name of Jesus.

55. No serpent shall control my life, in the name of Jesus.
56. Every serpent fired into my life, go back to your sender, in the name of Jesus.
57. Every dreaming-serpent, go back to your sender, in the name of Jesus.
58. Every serpent working in the root of my life, die, in the name of Jesus.
59. You serpent and scorpion of darkness delegated against my victory, die, in the name of Jesus.
60. I smash and scatter the heads of serpentine spirits, in the name of Jesus.
61. I break every covenant with the spirit of the python, in the name of Jesus.

62. Every serpent attached to my life, be roasted by fire, in the name of Jesus.

63. Every attraction of the serpent spirit to my life, be washed off by the blood of Jesus.

64. Every consultation with the powers of divination against my life, end in confusion, in the name of Jesus.

65. Every power of divination manipulating my destiny, be destroyed, in the name of Jesus.

66. Every evil oracle with my name, be consumed by fire, in the name of Jesus.

67. Every altar of the serpent erected against me, burn to ashes, in the name of Jesus.

68. I withdraw my name from every evil register and record file, in the name of Jesus.

69. Every linkage of the python spirit with my life, break to pieces, in the name of Jesus.

70. Every covenant formed on my behalf with serpent spirits by my ancestors/parents, break by the blood of Jesus.

71. I loose myself from every hold of the serpent, in the name of Jesus.

72. Every poison of the serpent in my life, come out, in the name of Jesus.

73. Every egg of the serpent in the vessel of my life, be burnt to ashes by the fire of God, in Jesus' name.

74. Every property of the serpent in my possession, vanish to return no more, in the name of Jesus.

75. Let the resting place of the serpent in my life receive the unbearable heat of the Almighty, in the name of Jesus.

76. Let the strongroom of the serpent in my life be destroyed by the fire of God, in the name of Jesus.

77. You the head of the serpent, be smashed to pieces by Holy Ghost fire, in the name of Jesus.

78. Fire of God, enter into my life and consume every stranger, in the name of Jesus.

79. Every poison of sexual immorality in my life, be paralysed,

in the name of Jesus.

80. Every activity of seduction in any area of my life, be paralysed, in the name of Jesus.

81. Every invisible programme of the serpent in my life, be destroyed, in the name of Jesus.

82. Let the ancestral altar of the serpent spirit in my family burn to ashes, in the name of Jesus.

83. Every unrepentant snake worshipper in my family, fall down and die, in the name of Jesus

CHAPTER FOUR

LET ME BE WISER THAN MY ENEMIES

LET ME BE WISER THAN MY ENEMIES

4

One of the greatest prayers you must pray is that God should make you wiser than your enemies. Victory begins when your wisdom surprises the enemy's wisdom. You are at a vantage point when you are wiser than your enemies. You can ask God to endow you with enough wisdom to overcome the enemy and sing the victor's song. Wisdom is a powerful weapon of war. The wisdom of God will enable you to tackle the enemy effectively and overcome every antic of the wicked one.

It is indeed true that you cannot avoid enemies. But you can become so endowed with wisdom as to spread confusion in the camp of the enemy. When you are wiser than your enemies, you have supremacy and divine edge over them. When you pray and greater wisdom is bestowed upon you, the strategy of the enemy will be rendered null and void. No matter how numerous your enemies are, God will demonstrate the supremacy of His power by making you wiser than they. Divine wisdom will make you stand out and enable you to climb the ladder of victory.

The moment you are wiser than your enemies you will begin to operate from the platform of victory, God will make diviners mad, the enemies will take a bow and you will experience sweatless victory. You will prevail, wisdom will raise your head above the head of all the enemies.

The following steps must be taken:

1. You must ask God to envelope you with the spirit of wisdom.
2. Ask God to make you wiser than your enemies as your victory depends on these prayer points.
3. Take cognizance of the fact that wisdom is the ladder to the realm of unchallengeable victory.
4. Spend a great deal of time on these prayer points.
5. Know that wisdom gives you a higher platform where victory is achieved with ease.

Take note of the following:

1. Maintain a close relationship with God.
2. Meditate on the Scriptures.
3. Maintain a prayerful lifestyle.
4. Manifest faith for victory over the enemy.

PRAYER SECTION

Confession: **Psalm 19:1-14:** *The heavens declare the glory of God; and the firmament sheweth his handywork. Day unto day uttereth speech, and night unto night sheweth knowledge. There is no speech nor language, where their voice is not heard. Their line is gone out through all the earth, and their words to the end of the world. In them hath he set a tabernacle for the sun, Which is as a bridegroom coming out of his chamber, and rejoiceth as a strong man to run a race. His going forth is from the end of the heaven, and his circuit unto the ends of it: and there is nothing hid from the heat thereof. The law of the Lord is perfect, converting the soul: the testimony of the Lord is sure, making wise the* *simple. The statutes of the Lord are right, rejoicing the heart: the commandment of the Lord is pure, enlightening the eyes. The fear of the Lord is clean, enduring for ever: the judgments of the Lord are true and righteous altogether. More to be desired are they than gold, yea, than much fine gold: sweeter also than honey and the honeycomb. Moreover by them is thy servant warned: and in keeping of them there is great reward. Who can understand his errors? cleanse thou me from secret faults. Keep back thy servant also from presumptuous sins; let them not have dominion over me: then shall I be upright, and I shall be innocent from the great transgression. Let the words of my mouth, and the meditation of my heart, be acceptable in thy sight, O Lord, my strength, and my redeemer.*

PRAYER POINTS

1. Praises
2. My Father, let my enemies make mistakse that would advance my course, in the name of Jesus.
3. I receive wisdom that my enemies cannot understand or comprehend, in the name of Jesus.
4. My Father, let my thinking be at a level higher than those of my contemporaries, in the name of Jesus.
5. Father, visit my dreams with spiritual revelations to move me forward, in the name of Jesus.
6. Father, give me the wisdom of Solomon, the eyes of Elisha, and the ears of Samuel, in the name of Jesus.
7. My Father, let the Holy Spirit expose to me the dribbling tactics of the enemies, in the name of Jesus.
8. My Father, let Your Spirit guide me, let Your love overshadow me and let Your light inspire me, in the name of Jesus.
9. Father, give me a listening ear for divine direction, in the name of Jesus.
10. My Father, you are the Light that shines on my path. Let Your light give me insight and understanding that would help me to make good decisions, in the name of Jesus.

11. Holy Spirit, You are my source of wisdom, guide me and direct me always, in the name of Jesus.

12. My Father, let me no longer see men after the flesh alone, give me a discerning eye, in the name of Jesus.

13. Holy Spirit, arise in Your illuminating power and envelope my life, in the name of Jesus.

14. Let the wisdom of the ancient fall upon me in the name of Jesus.

15. My Father, enlighten me in the radiance of Your Person, in the name of Jesus.

16. Let the spirit of divine wisdom settle upon me mightily, in the name of Jesus.

17. My mind, receive the spirit of wisdom, in the name of Jesus.

18. I counter every wisdom of darkness by the wisdom of heaven, in the name of Jesus.

19. Great wisdom of the Almighty, arise and envelope my life, in the name of Jesus.

20. My Father, give me a deep understanding of what is logical and true, in the name of Jesus.

21. My Father, give me a deep understanding of what is right and lasting, in the name of Jesus.

22. My Father, let my labours reflect Your insight and let the works of my hands magnetise success, in the name of Jesus.

23. My Father, Your wisdom is an eternity ahead of man. Give me the wisdom that no man can withstand, in the name of Jesus.

24. My Father, give me a mouth and a wisdom that will mesmerise and confuse my enemies, in the name of Jesus.

25. I bind and cast out every darkness in my mind, and I command ignorance to scatter, in the name of Jesus.

26. It is written, "Out of the mouth of babes and sucklings has Thou ordained strength," Father, ordain strength for my mouth, in the name of Jesus.

27. Holy Ghost, guide my going in, going out and going forward, in the name of Jesus.

28. My Father, show me Your ways and teach me Your paths, in the name of Jesus.

29. My Father, guide me in Your truth and teach me, in the name of Jesus.

30. Any power assigned to scatter my efforts, be disgraced, in the name of Jesus.

31. I receive uncommon anointing and discernment to move me forward, in the name of Jesus.

32. Holy Ghost and fire, bulldoze out of my ways, blockages by sorcerers and satanic diviners, in the name of Jesus.

33. I bind every track that the enemy is setting for me now and in the future, in the name of Jesus.

34. My Father, let me be at the right place at the right time, in the name of Jesus.

35. My Father, give me wisdom to stay on the right path always, in the name of Jesus.

36. I bind every hindrance, roadblock, trick and trap of the enemies designed to get me off course, in the name of Jesus.

CHAPTER FIVE

ENOUGH IS ENOUGH

ENOUGH IS ENOUGH

5

The only language which the enemy understands is violence. When you confront all the powers that confront you with violence, you will overcome. The powers that operate in this environment are powers that are deaf and dumb. They are so stubborn that they will not give up easily. Nothing will change unless you make use of the weapon of bombardment. You must get to a point where you declare enough is enough. You must fight aggressively until you battle the enemy to a standstill. Victory cannot be won by those who are lazy or complacent. To obtain unchallengeable victory you must pursue and overtake your enemy.

The picture of an overcomer or a conqueror is painted in **Psalm 18:37-40:**

> *I have pursued mine enemies, and overtaken them: neither did I turn again till they were consumed. I have wounded them that they were not able to rise: they are fallen under my feet. For thou hast girded me with strength unto the battle: thou hast subdued*

under me those that rose up against me. Thou hast also given me the necks of mine enemies; that I might destroy them that hate me.

This kind of battle is offensive rather than defensive. Instead of being pursued by your enemies, you must stand your ground and pursue them. Enough is enough prayers are meant for men and women who can no longer tolerate what the enemy is doing. Enough is enough prayers are prayers for those who have had enough and are no longer ready to give any room for the enemy to operate. These are prayers that will stop the evil tide and give you freedom to fulfill your destiny and live your life according to the design of the Almighty.

Enough is enough prayers are prayers said by a mad prophet who prays with holy aggression. These prayer points will enable you to confront the enemy fire for fire. They are prayers that will overthrow every evil king occupying the throne of your life. They will put an end to age-long problems and terminate the oppressive regime of the enemy. They will make every eater of flesh and drinker of blood to eat their own flesh and drink their own blood.

The prayer points will turn every victim to a victor. They will convert the pursed to the purser and make the prince who has been working barefoot to climb the horse of his destiny.

I have a warning for you at this point, do not start these prayer points unless you are ready to pound the enemy to submission.

PRAYER SECTION

Confessions: **Psalm 118:1:** *O give thanks unto the Lord; for he is good: because his mercy endureth for ever.*

Isaiah 49:24-25: *Shall the prey be taken from the mighty, or the lawful captive delivered? But thus saith the Lord, Even the captives of the mighty shall be taken away, and the prey of the terrible shall be delivered: for I will* *contend with him that contendeth with thee, and I will save thy children.*

Psalm 124:7: *Our soul is escaped as a bird out of the snare of the fowlers: the snare is broken, and we are escaped.*

Psalm 18:37-40: *I have pursued mine enemies, and overtaken them: neither did I turn again till they were consumed. I have wounded them that they were not able to rise: they are fallen under my feet. For thou hast girded me with strength unto the battle: thou hast subdued under me those that rose up against me. Thou hast also given me the necks of mine enemies; that I might destroy them that hate me.*

Isaiah 44:25: *That frustrateth the tokens of the liars, and maketh diviners mad; that turneth wise men backward, and maketh their knowledge foolish;*

PRAISE WORSHIP

1. Every bird of darkness working against my progress, fall down and die, in Jesus' name.
2. I arrest every evil bird fashioned against my breakthroughs, in the name of Jesus.
3. Every bird of darkness on assignments against my destiny, be roasted, in the name of Jesus.
4. I shall not be a candidate of the eaters of flesh and drinkers of blood, in Jesus' name.
5. Holy Ghost fire, barricade my life from the rage of satanic birds, in the name of Jesus.
6. My destiny, reject every bewitchment fashioned against me by the birds of darkness, in the name of Jesus.
7. Any power programming evils against me, using evil birds, be dismantled, in Jesus' name.
8. I fire back every arrow of evil birds, in the name of Jesus.
9. Thou power of familiar spirits that peep and mutter, I arrest your power, in Jesus' name.

10. Every habitation of witchcraft birds fashioned against my life, be desolate, in the name of Jesus.
11. My life, jump out of every inherited witchcraft cage, in the name of Jesus.
12. Holy Ghost fire, barricade my habitation from the rage of satanic birds, in the name of Jesus.
13. Power to disgrace every bird of darkness, come upon me now, in the name of Jesus.
14. My life, become untouchable to every bird of darkness, in the name of Jesus.
15. All my virtues swallowed by satanic birds, be vomited, in the name of Jesus.
16. Every monitoring bird of darkness fashioned against me, be disgraced, in the name of Jesus.
17. I shall destroy every company of satanic birds fashioned against me, in the name of Jesus.
18. Every witchcraft bird flying against my destiny shall fly no more, in Jesus' name.
19. Holy Ghost fire, burn away the memory of my life from the possession of every satanic bird, in the name of Jesus.
20. Every evil cry fashioned against my habitation at night, be silenced, in the name of Jesus.
21. O God, arise and let all my stubborn enemies scatter, in the name of Jesus.
22. Thou power of the night fashioned against me, be disgraced, in the name of Jesus.
23. Let the rod of the wrath of the Lord come upon every enemy of my progress, in the name of Jesus.
24. Let the angels of God invade them and lead them into darkness, in the name of Jesus.
25. Let the hand of the Lord turn against them day by day, in the name of Jesus.
26. Let their flesh and skin become old and let their bones be broken, in the name of Jesus.
27. Let them be compassed with gall and travail, in the name of Jesus.

28. Let Your angels hedge them about and block their paths, in the name of Jesus.
29. O Lord, make their chains heavy.
30. When they cry, shut out their cries, in the name of Jesus.
31. O Lord, make their paths crooked, in the name of Jesus.
32. O Lord, make their ways to be hewed with sharp stones, in the name of Jesus.
33. Let the power of their own wickedness fall upon them, in the name of Jesus.
34. O Lord, turn them aside and pull them in pieces.
35. O Lord, make their ways desolate.
36. O Lord, fill them with bitterness and let them be drunken with wormwood.
37. O Lord, break their teeth with stones, in the name of Jesus.
38. O Lord, cover them with ashes, in the name of Jesus.
39. O Lord, remove their souls from peace and let them forget prosperity, in the name of Jesus.
40. I crush under my feet all the evil powers trying to imprison me, in the name of Jesus.
41. Let their mouth be put in the dust, in the name of Jesus.
42. Let there be civil war in the camp of the enemies of my destiny, in the name of Jesus.
43. I release panic upon my full-time enemies, in the name of Jesus.
44. Let stubborn confusion come upon the headquarters of my enemies, in the name of Jesus.
45. I loose confusion upon the plans of my enemies, in the name of Jesus.
46. Every stronghold of darkness, receive acidic confusion, in the name of Jesus.
47. I loose panic and frustration on satanic orders issued against me, in the name of Jesus.
48. I command every evil power fighting against me to fight against and destroy one another, in Jesus' name.

CHAPTER SIX

CRUSHING
WICKEDNESS

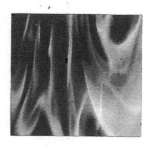

CRUSHING WICKEDNESS

6

WICKED POWERS HAVE A TERRIBLE AGENDA. The devil relishes wickedness. His agents are restless when they have no opportunity to unleash wickedness on mankind. When you allow evil powers to go to their warehouse and make use of their wicked weapons the result will be tragic.

Wickedness is an evil agenda that must not be allowed to see the light of day. The moment you allow demons to throw the bomb of wickedness into your camp, you may be crushed for life. The rule of the thumb, therefore, is crush wickedness before it crushes you. If there is anything you must tackle and crush totally, it is wickedness from the domain of dark powers.

If God opens your eyes to behold the agenda of wicked wasting powers you will decide to do everything that lies within your power to crush the totality of their agenda. The following are manifestation of wickedness to identify and crush:

1. Calamity.
2. Sudden mishaps.
3. Tragedy.
4. Untimely death.
5. Seeing apparitions.
6. Bad dreams.
7. Waking up to see marks on your body.
8. Sudden loss of job.
9. Cycle of misfortune.
10. Following evil patterns of your ancestors.
11. Unexplainable bad luck.
12. Wicked attacks.
13. Instances of your name being taken to fetish priests.
14. When things are kept on the floor or chain to harm you.
15. Occurrences that make you to shed tears or lament.
16. Violent attacks from household wickedness.
17. Destructive attacks from wickedness.
18. Whatever is sponsored to make you a victim of the arrow of untimely death.
19. Demonic incantations aimed at destroying your destiny.
20. An array of wicked attacks coming from all quarters.

You must raise a violent cry against arrows of wickedness. Take this prayer programme with holy anger. Decree death upon every wicked agent fighting against you. Pray until wickedness is totally crushed.

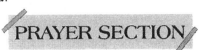

PRAYER SECTION

Confession: **Psalm 3:7:** *Arise, O Lord; save me, O my God: for thou hast smitten all mine enemies upon the cheek bone; thou hast broken the teeth of the ungodly.*

PRAISE WORSHIP

1. Let the teeth of the enemy over my life break, in the name of Jesus.

2. Every evil seed planted in my life by my place of birth, die, in the name of Jesus.

3. My glory, come out of the cage of evil location, in the name of Jesus.

4. Oh Lord, make all the rough places plain before me, in the name of Jesus.

5. Every ancient gate of my place of birth locking up my progress, hear the word of the Lord: lift up your heads and open, in the name of Jesus.

6. Every evil power of my place of birth, die, in the name of Jesus.

7. My glory, what are you doing in the valley? Arise and shine, in the name of Jesus.

8. Every satanic father and every satanic mother in the spirit realm, die, in the name of Jesus.

9. Let every covenant with the earth against my life be broken, in the name of Jesus.

10. Let every covenant with the sun, the moon and the stars against my life be broken, in the name of Jesus.

11. Let every covenant with the water against my life be broken, in the name of Jesus.

12. Everyone who has accepted witchcraft for my sake, be disgraced, in the name of Jesus.

13. Every power crippling against me, die, in the name of Jesus.

14. Oh Lord, release the rivers of life upon my dwelling, in the name of Jesus.

15. I shall not be a spiritual casualty, in the name of Jesus.

16. Oh Lord, take away my portions from casualty, in the name of Jesus.

17. My God, my life shall not be left with the wind, in the name of Jesus.

18. The meanderings of the enemy will not prosper in my life, in the name of Jesus.

19. Let the excesses of darkness be checked by fire, in the name of Jesus.

20. I break the law of death over my life, in the name of Jesus

21. Every covenant of death with this year, be broken, in the name of Jesus.

22. I am invisible to aggressive elements, in the name of Jesus.

23. My portion and water shall be secured, in the name of Jesus.

24. I destroy every magic in any house I have entered, in the name of Jesus.

25. Every evil power that has established authority in my family, be dismantled, in the name of the Jesus.

26. Wherever I go, satanic agents will not steal my portion, in the name of Jesus.

27. I command the sword of the Lord to rise against every enemy of my soul, in the name of Jesus.

28. Every biting demon, be silenced, in the name of Jesus.

29. Let the oil lost in my life be returned, in the name of Jesus.

30. I pull down every throne of iniquity, in the name of Jesus.

31. God will find rest in my life, in the name of Jesus.

32. Let the wall of challenges against my breakthroughs break, in the name of Jesus.

33. My neck shall not be broken by territorial spirits, in the name of Jesus.

34. Blood poured on the ground will not eat me up, in the name of Jesus.

35. My portion is not with the dead, in the name of Jesus.

36. Every medicine poured on the ground to subdue my life, I destroy you, in the name of Jesus.

37. I destroy the hand of every witchdoctor working against me, in the name of Jesus.

38. Any blood sacrifice against me, let the life in those blood be provoked to smite the enemies, in the name of Jesus.

39. Oh life that has been allowed to die through rituals against me, arise and strangulate your killers, in the name of Jesus.

40. I quench every anger energised through the land against me, in the name of Jesus.

41. I subjugate the power of witches, in the name of Jesus.
42. Every alignment of witches against my life, be destroyed, in the name of Jesus.
43. Every conglomeration of witches, be melted, in the name of Jesus.
44. I loosen my life from every witchcraft poisoning, in the name of Jesus.
45. I destroy the poison in my life, in the name of Jesus.
46. Every Haman assigned against my life, fall down and die, in the name of Jesus.
47. Every messenger of death assigned against my life, go back to your sender, in the name of Jesus.
48. Every agent of death inside my body, come out and die, in the name of Jesus.
49. Every gate of death assigned to swallow me, swallow your owner, in the name of Jesus.
50. Every plantation of death, die, in the name of Jesus.
51. Every stronghold of death on my mind and imagination, be pulled down, in the name of Jesus.
52. By the resurrection of the Lord Jesus Christ the power of death is broken upon my life, in Jesus' name.
53. Every string of death fashioned against my life, be neutralised by the blood of Jesus.
54. Every certificate of untimely death issued against my life, catch fire, in the name of Jesus.
55. I shall not die but live to declare the works of God, in the name of Jesus.
56. The number of my days shall be fulfilled, in the name of Jesus.
57. Every damaged organ in my body, be repaired by fire, in the name of Jesus.
58. My bones shall not be broken through accident, in the name of Jesus.
59. Every power that does not want to see me around, fall down and die, in the name of Jesus.

60. My soul shall not see corruption of death through sickness, accident or calamity, in the name of Jesus.

61. I drink the blood of Jesus. Let the life in it flow into every organ of my body, in the name of Jesus.

62. My blood, by the blood of Jesus, be inoculated and immunised against the invasion of death, in Jesus' name.

63. I eat of the flesh of Jesus and I receive life into my body, in the name of Jesus.

64. Every arrow of untimely death fashioned against my life, go back to your senders, in the name of Jesus.

65. Every power digging grave for me, enter therein, in the name of Jesus.

66. Vehicle of my transportation shall not become my coffin, in the name of Jesus.

67. I shall not journey into death, in the name of Jesus.

68. Every snare of death set up for my life, catch your owners, in the name of Jesus.

69. There shall be no sorrow of death in my family, in the name of Jesus.

70. Every shadow of death assigned against my life, scatter, in the name of Jesus.

71. Let the mark of the blood of Jesus wipe off every mark of death on my body, in the name of Jesus.

72. Every stronghold of untimely death fashioned against my life, be pulled down by fire, in the name of Jesus.

73. You wind of death, go back to your sender, in the name of Jesus.

74. Every spirit of depression and despair, die, in the name of Jesus.

75. Every wind of death, go back to your sender, in the name of Jesus.

76. Every satanic device to terminate my life, catch fire, in the name of Jesus.

77. Let the tokens of the liars to cut off my life be frustrated, in the name of Jesus.

78. Every pollution of death in the organ of my body, die, in the name of Jesus.
79. Let my blood be transfused with the blood of Jesus.
80. Every poison and contamination in my blood, be flushed out, in the name of Jesus.
81. Every tree of untimely death in my family line, my life is not your candidate, die, in the name of Jesus.
82. Every evil hunter of my soul, turn back and die, in the name of Jesus.
83. By the power in the blood of Jesus, I subdue death, oppression and violence, in the name of Jesus.
84. I am a mother of living children, in the name of Jesus.
85. I hide the lives of my children, in the name of Jesus.
86. Jesus has tasted death for my children to stay alive, in the name of Jesus.
87. I insure the lives of my children with the blood of Jesus.
88. I thwart all the decisions and plans of the enemy against my children, in the name of Jesus.
89. Oh Lord, shield my children against evil attacks, in the name of Jesus.
90. I envelope my children with divine covering, in the name of Jesus.
91. I withdraw the name of my children from the book of death, in the name of Jesus.
92. Father, protect my children from any kidnappers targeting them, in the name of Jesus.
93. Father, let Your fire consume every kidnapper targeting my children, in the name of Jesus.
94. I withdraw the names of my children from the book of kidnappers, in the name of Jesus.
95. Every evil gang-up against my children, scatter unto desolation, in the name of Jesus.
96. Oh Lord, deliver my children from the paw of the lion, in the name of Jesus.
97. My children, you will not answer the call of death, in the name of Jesus.

98. I insure the name of my children with the blood of Jesus.

99. *(Mention the name of your children and say:)* You will not go to the grave before me, in the name of Jesus.

100. Thou demon sending children to early grave, you will not locate any of my children, in the name of Jesus.

101. Father, deliver my children from any sickness that may want to claim their lives, in the name of Jesus.

102. Any portion in the body of my children infected with diseases, be cleansed by the blood of Jesus.

103. Every witch/wizard that wants to terminate the lives of my children, be roasted, in the name of Jesus.

104. Every harassment in the dream of my children, I stop you by fire, in the name of Jesus.

105. Every nightmare aimed at terminating the lives of my children, backfire, in the name of Jesus.

106. Arrows of untimely death fired into the lives of my children, backfire, in the name of Jesus.

107. Evil coffins, constituted for any of my children, burry your maker, in the name of Jesus.

108. Arrows of slow death fired into the body of my children, be removed by the blood of Jesus.

109. Power of the grave, I render you impotent in the lives of my children, in the name of Jesus.

110. Any poison eaten by my children, be neutralised by the blood of Jesus.

111. Any sickness planted into the body of my children while sleeping, be flushed out by the blood of Jesus.

112. Every enemy from my father's/mother's home that wants to kill my children, kill yourself now, in the name of Jesus.

113. Holy Ghost fire, make the lives of my children untochable, in the name of Jesus.

114. My children's names, be incubated by fire, in the name of Jesus.

115. Any power that does not want me to enjoy my children at old age, die, in the name of Jesus.

116. I will not bury any of my children, in the name of Jesus.

117. Father, elongate the lives of my children, in the name of Jesus.

118. Oh Lord, swallow up death for the victory of my children, in the name of Jesus.

1190. Power of rapid death, I transform you to rapid blessing for my children, in the name of Jesus.

120. Every incantation against my children, be converted to blessings, in the name of Jesus.

121. Father, deliver my children from the slaughter's slab, in the name of Jesus.

122. No secret cult will terminate the life of any of my children, in the name of Jesus.

123. Every witch that wants to suck the blood of my children, suck your own blood, in the name of Jesus.

124. My children, you are anointed for the top, in the name of Jesus.

125. Oh death, my children are not your candidates, in the name of Jesus.

126. Angels of elevation, locate my children, in the name of Jesus.

127. My children, you will not walk in the path of destruction, in the name of Jesus.

128. Collective death, my children will not partake you, in the name of Jesus.

129. My children, you shall live to see your children's children, in the name of Jesus.

130. My children, you are alive to fulfil divine agenda, in the name of Jesus.

131. Begin to thank God for answers to your prayers.

CHAPTER SEVEN

POWER AGAINST BATTLE EXTENDERS

POWER AGAINST BATTLE EXTENDERS

7

One of the strategies of the devil is to stretch battles until the fighter becomes weary. He devil knows that a lot of people give up too soon and would easily quit when it appears as if the time spent on the field of battle has got too long. The story of the children of Israel highlights the peril of discouragement, especially when weariness is brought in. The devil knows that the shorter the period of a battle. the greater your chances of winning. So, he stretches the time of conflict until you begin to get tired. When battles are prolonged, weariness will capture the heart of some victims. Other battles will set in and stubborn principalities will take change. You must deal decisively with any power that has vowed that your battle will not cease. You must pray fervently that any powers dribbling you on the field of battle must be paralysed.

You need to pray seriously if you notice the following:

1. Masquerading battles.
2. Battles that present the same manifestation.

3. Battles that trigger negative internal mechanisms within you.
4. The presence of the same pattern of ancestral problems.
5. Unexplainable provocation.
6. Chronic doubts.
7. Acute prayerlessness.
8. Mysterious apathy.
9. Acute immorality.
10. Curses being rained from every direction.
11. Being under the spell of mysterious foolishness.
12. Incomplete deliverance.
13. Laziness in the place of prayer.
14. Making personal efforts to prolong your battles without being aware that you are responding to a remote control antic.

There is always a sinister motive behind the extension of any battle by the devil. It is your responsibility to squash any attempt at extending your battles.

PRAYER SECTION

Scripture Reading: Numbers 13:23-33

Of the tribe of Asher, Sethur the son of Michael. Of the tribe of Naphtali, Nahbi the son of Vophsi. Of the tribe of Gad, Geuel the son of Machi. These are the names of the men which Moses sent to spy out the land. And Moses called Oshea the son of Nun Jehoshua. And Moses sent them to spy out the land of Canaan, and said unto them, Get you up this way southward, and go up into the mountain: And see the land, what it is; and the people that dwelleth therein, whether they be strong or weak, few or many; And what the land is that they dwell in, whether it be good or bad; and what cities they be that they dwell in, whether in tents, or in strong holds; And what the land is, whether it be fat or lean, whether there be wood therein, or not. And be ye of good courage, and bring of the fruit of the land. Now the time was the time of the firstripe grapes. So they went up, and searched the land from the wilderness of Zin unto Rehob, as men come to Hamath. And they ascended by the south, and came unto Hebron; where Ahiman, Sheshai, and Talmai, the children of Anak, were. (Now Hebron was built seven years before Zoan in Egypt.) And they came unto the brook of Eshcol, and cut down from thence a branch with one cluster of grapes, and they bare it between two upon a staff; and they brought of the pomegranates, and of the figs. The place was called the brook Eshcol, because of the cluster of grapes which the children of Israel cut down from thence. And they returned from searching of the land after forty days. And they went and came to Moses, and to Aaron, and to all the congregation of the children of Israel, unto the wilderness of Paran, to Kadesh; and brought back word unto them, and unto all the congregation, and shewed them the fruit of the land. And they told him, and said, We came unto the land whither thou sentest us, and surely it floweth with milk and honey; and this is the fruit of it. Nevertheless the people be strong that dwell in the land, and the cities are walled, and very great: and moreover we saw the children of Anak there. The Amalekites dwell in the land of the south: and the Hittites, and the Jebusites, and the Amorites, dwell in the mountains: and the Canaanites dwell by the sea, and by the coast of Jordan. And Caleb stilled the people before Moses, and said, Let us go up at once, and possess it; for we are well able to overcome it. But the men that went up with him said, We be not able to go up against the people; for they are stronger than we. And they brought up an evil report of the land which they had searched unto the children of Israel, saying, The land, through which we have gone to search it, is a land that eateth up the inhabitants thereof; and all the people that we saw in it are men of a great stature. And there we saw the giants, the sons of Anak, which come of the giants: and we were in our own sight as grasshoppers, and so we were in their sight.

PRAISE WORSHIP

1. Thanksgiving.
2. I receive aggressive reinforcement from the third heaven after the order of Daniel, in the name of Jesus.
3. Every Cain in my family line, you will not sacrifice me, in the name of Jesus.
4. Every witchcraft arrow from my ancestors, die, in the name of Jesus.
5. Arrows in the hand of household strongman, backfire, in the name of Jesus.
6. The enemy that came while I slept, die, in the name of Jesus.
7. Let my breakthroughs confuse my enemies, in the name of Jesus.
8. All evil rivers mocking my efforts, dry up, in the name of Jesus.
9. I set ablaze every satanic record about my life, in the name of Jesus.
10. Every house of shame constructed against me, scatter, in the name of Jesus.
11. Oh God, arise and send Your angels to go and perfect all that concerns my life, in the name of Jesus.
12. Every obstacle to my prayers, clear away, in the name of Jesus.
13. Every arrow of discouragement at the edge of my breakthroughs, die, in the name of Jesus.
14. Let my battles expire and let my tears cease, in the name of Jesus.
15. Every power that says my battle will not end, you are a liar, die, in the name of Jesus.
16. Every power that says I shall fight to the grave, you are a liar, die, in the name of Jesus.
17. Every evil arrow from satanic covens, backfire, in the name of Jesus.

18. Every 'Red Sea' on my way to prolong my battles, hear the word of the Lord, give way now, in the name of Jesus.
19. I will not end my life in shame, in the name of Jesus.
20. With fire from above, let satanic gates blocking my blessings roast, in the name of Jesus.
21. Host of heaven, arise, fight for me, in the name of Jesus.
22. Every power dragging my progress in the ground, die, in the name of Jesus.
23. Thunder of heaven, rage against every power planning my disgrace, in the name of Jesus.
24. Every power locking up my glory, die, in the name of Jesus.
25. My way, open, in the name of Jesus.
26. My virtues in the waters, come forth, in the name of Jesus.
27. My virtues under the earth, come forth, in the name of Jesus.
28. All the efforts of the enemies in my breakthroughs, be wasted, in the name of Jesus.

CHAPTER EIGHT

BREAKING THE DARK MYSTERY OVER YOUR LIFE

BREAKING THE DARK MYSTERY OVER YOUR LIFE

8

There are mysteries in life. Problems that the human eye cannot see abound. There are deep mysteries that academic professors can never understand. Life is a mystery. Many situations are complex. It is indeed true that some communities can be regarded as habitations of cruelty

Psalms 74:20 says:

> *Have respect unto the covenant: for the dark places of the earth are full of the habitations of cruelty.*

If you have listened to mysterious stories told by people, you will discover that the sky has been invaded by dark powers. You will also come to terms with the fact that certain ugly powers roam our beautiful cities. Dark creatures are here and there.

If you survey what is happening in the present world you will realise that we are confronted by a satanic abracadabra. Beloved, unless you are aided by the Almighty, the more you look, the less you will see. If you allow God to open the eyes of your understanding, you will be scared and shocked to your marrows. The mystery of darkness is at work. Wicked powers have turned a lot of things upside down. Beloved, the enemy is wickedly wicked and badly bad. An evil cloud is hanging over this generation. Many seas and rivers have been poisoned. The air which we breathe has been polluted. The food sold in the markets has been contaminated by dark powers.

There is an evil invasion over our calendar. Our leaders have been captured by the spirits of error. There are unseen evil altars in several homes. The divine wind of blessing has been halted by demonic umbrellas. The rain of blessing has been barricaded from falling by wicked mysterious powers. The only way you can come out from the evil umbrella is to fight and break dark mysteries over your life. You must halt every evil programme and put an end to the satanic agenda being unfolded against your destiny.

This prayer programme will alter the course of your journey and change your destiny for good. You need these prayer points if you have discovered that you are aiming at the wrong destination. You need these prayers if you are being controlled mysteriously. You need to pray like a wounded lion. Then if you actually want the powers behind dark mysteries to be subjected to a divine summersault that will put them out of circulation. This is a do or die battle. It is a battle you must fight and win.

Isaiah 9:6 says:

> *For unto us a child is born, unto us a son is given: and the government shall be upon his shoulder: and his name shall be called Wonderful, Counsellor, The mighty God, The everlasting Father, The Prince of Peace.*

PRAYER POINTS

Confession: **Psalm 74:20:** *Have respect unto the covenant: for the* *dark places of the earth are full of the habitations of cruelty.*

PRAISE WORSHIP

1. Every power that has formed an evil cloud over my head, scatter, in the name of Jesus.
2. Every wall of partitioning between me and my breakthroughs, break, in the name of Jesus.
3. Every evil mystery over my life, be destroyed, in the name of Jesus.
4. I resist the threat of death in my dream, in the name of Jesus.
5. Every evil dream that other people have had about me, I cancel it in the astral world, in the name of Jesus.
6. In the quietness of my spirit, oh Lord, open the gates of heaven, in the name of Jesus.
7. Oh Lord, open the gates of righteousness and put me inside, in the name of Jesus.
8. The poisons of the waters shall not affect me, in the name of Jesus.
9. Any evil wound that I carry, fall off my body, in the name of Jesus.
10. Oh flesh, I command the infirmity within you to break off, in the name of Jesus.
11. Every altar giving sickness its life, be broken, in the name of Jesus.
12. Let this month be my open door, in the name of Jesus.
13. Let my business bring forth honour, in the name of Jesus.
14. I shall not be numbered amongst the wasted, in the name of Jesus.
15. Oh Lord, defend my portion, in the name of Jesus.
16. Oh Lord, open up the environment for me, in the name of Jesus.
17. Every evil around me, break, in the name of Jesus.
18. I destroy the sharpened edge of the enemy, in the name of Jesus.

19. Every power drawing power from the heavens against me, die, in the name of Jesus.
20. I break every covenant with the sun, in the name of Jesus.
21. Whatever will make the sun to smite me by day, die, in the name of Jesus.
22. Let today be a strategic day in my life, in the name of Jesus.
23. Oh Lord, in situations in my life, I want to manifest the thunder of Your power, in the name of Jesus.
24. Oh Lord, make me the rod of Your power, in the name of Jesus.
25. Oh Lord, give my enemies a cup of trembling to drink, in the name of Jesus.
26. Oh Lord, give unto my enemies a cup of confusion to drink, in the name of Jesus.
27. Let the same Spirit that raised Jesus from the dead break my yokes now, in the name of Jesus.

Every destiny-paralysing power fashioned against my destiny, fall down and die, in the name of Jesus.

28. Let the rivers inside of me come alive, in the name of Jesus.
29. Let my dread be upon the earth, in the name of Jesus.
30. I command stubborn problems in my life to wither, in the name of Jesus.
31. Let heaven begin to defend me, in the name of Jesus.
32. Oh Lord, pour Your oil into my life and heal my roots, in the name of Jesus.
33. Oh Lord, hold back tomorrow from obstructing me, in the name of Jesus.
34. Oh Lord, set Your watch afresh over my life, in the name of Jesus.

35. Holy Ghost fire, challenge every stranger in my life, in the name of Jesus.
36. I release earthquake against my full-time enemies, in the name of Jesus.
37. Let God spit fire into the camp of my enemy today, in the name of Jesus.
38. Anything glorifying satan in my life, fall down and die, in the name of Jesus.
39. I rebuke every evil linkage with my life with any evil, in the name of Jesus.
40. I remove the portion of the serpent from my own life, in the name of Jesus.
41. Oh God, arise and let evil altars scatter, in the name of Jesus.
42. Whether the world goes up or down, my harvest shall continue, I shall prosper, in the name of Jesus.
43. Any power affecting the testimony of the Lord in my life, fall down and die, in the name of Jesus.
44. Time, you have no right to hurt me, in the name of Jesus.
45. Every strange imagination against me, I nullify you, in the name of Jesus.

CHAPTER NINE

DEALING WITH SATANIC ROBBERS

DEALING WITH
SATANIC ROBBERS
9

Just as there are robbers and thieves in the physical realm, there are robbers in the spiritual realm. Jesus declared categorically that the enemy has come to steal. Satan and his agents are ready to steal precious items and destinies at any given opportunity. Wherever satanic robbers find things of value, they go for robbery. Satanic robbers are more wicked than physical robbers.

The enemy who steals your books is a wicked enemy. But the enemy who steals your brain is an embodiment of wickedness. The enemy who steals your mattress is a bad one, but the enemy who steals your sleep is the most wicked enemy you can ever come across. The robber who steals your certificate is wicked, but the spiritual robber who steals your success is the greatest of all robbers.

The enemy who steals your clothes has an evil intention, but the one who robs you of your glory is the worst robber you can ever imagine. The enemy who steals your money is a bad enemy but the enemy who steals your means of getting money is a satanic robber indeed. The enemy who steals instruments which you use to carry out your projects is a common thief. But the enemy who steals your idea and your entire concept is a robber from the pit of hell.

The enemy who steals your car will surely prevent you from moving around, but the robber who steals your progress is the greatest robber of all. The thief who comes to your house to pack all your belongings is heartless. But, the thief who steals your virtue is a wicked satanic robber. The thief who breaks into your house and carts away all your musical instruments is a bad thief. But the thief who steals your joy and your ability to sing a new song is the most wicked robber you can ever imagine.

The thief who aims at physical things is not your friend at all. But the thief who steals your destiny is a satanic robber of monumental dimensions. You must therefore hate satanic robbers with perfect hatred. You must deal with satanic robbers and keep them out of business. If you want to enjoy your life and fulfill your destiny, you must locate satanic robbers and barricade your spiritual properties with the fire of the Holy Ghost. You must not suffer any satanic robber to live. The thief must be located, caught, punished and forced to vomit what he has eaten and restore what he has stolen. You must recover your stolen virtue and redeem what the enemy has captured. If you have to lose your voice while saying these prayer points, go ahead. This is your season of recovery. Make as many arrests as possible.

PRAYER SECTION

Confession: Psalm 91

Praise Worship

1.   Father, in the name of Jesus, I thank You for You are the

provider of good things in life.

2. I thank You for all You have given to me in this life, in the name of Jesus.

3. In the name of the Father, of the Son and of the Holy Spirit, I dedicate my life and all that belong to me to God, in the name of Jesus.

4. Father, let Your power keep the invasion of the enemy away from me, in the name of Jesus.

5. Let the power of God arise to deliver me and all that belong to me from the hands of the oppressors, in the name of Jesus.

6. Let the paths of the robbers assigned against my life be dark and slippery, in the name of Jesus.

7. All counsels to steal from me or rob me of my blessings, shall fail, in the name of Jesus.

8. Every sorrow assigned my portion, die, in the name of Jesus.

9. Every door opened to spiritual robbers in my life, be shut by fire, in the name of Jesus.

10. Any conscious or unconscious link between my life and any demon, be cut off by the blood of Jesus.

11. Any evil consequences of my father's house, appearing as spiritual robbery in my life, die, in the name of Jesus.

12. Every handwriting of theft and robbery on my forehead, be wiped out by the power in the blood of Jesus.

13. Every blood avenger of the past, be silenced by the blood of Jesus.

14. Let the craftiness of the wicked against my life be disappointed, in the name of Jesus.

15. The strongman of spiritual robbers assigned against my life, fall down and die, in the name of Jesus.

16. Let the finger of God be lifted up against every heart of stone assigned against me and my possessions, in the name of Jesus.

17. Let the wrath of God scatter the strong room of spiritual robbers assigned against my life, in the name of Jesus.

18. Let the sword of the Lord quench the uprising of losses and sorrow in my life, in the name of Jesus.

19. Let the powers sponsoring evil in life receive the judgement of fire of God, in the name of Jesus.

20. All satanic imagination aimed at stealing from me, die, in the name of Jesus.

21. Let all wicked imaginations against my life vanish into the air, in the name of Jesus.

22. All satanic imaginations against my destiny, backfire, in the name of Jesus.

23. By the power in the blood of Jesus, I cast down all thoughts of wickedness to steal and destroy my inheritance, in the name of Jesus.

24. All satanic counsels put together to rob me of my honour, scatter, in the name of Jesus.

25. All thoughts that desire my captivity, go into captivity, in the name of Jesus.

26. Let confusion of thoughts baptize the camp of my enemies, in the name of Jesus.

27. Any evil word spoken to destroy my inheritance, fall down and die, in the name of Jesus.

28. All enchantments put together for my downfall, scatter, in the name of Jesus.

29. Every evil dream assigned to rob me of my covenant rights, die, in the name of Jesus.

30. Let the gathering of thieves and robbers assigned against me be wasted, in the name of Jesus.

31. You strong wind from the presence of God, arise and waste the wasters assigned against my inheritance, in the name of Jesus.

32. Every rage of theft and robbery rising up against my life, be still, in the name of Jesus.

33. Let the camp of spiritual robbers be visited with thunder and storm, in the name of Jesus.

34. Wherever spiritual robbers are gathered against me, oh

God, arise and set them against themselves, in the name of Jesus.

35. Let the killers of inheritance assigned against my life begin to hear strange voices to destroy themselves, in the name of Jesus.

36. Let God arise and let His voice thunder to destroy my oppressors, in the name of Jesus.

37. I refuse to become the captive of the mighty, in the name of Jesus.

38. I receive power from on high to overcome all siege of the enemy, in the name of Jesus.

39. Let all evils within and around me begin to bow to me by fire, in the name of Jesus.

40. Let the knees of spiritual thieves bow to the name of Jesus in my life, in the name of Jesus.

41. Let the fire of God dislodge the community gatekeepers that open doors to thieves and robbers in my life, in the name of Jesus.

42. Let territorial gatekeepers be driven away from my territory by the blood of Jesus.

43. Let the blood of Jesus be invoked on my inheritance and let no one be able to desire my portions in the name of Jesus.

44. By the blood of Jesus, I reclaim all my lost grounds in possessions, priviledges and finances, in Jesus' name.

45. I decree a seven-fold restoration of all that has been stolen from me, in the name of Jesus.

46. Any power that has swallowed my inheritance, vomit it by fire, in the name of Jesus.

47. By the blood of Jesus, no spiritual robbers shall invade my life again, in the name of Jesus.

48. My life and goods are preserved by the blood of Jesus, in the name of Jesus.

49. Let sorrow and tears be wiped out of my inheritance, in the name of Jesus.

50. Let my land begin to experience rest, peace and joy, in the name of Jesus.

51. By the blood of Jesus, let my land be healed from sicknesses and diseases, in the name of Jesus.

52. Let death visit eaters of good things in my life, in the name of Jesus.

53. Any evil tongue arising against my increase, be cut off, in the name of Jesus.

54. I use the blood of Jesus to redeem by days, in the name of Jesus.

55. I use the blood of Jesus to redeem my nights from destruction that walks at night, in the name of Jesus.

56. Let the earth begin to yield its increase unto me, in the name of Jesus.

57. Let me receive divine wisdom to overcome the craftiness of destroyers, in the name of Jesus.

58. Let the fire of God surround my life and property, in the name of Jesus.

59. Sudden destruction will not locate my habitation, in the name of Jesus.

60. All conscious and unconscious appointments with thieves and robbers, die, in the name of Jesus.

61. I shall not walk into destruction, in the name of Jesus.

62. Oh Lord, let Your angels in legions preserve me and my properties, in the name of Jesus.

63. Let the thunder of God scatter any gathering aimed at stealing God's possession in my life, in Jesus' name.

64. Every counsel of the spirit of Ahitophel against my life and possessions, die, in the name of Jesus.

65. Gates and doors of robbery instituted against my possessions, be closed by the blood of Jesus.

66. Any power assigned to trouble the peace of my life, fall down and die, in the name of Jesus.

67. Any evil conspiracy against my inheritance, scatter, in the name of Jesus.

68. I shall not die, the number of the days of my life shall be fulfilled, in the name of Jesus.

69. Oh God, arise and promote Your glory in my life, in the name of Jesus.
70. Begin to thank God for answers to your prayers.

PRAYER SECTION

Confession: **Proverbs 4:18:** *But the path of the just is as the shining light, that shineth more and more unto the perfect day.*

PRAISE WORSHIP

1. Any power hindering the free flow of the power of God in my life, loose your hold and die,, in the name of Jesus.
2. Oh God, arise and let my adversaries be clothed with shame and disgrace, in the name of Jesus.
3. Every generational bondage blocking the light of my glory break by the power in the blood of Jesus.
4. Every evil wind assigned to be blowing favour away from me scatter and die, in the name of Jesus.
5. Every evil power assigned to be blowing blessings away from me, die, in the name of Jesus.
6. Every ancient evil gate shutting favour away from me, crash into pieces, in the name of Jesus.
7. Every evil wind blowing my opportunity away, hear the word of the Lord: Enough is enough, die, in Jesus' name.
8. Every evil chain limiting my moving forward, break into pieces, in the name of Jesus.
9. Every witchcraft manipulation of my star, die, in the name of Jesus.
10. Let the fire of God destroy any evil deposit in any part of my body, in the name of Jesus.
11. Powers assigned to be cutting short my blessings, your time is up. Die, in the name of Jesus.
12. Every strongman of my father's house assigned against good opportunities in my life, receive confusion and let me go, in the name of Jesus.

13. Every evil power fragmenting my blessings, scatter and die, in the name of Jesus.

14. Any evil act carried out on the day of my naming ceremony that is now affecting the star of my life, be reversed and die, in the name of Jesus.

15. You destroyers of opportunities, my life is not your candidate, die, in the name of Jesus.

16. Oh God, arise and let my name be too hot for the enemy to handle, in the name of Jesus.

17. Every spirit of Herod assigned against my blessings, fall down and die, in the name of Jesus.

18. I charge my blessings with the fire of the Holy Ghost; they are untouchable for the enemy, in the name of Jesus.

19. By the power in the blood of Jesus, I shall not miss good opportunities, in the name of Jesus.

Every destiny-paralysing power fashioned against my destiny, fall down and die, in the name of Jesus.

20. Any evil attached to my name against my blessings, be cut off and die, in the name of Jesus.

21. Let my name become poison in the mouth of my enemies, in the name of Jesus.

22. Anything attached to my name scarring opportunities away from me, die, in the name of Jesus.

23. Let the mentioning of my name bring favour into my life, in the name of Jesus.

24. My name, hear the word of the Lord: You will no longer scar opportunities away from me, in Jesus' name.

25. Every evil lot assigned against my blessings, die, in the name of Jesus.

26. Blood of Jesus, begin to speak favour into my life, in the

name of Jesus.

27. Every mountain blocking the paths to my promised land, clear away by fire, in the name of Jesus.
28. My hands shall not pull down my glory, in the name of Jesus.
29. After the order of the tomb of Jesus, let every evil stone on the road to my breakthroughs be rolled away, in the name of Jesus.
30. Good opportunities that have ever passed my life, reappear by fire, in the name of Jesus.
31. All opportunities coming to me shall become wells of blessings, in the name of Jesus.
32. My labour shall not bring sorrow into my life, in the name of Jesus.
33. Every evil associated with the labours of my hand, your time is up, be cut off by fire, in the name of Jesus.
34. Any evil wind on assignment against my blessings, go back to your senders, in the name of Jesus.
35. I command peace upon all stormy issues in my life, in the name of Jesus.
36. By the blood of Jesus, I secure all my goodly portions in Christ Jesus.
37. Let the hedge of fire and the hedge of the blood of Jesus be built round me and all that belongs to me, in the name of Jesus.
38. I soak my opportunities in the pool of the blood of Jesus.
39. Every wall of Jericho around my opportunities, crumble, in the name of Jesus.
30. Henceforth, no power shall abort my opportunities, for I bear in my body the mark of the Lord Jesus Christ.

CHAPTER TEN

DEALING WITH
THE ABORTION
OF OPPORTUNITIES

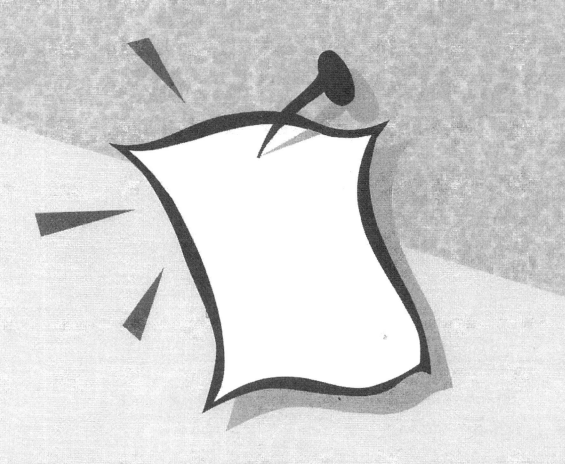

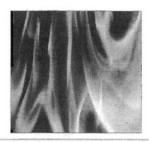

DEALING WITH
THE ABORTION
OF OPPORTUNITIES
10

A single opportunity can change your situation. The loss of one opportunity can make you miserable for life. The abortion of opportunities is unpleasant. Every power that is trying to abort good opportunities in your life must be dealt with. The devil operates through demonic spies. Powers of darkness know the difference that opportunities can make. Hence, demonic agents are busy working vigorously towards the abortion of opportunities.

This prayer programme is meant for:

1. Those who have discovered that good opportunities slip through their hands.
2. Those who have gained nothing from their best opportunities.
3. Those who have discovered that certain powers are busy scattering their opportunities.
4. Men and women who have witnessed the frittering away of golden opportunities.

5. When you know that there are wicked powers swallowing opportunities.
6. Those who have been given wonderful promises but no fulfillment of anyone.
7. Those who have been in the condors of power but unable to harness any gain.
8. Men and women who discover that the opportunities that have made their colleagues to prosper have made them to be worse off.
9. Those who have discovered that they are constantly missing good opportunities.
10. When you discover that opportunities are withdrawn whenever it comes to your turn.
11. When you notice that ancient ancestral gates have been locked against members of your family.
12. When you notice that your family name constantly withdraws good opportunities from you.
13. When you notice that each time you are about to benefit from your opportunity some powers provoke you and consequently disqualify you.
14. When your portion is taken and given to another person.
15. When there are stumbling blocks between you and your opportunities.
16. When you discover that no opportunity has ever benefited you.
17. When you sense opportunity famine.
18. When you are kept far away from the land of your opportunities.
19. When you are suddenly deleted from the list of those who are supposed to benefit from a particular opportunity.
20. When your opportunities are swallowed by the power of the emptiers

You need to pray fervently against the power that aborts opportunities. The prayer points will change your situation.

BINDING THE STRONGMAN

The strongman can be likened to a brigade commander in change of a large number of evil spiritual solders. He stands for the principality in change of a territory and is the demonic personality who takes charge of a particular situation. He is generally armed to take control of a particular situation. To deal with him you must know what you are doing.

Fighting against the strongman is no child's play. When any battle gets to his level the warrior has a serious battle in his hands. The conditions of several people have proved stubborn simply because a strongman is in charge. The weapon needed to fight him is a serious one. When you are fighting him you shouldn't expect the battle to be over in a split second. When the enemy has taken your cease to the table of the strongman, you must be prepared to fight until the strongman is defeated and victory is yours.

This particular prayer programme is a result-oriented one. There are seven prayer segments that can run for seven days. It is not a programme you can pursue half-way. The Holy Ghost has meticulously addressed every area of the prayer to give you decisive victory over the strongman who is an experienced war monger. You cannot go to his territory with toy guns, when he is armed to the teeth with sophisticated machines. Binding the strongman is not a joke, it is not what can be done by prayerless folks. To bind him is to get to the height of warfare. You must be fully prepared as you commence this prayer programme. You must pray with holy aggression. If you take this prayer programme to the end, the victory you will obtain will amaze you. Take note of the dreams and revelations, God will give you after each prayer session.

This is one of the greatest prayer programmes you can handle. Each prayer point will give birth to fantastic testimonies. Go

Dr. D. K. Olukoya

through the prayer points meant for each day without omitting anyone.

 PRAYER SECTION

Confession: (Matthew 12:29) Or else how can one enter into a strong man's house, and spoil his goods, except he first bind the strong man? and then he will spoil his house.

PRAISE WORSHIP

 DAY 1

1. I take authority over and order the binding of every strongman in every department of my life. I bind and paralyse every strongman attached to any specific problem that I have, in the name of Jesus.
2. I withdraw and take back all my properties in the possession of the strongman, in the name of Jesus
3. I bind and paralyse every strongman of death and hell, in Jesus' name.
4. I receive the mandate to release my children from the prison of any strongman, in the name of Jesus.
5. I release myself from the hold of any sexual strongman, in the name of Jesus.
6. You the strongman of my ancestors, release my blessings in your hands, in the name of Jesus
7. I take authority over and bind the strongman attached to my marriage, in the name of Jesus.
8. I bind every strongman from my father's and mother's sides attached to my marital life, in the name of Jesus.
9. I bind and paralyse every strongman of fear in my life, in the mighty name of Jesus
10. I take authority over and order the binding of the strongman of financial failure.
11. I bind every strongman holding my privileges and rights captive, in Jesus' name.

12. I bind, plunder and render to naught every strongman assigned to my marital life in Jesus' name.
13. Let all multiple strongman operating against me be paralysed, in Jesus' name.
14. I bind the strongman attached to the life of . . . *(mention the name of the person)*, from keeping him/her from receiving Jesus Christ as his/her Lord and Saviour, in the name of Jesus.
15. I release myself from the hold of any evil strongman, in the name of Jesus.
16. I disgrace the strongman delegated by satan over my life, in the name of Jesus
17. You strongman of evil imagination paralysing the good things in my life, be paralysed, in the name of Jesus.
18. All the good thoughts that the strongman has paralysed in my life, receive life and be restored into my life, in the name of Jesus
19. I bind, plunder and render to naught every strongman assigned to my womb, reproductive system and marital life, in Jesus' name.
20. I bind the strongman behind my spiritual blindness and deafness and paralyse his operations in my life, in Jesus' name.
21. Let the stubborn strongman delegated against me fall down to the ground and become impotent, in the name of Jesus.
22. I bind the strongman over my life, in the name of Jesus.
23. I bind the strongman over my family, in the name of Jesus.
24. I bind the strongman over my blessings, in the name of Jesus.
25. I bind the strongman over my business, in the name of Jesus.
26. I bind and render useless every strongman assigned to my womb, reproductive system and marital life, in the name of Jesus.
27. I bind every strongman delegated to hinder my progress, in the name of Jesus

28. I bind and paralyse the strongman delegated to disgrace me, in the name of Jesus.
29. Let the backbone of the strongman in charge of each problem be broken, in the name of Jesus.
30. Let the stubborn strongman delegated against me and my career fall down to the ground and become impotent, in the name of Jesus.

DAY 2

1. Let the stubborn strongman delegated against me fall down to the ground and become impotent, in the name of Jesus.
2. Any satanic strongman keeping my blessings fall down and die, I recover my goods back now, in the name of Jesus.
3. You strongman of destiny destruction, loose your hold over my destiny, fall down and die.
4. You strongman of body destruction loose your hold over my body, fall down and die.
5. Every strongman and associated spirits of financial collapse, receive the hailstones of fire and be roasted beyond remedy, in Jesus' name.
6. Let the finger of God unseat my household strongman, in the name of Jesus.
7. I bind the strongman in my life and I clear my goods from fis possession, in the name of Jesus.
8. You strongman of body destruction, be bound, in Jesus' name.
9. You strongman of mind destruction, be bound, in Jesus' name.
10. You strongman of financial destruction, be bound, in Jesus' name.
11. Every strongman of bad luck attached to my life, fall down and die, in Jesus' name
12. I bind every strongman having my goods in his possessions, in the name of Jesus.
13. I bind and paralyse every strongman of death and hell, in

the name of Jesus.

14. You evil strongman attached to my destiny, be bound, in Jesus' name.

15. I paralyse every territorial strongman operating evil programme in......... hospital or clinic, in the name of Jesus.

16. I bind and plunder the goods of every strongman attached to my marriage, in the name of Jesus.

17. Let the stubborn strongman delegated against me and my career fall down to the ground and become impotent, in the name of Jesus.

18. Let the stubborn strongman delegated against me fall down to the ground and become impotent, in the name of Jesus.

19. I release my money from the house of the strongman, in the name of Jesus.

20. I bind every strongman delegated to hinder my progress, in the name of Jesus.

21. Every strongman of my father's house, die, in the name of Jesus.

22. Every strongman assigned by the evil powers of my father's house against my life, die, in the name of Jesus.

23. I command the shrine of the strongman in my family to be consumed with the fire of God, in the name of Jesus.

24. You strongman from my father's side, you strongman from my mother's side, begin to destroy yourselves, in the name of Jesus

25. You strongman of body destruction, loose your hold over my body, fall down and die, in the name of Jesus.

26. Every strongman and associated spirits of financial collapse, receive the hailstones of fire and be roasted beyond remedy, in Jesus' name.

27. Let the finger of God unseat my household strongman, in the name of Jesus.

28. I bind the strongman in my life and I clear my goods from his possession, in the name of Jesus.

29. You strongman of mind destruction, be bound, in Jesus' name.

30. You strongman of financial destruction, be bound, in Jesus' name.

DAY 3

1. Every strongman of bad luck attached to my life, fall down and die, in Jesus' name
2. I bind every strongman militating against my home, in the name of Jesus
3. I bind and paralyse every strongman of death and hell, in the name of Jesus
4. You evil strongman attached to my destiny, be bound, in Jesus' name
5. Every strongman of my father's house, die, in the name of Jesus
6. Every strongman assigned by the evil powers of my father's house against my life, die, in the name of Jesus
7. Every strongman assigned to weaken my faith, catch fire, in the name of Jesus
8. I bind and render to nothing all the strongmen that are currently troubling my life, in the name of Jesus.
9. Let the backbone of the stubborn pursuer and strongman break, in the name of Jesus.
10. I bind every strongman having my goods in his possessions, in the name of Jesus.
11. I clear my goods from the warehouse of the strongman, in the name of Jesus
12. I withdraw the staff of the office of the strongman delegated against me, in the name of Jesus
13. I bind every strongman delegated to hinder my progress, in the name of Jesus.
14. I bind the strongman behind my spiritual blindness and deafness and paralyse his operations in my life, in the name of Jesus.
15. Let the stubborn strongman delegated against me fall down to the ground and become impotent, in Jesus' name

16. I command the armour of the strongman to be roasted completely, in the name of Jesus.
17. I release myself from the hold of any religious spirit strongman, in the name of Jesus
18. Every power siting on my divine promotion, clear away, in the name of Jesus.
19. My glory, my head, arise and shine, in the name of Jesus.
20. Every strongman behind poison of darkness in my body, come out now, in the name of Jesus.
21. Let the altars of affliction of the strongman assigned against my life, catch fire, in the name of Jesus.
22. Every strongman behind stubborn problems in my life, die, in the name of Jesus.
23. Every power behind the strongman of persistent problems in my life, die, in the name of Jesus.
24. Every strongman behind yokes acquired in the dreams, die, in the name of Jesus.
25. Every strongman behind plantation of infirmity in my family, die, in the name of Jesus.
26. Every strongman behind mocking yokes in my life, die, in the name of Jesus.
27. Let the habitation of cruelty assigned against me by the strongman of my father's house die, in the name of Jesus.
28. Every strange garment put on my spiritual body by the strongman, catch fire, in the name of Jesus.
29. Angels of God, gather your arrows and attack every strongman attached to my destiny, in the name of Jesus.
30. Every witchcraft judgement against me, scatter, in the name of Jesus.

DAY 4

1. Demonic pillars supporting every strongman assigned to my life, crumble, in the name of Jesus.
2. I will not die before my glory appears, in the name of Jesus.
3. Let the power in the name of Jesus, the name that is higher

than all names, wipe out evil names of the strongman, in the name of Jesus.

4. Every witchcraft operation during my naming ceremony, die, in the name of Jesus.
5. I soak my name in the blood of Jesus.
6. I receive power to divide my Red Sea, in the name of Jesus.
7. After the order of Daniel, Oh Lord, deliver me from satanic lions, in the name of Jesus.
8. Thou altar of affliction, die, in the name of Jesus.
9. Power to be singled out for favour, fall upon me now, in the name of Jesus.
10. Every wicked conspiracy against my God-given dream, scatter, in the name of Jesus.
11. Every decision to slay me because of my dreams and visions, backfire, in the name of Jesus.
12. In the presence of those saying, 'We shall see what will become of his dreams,' the God of Joseph shall land me on the throne, in the name of Jesus.
13. You wicked conspirators, wait and see what shall become of my dreams. My God shall arise on my behalf, in the name of Jesus.
14. By the power that made the boasts of Joseph's brothers expire, O Lord, complete your work in my life, in the name of Jesus.
15. You enemies of progress breathing fire against the pregnancy of God for my life, expire, in the name of Jesus.
16. The dream of God for my life shall not be slaughtered. O God, arise and manifest my dreams in full, in the name of Jesus.
17. My cry, provoke angelic violence against any strongman assigned to my life, in the name of Jesus.
18. Every plantation of failure in my foundation, die, in the name of Jesus.
19. Foundational witchcraft yoke, break, in the name of Jesus.
20. Every negative power flowing from my foundation to kill my destiny, die, in the name of Jesus.

21. Every dog of witchcraft barking against me, die, in the name of Jesus.
22. Every altar of witchcraft, I tear you down, in the name of Jesus.
23. Every assembly of witchcraft working against me, scatter, in the name of Jesus.
24. Every seed of witchcraft in my life, die, in the name of Jesus.
25. Every dream sponsored by witchcraft, die, in the name of Jesus.
26. Every power troubling my star, die, in the name of Jesus.
27. I declare war on every enchantment, in the name of Jesus.
28. O confidence of the wicked, be broken, in the name of Jesus.
29. Every serpent and scorpion of affliction, die, in the name of Jesus.
30. Every wicked plantation in the garden of my life, die, in the name of Jesus.

DAY 5

1. Every evil association working against me, O Lord, thunder upon them, in the name of Jesus.
2. I go from strength to strength by the power in the blood of Jesus.
3. Every evil power summoning my spirit, die, in the name of Jesus.
4. Every root of witchcraft in my family line, die, in the name of Jesus.
5. Every communal bondage limiting my breakthroughs, die, in the name of Jesus.
6. Every spell and enchantment, clear off, in the name of Jesus.
7. Every evil malpractice over my family, be crushed, in the name of Jesus.
8. Every witchcraft marine power, be crushed to pieces, in the

name of Jesus.

9. Every witchcraft agenda in my life, be destroyed, in the name of Jesus.

10. Every power using my life as a dumping bin, scatter, in the name of Jesus.

11. Every resurrection of affliction, die, in the name of Jesus.

12. Every evil game plan over my success, die, in the name of Jesus.

13. Every manufacturer of yokes, die, in the name of Jesus.

14. Every pregnancy of sorrow and setbacks, die, in the name of Jesus.

15. Every demonic set up against me, scatter, in the name of Jesus.

16. Every satanic imprisonment over my life, break away, in the name of Jesus.

17. Every satanic remote control against me, catch fire, in the name of Jesus.

18. Every power sponsoring repeated problems in my life, die, in the name of Jesus.

19. Let the voice of destruction be heard in the camp of every oppressor, in the name of Jesus.

20. Every wicked spirit working against my family, loose your hold and die, in the name of Jesus.

21. Let every satanic manipulating altars and their attending priests scatter, in the name of Jesus.

22. Every satanic yoke in my life, break, in the name of Jesus.

23. Every evil load heaped on my progress, clear away, in the name of Jesus.

24. Every satanic prayer against my destiny, scatter, in the name of Jesus.

25. Every evil-hindering-force militating against me, scatter by fire, in the name of Jesus.

26. Every witchcraft padlock hanging against my life, be smashed to pieces, in the name of Jesus.

27. Every witchcraft engagement over my success, break, in the name of Jesus.

28. Every demonic claim on my life, break, in the name of Jesus.
29. Every power of stagnation and limitation over my life, be destroyed, in the name of Jesus.
30. Every tree of failure in my lineage, be cut off, in the name of Jesus.

DAY 6

1. Every pin-up of witchcraft in my family, be destroyed, in the name of Jesus.
2. Every evil covenant working against me, break, in the name of Jesus.
3. Every witchcraft agenda for my life, be frustrated, in the name of Jesus.
4. Every witchcraft register bearing my name, catch fire, in the name of Jesus.
5. Every evil document against my life, be consumed by fire, in the name of Jesus.
6. Every evil informant assigned against my life, fall down and die, in the name of Jesus.
7. Every evil image carved in my name, catch fire, in the name of Jesus.
8. Every witchcraft authority over my life, break, in the name of Jesus.
9. Every evil tree planted against my freedom, be uprooted, in the name of Jesus.
10. Every curse of limitation in my life, be destroyed by fire, in the name of Jesus.
11. Every satanic road block, clear off by fire, in the name of Jesus.
12. Every millipede concoction working against my life, die, in the name of Jesus.
13. Every Beelzebub web cast over my life, clear off, in the name of Jesus.
14. Every satanic prophecy against my destiny, be nullified, in

the name of Jesus.

15. Every witchcraft concourse against my life, be crushed to pieces, in the name of Jesus.

16. Every backbone of disfavour, break, in the name of Jesus.

17. I crush every witchcraft lion roaring against my favour, in the name of Jesus.

18. Every gate of evil delay, be broken, in the name of Jesus.

19. Every chain and shackle of limitation upon my life, break, in the name of Jesus.

20. Disappeared helpers, reappear to move my destiny forward, in the name of Jesus.

21. I stop my stoppers by fire, in the name of Jesus.

22. O God, arise and set my feet in a large room, in the name of Jesus.

23. Thou power of vain-labour, die, in the name of Jesus.

24. Every power wasting my efforts, die, in the name of Jesus.

25. Power of hard-labour assigned against my life, die, in the name of Jesus.

26. Anointing for turn-around breakthroughs, come upon my life, in the name of Jesus.

27. Thou mantle of divine accelerator, fall upon my life, in the name of Jesus.

28. O God, arise and confound the wicked, in the name of Jesus.

29. O God, arise and ordain terrifying noises against my oppressors, in the name of Jesus.

30. Power-base of witchcraft in my place of birth, die, in the name of Jesus.

31. Every witchcraft meeting summoned for my sake, scatter, in the name of Jesus.

DAY 7

1. Every agent of darkness peeping into the spiritual world against me, receive blindness, in the name of Jesus.

2. O God, arise and cut off every agent of darkness calling my

life into any cauldron, in the name of Jesus.

3. Thou power of God, locate and destroy every spiritual pot assigned against my life, in the name of Jesus.

4. Every astral projection against my life, I cut you off, in the name of Jesus.

5. O creation, arise in battle against every agent of darkness attached to my life, in the name of Jesus.

6. Foundational yokes, foundational bondage, break, in the name of Jesus.

7. Foundation of marital distress, break, in the name of Jesus.

8. Every embargo on my glory from the womb, die, in the name of Jesus.

9. By the power that drown Pharaoh, let my stubborn problems, die, in the name of Jesus.

10. By the power that disgraced Goliath, let my stubborn problems, die, in the name of Jesus.

11. Holy Ghost fire, arise, attack my mountain, in the name of Jesus.

12. Every witchcraft incantation against my destiny, die, in the name of Jesus.

13. Every trouble of the night, bow to the name of Jesus.

14. Angels of God, scatter all those plotting against my destiny, in the name of Jesus.

15. Every demonic dragon working against my life, die, in the name of Jesus.

16. Thou terror of the night, scatter before me, in the name of Jesus.

17. I have dominion over every satanic challenge, in the name of Jesus.

18. I confront every witchcraft challenge by the power of God, in the name of Jesus.

19. Thou oppressor and thy weapons, drown in your own Red Sea, in the name of Jesus.

20. I cancel every weapon of discouragement, in the name of Jesus.

21. Holy Ghost, arise and link me with those who will bless me, in the name of Jesus.
22. Fire of God, shatter blindness and darkness in my life, in the name of Jesus.
23. My body, refuse to cooperate with every arrow of darkness, in the name of Jesus.
24. Every witchcraft broom sweeping away my blessings, die, in the name of Jesus.
25. Every yoke manufacturer, die with your yoke, in the name of Jesus.
26. Every satanic investment in my life, be wasted, in the name of Jesus.
27. Let my life experience divine acceleration, in the name of Jesus.
28. Satanic agenda for my life, vanish, in the name of Jesus.
29. Every satanic pregnancy for my life, die, in the name of Jesus.

CHAPTER ELEVEN

KILLING GLORY KILLERS

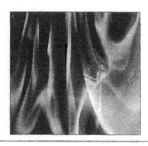

KILLING
GLORY KILLERS

11

Your God-given glory is your greatest asset. When you lose your glory you have lost your greatest possession. There are certain powers in the demonic kingdom whose goal is to locate, destroy and bury your glory. If you allow them powers to carry out their activities unhindered, they will swallow your glory completely and leave your life empty.

The nature of your glory:

1. Your glory is your strength.
2. It is your virtue.
3. It is your uniqueness.
4. It is what makes you outstanding.
5. It is what distinguishes you from the crowd.
6. It is your value.
7. It is the plus factor in your life.
8. It is the positive factor that makes you important wherever you find yourself.
9. It is the factor that makes you useful and indispensable.

10. It is the high point of your life.
11. It is your divine endowment.
12. It is the seed of your destiny.
13. It is what makes your relevant in your generation.
14. It is what marks you out among the masses.
15. It is the agent of your promotion.
16. It is what earns you reward among men.
17. It is what makes you someone who cannot be pushed aside.
18. It is what make your opinion counts.

The greatest thing you can do is to discover your glory and pray for its restoration. You must guard it jealously. You must not allow demonic agents to tamper with your glory. It is true that the devil goes about looking for any glory he can kill and bury, it is your duty to hinder glory killers to perform their enterprise.

You need these prayer points if you have ever discovered that some powers are attacking your glory. You must pray fervently if you have discovered that demonic agents are gradually turning your glory to shame. The moment you identify glory killers, there are certain weapons, you must make use of.

What you must do:

1. Recognise the activities of glory killers.
2. Identify the powers behind attacks on your glory.
3. Decide to kill them before they kill your glory.
4. Make use of the weapon of aggression.
5. You must deal with all categories of glory killers.
6. You must destroy their weapons.
7. Command them to restore what they have stolen from you.
8. Be filled with the Holy Spirit.
9. Be merciless when dealing with glory killers.
10. Let your faith be strong.
11. Make use of the weapon of praises.

PRAYER SECTIONS

Confession: **Psalms 27:6** *And now shall mine head be lifted up above mine enemies round about me: therefore will I offer in his tabernacle sacrifices of joy; I will sing, yea, I will sing praises unto the LORD.*

PRAISE WORSHIP

1. Rage of blood drinkers of the night, die, in the name of Jesus.
2. Every opposition to my full-scale laughter, scatter, in the name of Jesus.
3. Goliath that stopped my parents, hear the word of the Lord: My life is not your candidate, in the name of Jesus.
4. Anti-destiny internal chains, break by fire, in the name of Jesus.
5. Power to rise above my enemies, fall upon me, in the name of Jesus.
6. Yoke of sluggish progress, break, in the name of Jesus.
7. Circle of trouble, break by fire, in the name of Jesus.
8. Fire of breakthroughs, burn in my destiny, in the name of Jesus.
9. My Father, open doors of uncommon results for me, in the name of Jesus.
10. My Father, move in my life to make me great, in the name of Jesus.
11. Oh God, arise and scatter all financial torments assigned against me, in the name of Jesus.
12. Oh heavens, open over my destiny, in the name of Jesus
13. The glory killer of my father's house, let me go, in the name of Jesus.
14. Earth, hear the word of the Lord, swallow every enchanter assigned against me, in the name of Jesus.
15. Crystal ball of the enemies, explode in their faces, in the name of Jesus.
16. Any power calling for my head before evil mirrors, die with

the mirror, in the name of Jesus.

17. Head of my father's house, go back to the Red Sea, in the name of Jesus.

18. Messengers of frustration, carry your message back to your sender, in the name of Jesus.

19. Messengers of affliction, release your affliction on your sender, in the name of Jesus.

20. Problems caused by enchantment, pack your load and go, in the name of Jesus.

21. Every chain limiting my favour, break, in the name of Jesus.

22. Infirmity, fall away from my life, in the name of Jesus.

23. Every bondage against my brain, break, in the name of Jesus.

24. I break the law of death over my life, in the name of Jesus.

25. Every consultation of sorcerers against me, scatter, in the name of Jesus.

26. Every power harbouring enchantment against me, die, in the name of Jesus.

27. Sun, moon and stars, vomit every enchantment against my life, in the name of Jesus.

28. Enchantment, you will not settle down in my life, in the name of Jesus.

29. Every magic poured on the ground to subdue my life, backfire, in the name of Jesus.

30. Every power that weakens my spiritual anointing, die, in the name of Jesus.

31. Masquerades assigned to sleep in my house, die, in the name of Jesus.

32. O sun, arise and smite every evil assigned against me, in the name of Jesus.

33. My Father, whatsoever You have not planted in my life, let it catch fire, in the name of Jesus.

34. My Father, appear in my situation by fire, in the name of Jesus.

35. Father Lord, my times are in Thine hand. Deliver me from the hand of the enemies and from those that persecute me,

in the name of Jesus.

36. Let my destiny be rescued from the hands of my enemies, in the name of Jesus.

37. Every wicked gadget assigned against my destiny, scatter, in the name of Jesus.

38. I remove my name from any demonic calendar, in the name of Jesus.

39. Whatsoever the enemy has programmed into the sun, the moon and the stars concerning my life, I command them to scatter, in the name of Jesus.

40. Every evil pronouncement in the sun, the moon and the stars against my destiny, scatter, in the name of Jesus.

41. Any evil incubated by the enemy into this year for my life, backfire, in the name of Jesus.

42. Any quota of disaster designed for me and my family this year, die, in the name of Jesus.

43. Any astral altar raised against my destiny, catch fire, in the name of Jesus.

CHAPTER TWELVE

SILENCING ENEMIES OF MY NEW SONGS

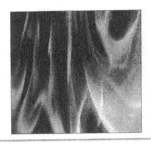

SILENCING ENEMIES OF MY NEW SONGS

12

There are powers that specialise in attacking testimonies. These powers hate to see you happy. Their major goal is to push you into the river of Babylon and make you to hang every instrument of music. Some powers are angry when you are about singing a new song. They will rather have you go through seasons of discouragement without any reason to sing a new song. Beloved, there are enemies who have vowed that there will be no sound of music or joy in your habitation. Such powers want you to get to the edge of your breakthroughs without smelling any blessing.

Enemies of your new song will do the following:

1. ....Push you into mistakes or errors that will erase your chances of singing a new song.
2. ....Trigger tragedies that will make you mourn.
3. ....Make you take God for granted.
4. ....Steal your faith.
5. ....Dim your hope.

6. ....Push you into frustration.
7. ....Throw you into a situation where you do not see any reason for singing a new song.

To deal with the satanic agenda you must cultivate the habit of singing new songs at all times. Make sure that sounds of music will not depart from your habitation, and the praise of the Almighty will not depart from your mouth. You must locate every enemy of your new song and command them to be busy with useless assignments. You must learn how to sing new songs from the depth of your heart at all times. You must learn how to sing in the spirit and sing with your own understanding. You must learn how to identify what the enemy is trying to do to hinder you from singing your song and dancing your dance. You need to pray that whatever will sentence you to mourning, murmuring and complaining should be consumed by the fire of the Holy Ghost. You need to learn how to make a joyful noise unto the Lord.

The following steps must be taken:

1. Silence the enemy of your new song before you are silenced.
2. Deal with every power that has been assigned to steal your song.
3. Deal with internal agents positioned secretly to prevent you from singing a new song and let the joy of the Lord be your strength.
4. Learn how to be happy at all times.
5. Keep the flag of your faith flying.
6. Launch a violent attack against powers that are bent on keeping you from singing your song of victory.
7. Pray until joy flows from your heart and a new song of victory from within.
8. Keep singing until the enemy flees.

PRAYER SECTION

Confession: **Psalms 2:** *Why do the heathen rage, and the people imagine a vain thing? The kings of the earth set themselves, and the rulers take counsel together, against the Lord, and against his anointed, saying, Let us break their bands asunder, and cast away their cords from us. He that sitteth in the heavens shall laugh: the Lord shall have them in derision. Then shall he speak unto them in his wrath, and vex them in his sore displeasure. Yet have I set my king upon my holy hill of Zion. I will declare the decree: the Lord hath said unto me, Thou art my Son; this day have I begotten thee. Ask of me, and I shall give thee the heathen for thine inheritance, and the uttermost parts of the earth for thy possession. Thou shalt break them with a rod of iron; thou shalt dash them in pieces like a potter's vessel. Be wise now therefore, O ye kings: be instructed, ye judges of the earth. Serve the Lord with fear, and rejoice with trembling. Kiss the Son, lest he be angry, and ye perish from the way, when his wrath is kindled but a little. Blessed are all they that put their trust in him.*

PRAISE WORSHIP

1. Thank God that you are alive and thank Him for the blessings of prayer.
2. Take authority over the piritual environment of where you are.
3. Blood of Jesus, wash away my iniquities right now, in the name of Jesus.
4. Let every obstacle blocking answers to my prayers be removed, in the name of Jesus.
5. I declare and proclaim that this is my year of new song, in the name of Jesus.
6. I command every Hamaan working against my new song and unexplained celebrations to hang and die, in the name of Jesus.
7. Every enemy, like Hamaan, of my destiny, you shall end your life in frustration, confusion and shame, in the name of Jesus.

8. Every ministry of Hamaan working against my greatness, expire on your own tree, in the name of Jesus.

9. I proclaim aloud that no weapon fashioned against me shall prosper, in the name of Jesus.

10. Every evil plan by unfriendly friends targeted against my destiny, scatter, in the name of Jesus.

11. The plans of witchcraft jealousy and envy of my father's house and of my mother's house, catch your senders, in the name of Jesus.

12. Evil powers of my father's house and of my mother's house on my life and ministry be broken, in the name of Jesus.

13. Every witchcraft plan assigned against my glory this year, scatter, in the name of Jesus.

14. You witchcraft hunters assigned against my star, fall down and die, in the name of Jesus.

Every destiny-paralysing power fashioned against my destiny, fall down and die, in the name of Jesus.

15. Every power assigned to drain my glory, be frustrated, in the name of Jesus.

16. Any gathering assigned to stop my new song this year, scatter, in the name of Jesus.

17. Every incantation, divination and evil shrine of my father's house, assigned against my life, die, in the name of Jesus.

18. Any power planning untimely death for me this year, die in my place, in the name of Jesus.

19. Every rule contrary to the rule of God for my life this year, be overruled, in the name of Jesus.

20. Every ancestral covenant and remote control over my destiny, break, in the name of Jesus.

21. Let the enemies from my father's house and from my mother's house, be disappointed, in the name of Jesus.
22. Every serpent and scorpion planted around my life and ministry, catch fire, in the name of Jesus.
23. Every ancestral root of problems in my life, burn to ashes, in the name of Jesus.
24. Every arrow fired to quench my destiny, go back to your sender, in the name of Jesus.
25. Let confusion come upon the camps of my enemies now, in the name of Jesus.
26. No matter the situation I'm facing, I shall become what God has made me to be, in the name of Jesus.
27. Every evil power fighting against my future and glory, fall down and die, in the name of Jesus.
28. By the blood of Jesus, I receive deliverance from every household attack, in the name of Jesus.
29. By the blood of Jesus, I receive deliverance from evil foods and drinks, in the name of Jesus.
30. By the blood of Jesus, I receive deliverance from my family strongman, in the name of Jesus.

CHAPTER THIRTEEN

BURY YOUR HAMAN

13

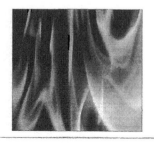

BURY
YOUR HAMAN

13

ny power that is waging war against a true child of God is writing a quick letter of its obituary. Wicked powers must not be spared. They deserve quick and final burial. Everyone who is destined for greatness has a secret Haman lurking in dark places to inflict injury on him. The devil has set up lots of Hamans to bury the glory of God's people, steal precious virtues and destroy treasures that will make you great in life. You need to bury your Haman.

You must not suffer your Haman to live. He must be located, paralysed and forced to do repeated summersaults until he is confirmed dead. The ministry of Haman must be terminated. His activities must be stopped, his goals must be destroyed. You must not allow the enemy of your progress to prosper in his demonic mission. You must destroy Haman before he destroys you. You need these prayer points if:

1. Your destiny is colourful
2. Your star is unique.

3. You are supernaturally endowed to function in the realm of glory.
4. You are a threat to the kingdom of darkness.
5. Your goals and aspirations are making the enemy sad.
6. The destiny of several people are attached to your destiny.
7. You have discovered that you have a unique role to play in your generation.
8. The power of your father's house has instigated revolt against your progress.
9. The enemy is angry because your moment of breakthrough is near.
10. Power of the dark kingdom are ganging up against you.
11. The enemy is fighting you because your life is a symbol of hope for the hopeless.
12. God has made you a helper to many in this generation.

If these describe your condition, you cannot escape attacks from Haman. The fact that you are attacked does not mean that Haman will win. To tackle him, you must take the following steps:

1. Put on the armour of faith.
2. Put on the regalia of a fighter.
3. Use the weapon of consistent bombardment.
4. Make up your mind that every Haman that wants you to die must die.
5. Command your Haman to be destroyed by his own weapons.
6. Decree that your Haman must hang, using the weapon he has constructed for you.
7. Pray like a wounded lion.
8. Issue the cry of vengeance against your Haman.
9. Command angels that have no mercy to invade the camp of Haman and perform utter destruction.
10. Kill and bury your Haman.

Beloved, the prayer points in this programme have been vomited by the Holy Ghost to give you victory over your Haman. This is the day that God will give you the head of your Haman and the head of your Goliath. Pray and your testimony will spread disaster in the camp of the enemy.

PRAYERS SECTION

Confession: **Revelation 13:10:** *He that leadeth into captivity shall go into captivity: he that killeth with the sword must be killed with the sword. Here is the patience and the faith of the saints.*

PRAISE WORSHIP

PRAYER POINTS

1. Thank the Lord for He is the only One that answers prayers.
2. Every Haman assigned against my life, fall down and die, in the name of Jesus.
3. Every messenger of death assigned against my life, go back to your sender, in the name of Jesus.
4. Every agent of death inside my body, come out and die, in the name of Jesus.
5. Every gate of death assigned to swallow me, swallow your owner, in the name of Jesus.
6. Every plantation of death, die, in the name of Jesus.
7. Every stronghold of death on my mind and imagination, be pulled down, in the name of Jesus.
8. By the resurrection of the Lord Jesus Christ the power of death is broken upon my life, in the name of Jesus.
9. Every string of death fashioned against my life, be neutralised by the blood of Jesus.
10. Every certificate of untimely death issued against my life, catch fire, in the name of Jesus.
11. I shall not die but live to declare the works of God, in the

name of Jesus.

12. The numbers of my days shall be fulfilled, in the name of Jesus.

13. Every damaged organ in my body, be repaired by fire, in the name of Jesus.

14. My bones shall not be broken through accident, in the name of Jesus.

15. Every power that does not like to see me around, fall down and die, in the name of Jesus.

16. My soul shall not see corruption of death through sickness, accident or calamity, in the name of Jesus.

17. I drink the blood of Jesus. Let the life in the blood of Jesus flow into every organ of my body, in the name of Jesus.

18. My blood, by the blood of Jesus, be inoculated and immunised against the invasion of death, in the name of Jesus.

Every destiny-paralysing power fashioned against my destiny, fall down and die, in the name of Jesus.

19. I eat of the flesh of Jesus, and I receive life into my body, in the name of Jesus.

20. Every arrow of untimely death fashioned against my life, go back to your senders, in the name of Jesus.

21. Every power digging grave for me, enter therein, in the name of Jesus.

22. The vehicle of my transportation shall not become my coffin, in the name of Jesus.

23. I shall not journey into death, in the name of Jesus.

24. Every snare of death set up for my life, catch your owners, in the name of Jesus.

25. There shall be no sorrow of death in my family, in the name of Jesus.
26. Every shadow of death assigned against my life, scatter, in the name of Jesus.
27. Let the mark of the blood of Jesus wipe off every mark of death on my body, in the name of Jesus.
28. Every stronghold of untimely death fashioned against my life, be pulled down by fire, in the name of Jesus.
29. You wind of death, go back to your sender, in the name of Jesus.
30. Every spirit of depression and despair, die, in the name of Jesus.
31. Every wind of death, go back to your sender, in the name of Jesus.
32. Every satanic device to terminate my life, catch fire, in the name of Jesus.
33. Let the tokens of the liars assigned to cut off my life be frustrated, in the name of Jesus.
34. Every pollution of death in any organ of my body, die, in the name of Jesus.
35. Let my blood be transfused with the blood of Jesus.
36. Every poison and contamination in my blood, be flushed out, in the name of Jesus.
37. Every tree of untimely death in my family line, my life is not your candidate, die, in the name of Jesus.
38. Every evil hunter of my soul, turn back and die, in the name of Jesus.
39. By the power in the blood of Jesus, I subdue death, oppression and violence, in the name of Jesus.
40. O God, I thank You for giving me life to replace death.

CHAPTER FOURTEEN

PULLING DOWN STRONGHOLDS

14

PULLING DOWN STRONGHOLDS

14

One of the toughest problems to deal with is the demonic stronghold. There are ordinary problems and there are deep problems. However, when a particular problem has been erected and fortified by stubborn strongholds victims will struggle every moment of their lives. What most people go through today are problems that are put in place by the enemy using strong pillars. To pull down such stubborn pillars can be very difficult, more so when you are merely chasing shadow. Prayers for pulling down strongholds are uncommon prayers that must be handled with the highest degree of fervency. Strongholds of darkness are responsible for the knotty problem that people go through day in day out.

2 Corinthians 10:5 says:

> *Casting down imaginations, and every high thing that exalteth itself against the knowledge of God, and bringing into captivity every thought to the obedience of Christ;*

You need these prayer points when your problems are compounded, when you keep going through circular problems, when you suddenly discover that you are in the midst of problem and there is no amount of breather, when every season of your life is characterised by tragedies, terrible mishaps and problems sponsored by the kingdom of darkness.

You need them when you go through days, weeks and years without a single testimony, when thoughts of committing suicide invade your heart, when you want to put an end to all forms of satanic revival that have erupted in your life, when your destiny is floating upon the ocean of life.

You need these prayer points when you are completely immersed in the mud of satanic captivity, when you discover that your destiny is completely buried, when you discover that you have become a shadow of your real self. Beloved, as far as this prayer points are concerned you must keep on praying until the stronghold of darkness collapses and you are free to pursue your God-given agenda. You must pray until every stubborn foe is vanquished, until your testimony is full. The strongholds of darkness must not prevail over you.

PRAYERS SECTION

Confessions: **2 Corinthians 10:5:** *Casting down imaginations, and every high thing that exalteth itself against the knowledge of God, and bringing into captivity every thought to the obedience of Christ.* **Proverbs 10:22:** *The blessing of the Lord, it maketh rich, and he addeth no sorrow with it.* **Proverbs 4:18:** *But the path of the just is as the shining light, that shineth more and more unto the perfect day.* **Exodus 7:1:** *And the Lord said unto Moses, See, I have made thee a god to Pharaoh: and Aaron thy brother shall be thy prophet.* **Psalm 82:6:** *I have said, Ye are gods; and all of you are children of the most High.* **Psalm 110:1-3:** *The Lord said unto my Lord, Sit thou at my right hand, until I make thine enemies thy footstool. The Lord shall send the* *rod of thy strength out of Zion: rule thou in the midst of thine enemies. Thy people shall be willing in the day of thy power, in the beauties of holiness from the womb of the morning: thou hast the dew of thy youth.*

PRAISE WORSHIP

PRAYER POINTS

1. Thank the Lord for He is the only One that answers prayers.
2. Any power within and around me, that is hindering the manifestation of the power of God in my life, die, in the name of Jesus.
3. All ye my adversaries, be clothed with shame and disgrace, in the name of Jesus.
4. Every ancestral bondage affecting my life negatively, die, in the name of Jesus.
5. Every evil wind assigned to be blowing away my breakthroughs, die, in the name of Jesus.
6. Every evil power assigned to be blowing away my breakthroughs, be crushed to pieces, in the name of Jesus.
7. Every ancient iron gate that does not want to let me go, be dismantled, in the name of Jesus.
8. Every evil wind blowing away my blessings, die, in the name of Jesus.
9. Every evil chain, limiting my glory, break by fire, in the name of Jesus.
10. Every evil manipulation of my star, die, in the name of Jesus.
11. Every evil deposit in my life limiting my success, die, in the name of Jesus.
12. Every power assigned to be cutting short my blessings, die, in the name of Jesus.
13. Every satanic taskmaster fashioned against my success, die, in the name of Jesus.
14. I reject fragmented blessings, in the name of Jesus.

15. Any evil done on my naming ceremony day that is now affecting my moving forward, die now, in the name of Jesus.
16. You destroyer of blessings, loose your hold upon my life, in the name of Jesus.
17. Let my name become too hot for the enemy to handle, in the name of Jesus.
18. Every Herod assigned against my blessings, die, in the name of Jesus.
19. Any evil assigned to my name, die, in the name of Jesus.
20. I wrestle my name from the hand of the wicked, in the name of Jesus.
21. I receive a name from heaven, in the name of Jesus.
22. Any evil attachment to my name, die, in the name of Jesus.
23. Every evil lot assigned against my blessings, die, in the name of Jesus.

Every destiny-paralysing power fashioned against my destiny, fall down and die, in the name of Jesus.

24. Every destruction mountain erected on the path to my breakthroughs, scatter, in the name of Jesus.
25. I shall not use my hands to pull down my blessings, in the name of Jesus.
26. Every evil stone placed on my breakthroughs, let thunder fire from heaven strike you to pieces, in the name of Jesus.
27. Any good opportunity stolen into the rivers, come back by fire, in the name of Jesus.
28. Every evil within and around me associated with my progress, be cut off by fire, in the name of Jesus.
29. Where is the God of Elijah? Arise and deliver me from the power of the oppressors, in the name of Jesus.

30. Every evil hand assigned to be oppressing me, be cut off by fire, in the name of Jesus.
31. Every load of oppression in my life, go back to your senders, in the name of Jesus.
32. Let the Spirit of God lift up a standard against every oppression fashioned against my life, in the name of Jesus.
33. Every kingdom of oppression assigned against my life, scatter unto desolation, in the name of Jesus.
34. Every word of oppression spoken against my life, backfire, in the name of Jesus.
35. Every power oppressing my life, receive double destruction, in the name of Jesus.
36. Every tree of oppression planted in my life, be cut off by fire, in the name of Jesus. ·
37. I shall not fall into the hand of the oppressors, in the name of Jesus.
38. Every force of oppression assigned against my breakthroughs, die, in the name of Jesus.
39. The son of wickedness shall not torment me, in the name of Jesus.
40. Every oppressor, die, in the name of Jesus.
41. Let the habitation of oppression in my life become desolate, in the name of Jesus.
42. Every power of the oppressor assigned to be following after the goodness of my life, your time is up, die, in the name of Jesus.
43. Let the Holy Ghost set a standard of freedom for my life, in the name of Jesus.
44. Affliction shall not rise again in my life, in the name of Jesus.
45. Every power that does not want to let me go, fall down and die, in the name of Jesus.
46. Every seed of oppression in the labour of my hands, die, in the name of Jesus.
47. You mountain of oppression, scatter, in the name of Jesus.

48. Every evil stronghold assigned against my life, be disgraced, in the name of Jesus.
49. O God, arise and make my life a mysterious wonder, in the name of Jesus.
50. Thank God for answers to your prayers.

CHAPTER FIFTEEN

WHERE IS THE LORD GOD OF ELIJAH

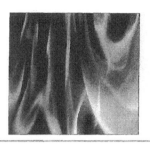

WHERE IS THE LORD GOD OF ELIJAH?

15

here are various levels of prayers. There are prayer patterns that have constituted threats to the kingdom of darkness. One of such prayers centres on evoking the Lord God of Elijah to swing into action.

The Lord God of Elijah is the God that answereth by fire. He is the God of instant judgment. He is the God who appears with the manifestation of the consuming fire. The Lord God of Elijah is the God who thunders and roars against the kingdom of darkness. He is the God who shall suddenly appear and inflict unforgettable injury upon the enemy of your destiny. He is the God who appears and shakes heaven and earth. When He comes into a situation, every agenda of darkness is annihilated. When He speaks from His holy temple, the whole earth will be silent.

You need to invoke the power of the Lord God of Elijah when you are sick and tired of the evil onslaughts of the kingdom of darkness. This prayer programme is needed by men and women who want God to appear suddenly and intervene in their situations. It will prove invaluable for those who desperately seek divine answers to their problems.

It is a powerful battle cry for those who have an eye on winning victory at all cost. When you declare, "Where is the Lord God of Elijah? "You are automatically sounding the battle cry that the Lord responds to. The God who answers by fire will prove Himself. You will experience dumbfounding miracles. To provoke the Lord God of Elijah you must continue with your prayer efforts until He appears with His chariot of fire.

PRAYER SECTION

Confessions: 2 Kings 2:14: *And he took the mantle of Elijah that fell from him, and smote the waters, and said, Where is the Lord God of Elijah? and when he also had smitten the waters, they parted hither and thither: and Elisha went over.*

PRAYER POINTS

1. Where is the Lord God of Elijah? Arise and disgrace my disgrace, in the name of Jesus.
2. Where is the Lord God of Elijah? Arise and pursue my pursuers, in the name of Jesus.
3. Where is the Lord God of Elijah? Arise and divide my Jordan, in the name of Jesus.
4. Where is the Lord God of Elijah? Arise and make me a mysterious wonder, in the name of Jesus.
5. Where is the Lord God of Elijah? Arise and make my way plain before my face, in the name of Jesus.
6. Where is the Lord God of Elijah? Arise and empower me for uncommon breakthroughs, in the name of Jesus.
7. Where is the Lord God of Elijah? Arise and scatter every Jezebel assigned against me, in the name of Jesus.
8. Where is the Lord God of Elijah? Move me forward by fire, in the name of Jesus.

9. O God, arise by Your power and make a way for me where there is no way, in the name of Jesus.

10. O God, arise by Your power and let my uncommon prosperity manifest, in the name of Jesus.

11. Every evil head raised to suppress me, I pull you down by the power of the God of Elijah, in the name of Jesus.

12. Every Hamaan power assigned to threaten my existence, die, in the name of Jesus.

13. Every Hamaan power monitoring my life, loose your power, in the name of Jesus.

14. Every power that is consulting witches because of me, be disgraced, in the name of Jesus.

15. Any power bewitching my star, fall down and die, in the name of Jesus.

Every destiny-paralysing power fashioned against my destiny, fall down and die, in the name of Jesus.

16. My Father, cause my heavens to open, in the name of Jesus.

17. O God of possibilities, empower my life above the desires of my enemies, in the name of Jesus.

18. Let the rain of my breakthroughs begin to fall, in the name of Jesus.

19. O God of Elijah, arise and provoke my showers of breakthroughs, in the name of Jesus.

20. O God of Elijah, arise and provoke my rain of uncommon breakthroughs, in the name of Jesus.

21. O God of Elijah, arise and provoke my Jordan to divide, in the name of Jesus.

22. Spiritual weakness, I cast you out of my life forever, in the name of Jesus.

23. Every power organised to embarrass me, be scattered by fire, in the name of Jesus.

24. I use the padlock of heaven to lock sorrow and disappointments, in the name of Jesus.

25. Any particular house in my place of birth cooking my destiny, catch fire, in the name of Jesus.

26. O wind, reverse any curse issued against me and bring me blessings, in the name of Jesus.

27. Invisible hands troubling my life, God of Elijah, arise by fire and roast them, in the name of Jesus.

28. Every power sitting on my destiny, O God, arise and punish them today, in the name of Jesus.

29. Powers perverting my destiny, fire from heaven, destroy them, in the name of Jesus.

Every destiny-paralysing power fashioned against my destiny, fall down and die, in the name of Jesus.

30. Thrones of darkness legislating against me, scatter, in the name of Jesus.

31. Every stone placed on my moving forward, scatter, in the name of Jesus.

32. Every witchcraft installation assigned to stop me, I stop you before you stop me, in the name of Jesus.

33. In this month, my turn-around shall break forth, in the name of Jesus.

34. The light of God shall shine upon my ways, in the name of Jesus.

35. Disappointment, frustration and discouragement shall

melt away, in the name of Jesus.

36. Every wave of adversity and tragedy shall be silenced, in the name of Jesus.
37. This month, there shall be divine manifestation of the exchange of power to favour me, in the name of Jesus.
38. Every troublesome situation shall bow before me, in the name of Jesus.
39. Every cloud of darkness covering my star shall melt away like cloud before the sun, in the name of Jesus.
40. I shall recover my stolen treasures, in the name of Jesus.
41. Every delay or limitation shall become a story of the past, in the name of Jesus.
42. Every evil bird flying against my destiny shall be shot down suddenly, in the name of Jesus.

SECTION 2

OBTAINING YOUR PORTION

CHAPTER ONE

INTERVIEW SUCCESS

1

1

INTERVIEW SUCCESS

1

Prayer points for success at important interviews must be handled with utmost seriousness. You must handle the spiritual aspect of any interview before you go there. Wisdom and ultimate success belong to God. When you spend time and prayed before going for an important interview the whole process will be achieved with ease.

During an interview various personalities are involved. However, when you allow God to take charge by handling every aspect of the interview over to Him through prayer, success is sure. The truth is that over 50 per-cent of the success you anticipate is often achieved at the place of prayer. Prayer opens the door of favour, gives you wisdom to answer questions with the wisdom of God and takes charge of the atmosphere during the interview.

When you pray yourself into the realm of favour, you will speak the right word at the right time and experience favour from members of the interview panel. When you secure the release of success from the spiritual realm, it will be delivered unto you with ease. Even if you are not able to answer every question right, the favour of the Almighty will earn you a place among the whole lot.

This prayer programme will prove invaluable:

1. When you are going for a job interview.
2. When you are attending a promotion interview.
3. When you are going to attend an admission interview.
4. When you are going for a contract interview.
5. When you want to appear before a selection board.
6. When you are in the midst of several competitors.
7. When decisions are about being taken to favour you.
8. When you want to achieve success at all costs.
9. When you need divine intervention.
10. When you know that your efforts are not just enough.
11. When you need someone to put in a word for you.
12. When you have dreams that bother on the fact that your success is threatened.
13. When you want God to distinguish you as an outstanding candidate.

Just three things to keep in mind.

1. Adequate preparation.
2. Confidence.
3. Absolute faith in God.

With this prayer point, success is yours, your success will become a reference point, and you will prove to the whole world that with God all things are possible.

Mark 9:23 says:

> *Jesus said unto him, If thou canst believe, all things are possible to him that believeth.*

PRAYER SECTION

Confessions: **Mark 9:23:** *Jesus said unto him, If thou canst believe, all things are possible to him that believeth.* **Psalm 75:6** *For promotion cometh neither from the east, nor from the west, nor from the south.* **2 Corinthians 9:8** *And God is able to make all grace abound toward you; that ye, always having all sufficiency in all things, may abound to every good work:* **Philipians 4:13:** *I can do all things through Christ which strengtheneth me.*

Praise Worship

 PRAYER POINTS

1. Father Lord, help me to dress for success, in the name of Jesus
2. Oh Lord, let the anointing for excellence and boldness come upon me as I prepare for this interview, in the name of Jesus.
3. Holy Spirit, open my eyes to know and deal with any weakness in preparing for this interview, in the name of Jesus.
4. Holy Spirit, help me to know how to respond to those who will interview me, in the name of Jesus.
5. I reject every fear of man as I go to this interview, in the name of Jesus.
6. Father Lord, bring me into great favour with all those who will decide on my application, in the name of Jesus.
7. Father Lord, let there be supernatural re-arrangement if this is what will move me forward, in the name of Jesus.
8. I command divine favour to rest upon me as I sit before those who will interview me, in the name of Jesus.
9. Oh Lord, let every impossible situation in my life be converted to divine possibility, in the name of Jesus.
10. I receive the strength and courage of the Lord as I face my interview, in the name of Jesus.

11. I bind and paralyse every strongman delegated to hinder my breakthrough, in the name of Jesus.

12. Oh Lord, let me find favour wherever I go, in the name of Jesus.

13. I bind and paralyse every monitoring spirit and evil followers, in the name of Jesus.

14. I bind and paralyse every spirit of demonic antagonism, in the name of Jesus.

15. I bind and paralyse every spirit of demonic thought and unreasonable interviews, in the name of Jesus.

16. I bind and paralyse every spirit of useless questions, in the name of Jesus.

17. I bind and paralyse every spirit of confusion, in the name of Jesus.

18. I reject every curse of failure, in the name of Jesus.

19. I reject every counsel of the enemies, in the name of Jesus.

20. I command success into my life, in the name of Jesus.

21. Holy Spirit, help me in all my undertakings, in the name of Jesus.

22. Oh Lord, let every hindrance and barrier to my progress be destroyed, in the name of Jesus.

23. Oh Lord, clothe me with honour and glory, in the name of Jesus.

24. Oh Lord, let the glory of Your presence accompany me to the interview room, in the name of Jesus.

25. I bind and paralyse every demon spirit of bad luck, in the name of Jesus.

26. Every demonic battle at the edge of my breakthrough, die, in the name of Jesus.

27. Every weapon of bewitchment, be roasted, in the name of Jesus.

28. Every hold of the spirit of almost-there, be broken, in the name of Jesus.

29. I bind and paralyse every spirit of profitless hardwork, in the name of Jesus.

30. I bind and paralyse every spirit of labour loss, in the name of Jesus.
31. Anointing to excel, come upon my life, in the name of Jesus.
32. I decree open heaven upon my life, in the name of Jesus.
33. I release my life form the spirit of failure, in the name of Jesus.
34. I receive wisdom and power to surpass all competitors, in the name of Jesus.
35. I receive divine prudence that leads to success, in the name of Jesus.
36. Thank God for answers to your prayers.

CHAPTER TWO

PRAYER POINTS TO SECURE CONTRACTS

2

PRAYER POINTS TO SECURE CONTRACTS

2

When favour is bestowed upon your labour, the consequences are unimaginable. Success and prosperity come from above. You need a great deal of efforts to secure contracts that will change your situation. Children of the devil do all sorts in of orders to secure contracts and succeed in their business endeavors. The truth is that the God of possibilities is the only One who can so overshadow your life with favour that you will be the preferred candidate when people are hustling for beneficial contracts.

Picture in your mind's eye the particular place where you need contracts. Be assured of the fact that God is the Alpha and Omega of the establishment and workplace. When you make use of this prayer programme favour will speak for you. Those who are to give out the contracts will be restless until they give the contracts to you.

This prayer programme will, among other things:

1.   Open the door of favour for you.
2.   Lead you to where beneficial contracts can be found.
3.   Remove any cobweb limitation against the contract.
4.   Raise voices that will favour you when contracts are to be given out.
5.   Attack every power in the spiritual realm attacking your contracts.
6.   Give you wisdom to handle problems relating to bribery and corruption.
7.   Make you to be singled out when there are too many people bidding for the same contract.
8.   Keep you in the memory of those who have been earmarked by God to favour you with the signing of the contract.
9.   Give you wisdom to quote appropriately for the contract.
10. Grant you divine help throughout the process of executing the contract.
11. Destroy agents of waste and contract failure.
12. Endow you with the spirit of excellence.
13. Make your performance a reference point as far as your success is concerned.
14. Finally, you must vow to give glory to God at the end of the execution of the contract.

PRAYER SECTION

Confessions: **Romans 8:32:** *He that spared not his own Son, but delivered him up for us all, how shall he not with him also freely give us all things?* **Psalm 18:29**: *For by thee I have run through a troop; and by my God have I leaped over a wall.* **Jeremiah 32:17**: *Ah Lord God! behold, thou hast made the heaven and the earth by thy great power and stretched out arm, and there is nothing too hard for thee.* **Deut. 28:13**: *And the Lord shall make thee the head, and not the tail; and thou shalt be above only, and thou shalt not be beneath; if that thou hearken unto the* commandments of the Lord thy God, which I command thee this day, to observe and to do them. **Proverbs 21:1**: *The king's heart is in the hand of the Lord, as the rivers of water: he turneth it whithersoever he will.* **Proverbs 11:27**: *He that diligently seeketh good procureth favour: but he that seeketh mischief, it shall come unto him.* **Zechariah 12:10**: *And I will pour upon the house of David, and upon the inhabitants of Jerusalem, the spirit of grace and of supplications: and they shall look upon me whom they have pierced, and they shall mourn for him, as one mourneth for his only son, and shall be in bitterness for him, as one that is in bitterness for his firstborn.*

Praise Worship

 PRAYER POINTS

1. Thank the Lord because His season of promotion has come.
2. I bind every fear of rejection, in the name of Jesus.
3. I receive God's favour and that of those who will decide on this contract, in the name of Jesus.
4. Oh Lord, catapult me to greatness as You did for Joseph in the land of Egypt, in the name of Jesus.
5. Oh Lord, let Your favour go with me everywhere I go, in the name of Jesus.
6. Father Lord, make all my contracts and business proposals find favour in the sight of my helpers, in the name of Jesus.
7. Oh Lord, let whosoever means to help me receive help to help me, in the name of Jesus.
8. My helpers will not change their minds towards me, in the name of Jesus.
9. Oh Lord, let me find favour, compassion and goodwill with my helpers, in the name of Jesus.
10. I command my contract being caged by the enemy to be released by fire, in the name of Jesus.
11. Oh Lord, give me supernatural breakthrough in my present contract proposal, in the name of Jesus.

12. Every door of breakthrough that has been closed against my life, open by fire, in the name of Jesus.

13. Every power that wants to nullify good things in my life, die, in the name of Jesus.

14. I release all my contracts and goodness that have been tied down by the spirit of wickedness, in Jesus' name.

15. All my confiscated blessings, be released by fire, in the name of Jesus.

16. Every evil power diverting the benefits of my life, fall down and die, in the name of Jesus.

17. I paralyse the handiwork of household enemies and envious agents concerning this contract, in Jesus' name.

18. You devil, take your legs away from the top of this contract, in the name of Jesus.

CHAPTER THREE

SPEEDY PROMOTION

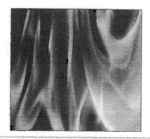

SPEEDY PROMOTION

3

Your altitude in life depends on your attitude. The height you attain is directly proportional to your prayer temperature. Speedy prayers will produce speedy promotion. When you tarry long in the realm of prayer you will experience supernatural exploits. You can determine the speed that you will be promoted in life.

The prayer programme in this section will link you to the realm of accelerated promotion. You can fast-track your promotion and make things happen beyond human imagination. The mystery of speedy promotion can become an experience you cherish. The Bible makes it crystal clear that God is the source of promotion.

Psalms 75:6 says:

> *For promotion cometh neither from the east, nor from the west, nor from the south.*

When you enjoy the benefits of divine promotion no power on earth will be able to limit them. Your promotion comes from the throne of the Almighty and its speed will reflect God's unlimited ability. When God promotes you, your promotion will be extraordinary. God does not need anyone to assist you before He promotes you. Once your promotion has been decreed in heaven, it will be established here on earth. No one can stand in the way of God when he moves. Immediately heaven signs your letter of promotion your life shall break forth and you will experience multiple promotions.

Isaiah 58:8 says:

> *Then shall thy light break forth as the morning, and thine health shall spring forth speedily: and thy righteousness shall go before thee; the glory of the LORD shall be thy rereward.*

The mystery of divine compensation operates through supernatural principles. Even if you have been denied the promotion due to you, God will step into your case and the officers that are above you will bend backward over to place you where you belong.

Beloved, you need speedy promotion when:

1. The spirit of the tail has plagued your destiny.
2. When you discover that you have remained at the back while your contemporaries have been moved above you.
3. When you discover that you have been marking time on the same spot for a very long time.
4. When you are ashamed of being at the rear.
5. When people with whom you started have taken giant strides.
6. When you have put in so much without being adequately rewarded.
7. When you have struggled unsuccessfully to make it in life.
8. When you have constantly lived from hand to mouth.

9. When the powers of your fathers house have kept you in a backward position.
10. When your hard-work is unnoticed and unrewarded.
11. When the spirit of the snail has plagued your destiny.
12. When you have been given a loud official title without any corresponding benefit.
13. When you have discovered that demoting powers are working seriously against your promotion.
14. When you have noticed that your promotion has been mysteriously kept on hold.
15. When you desire speedy promotion.

Beloved, this prayer programme will make a difference in your life. It will take you to the realm of destiny fulfilment. Speedy promotion will announce the awesome power of God and portray His glory in your life. Uncommon promotion will be your lot as you vigorously pursue this prayer programme.

PRAYER SECTION

Confessions: **Isaiah 58:8**: *Then shall thy light break forth as the morning, and thine health shall spring forth speedily: and thy righteousness shall go before thee; the glory of the LOrd shall be thy rereward.* **Hebrews 2:3:** *How shall we escape, if we neglect so great salvation; which at the first began to be spoken by the Lord, and was confirmed unto us by them that heard him.* **Jeremiah 29:11:** *For I know the thoughts that I think toward you, saith the LOrd, thoughts of peace, and not of evil, to give you an expected end.* **Luke 18:8:** *I tell you that he will avenge them speedily. Nevertheless when the Son of man cometh, shall he find faith on the earth?* **Psalm 102:2** : *Hide not thy face from me in the day when I am in trouble; incline thine ear unto me: in the day when I call answer me speedily.* **Mark 9:23:** *Jesus said unto him, If thou canst believe, all things are possible to him that believeth.* **Psalm 75:6:** *For promotion cometh neither from the east, nor from the west, nor from the south.* **2 Corinthians 9:8:** *And God is able to make all grace abound toward you; that ye, always having all sufficiency in all things,* *may abound to every good work. **Philip. 4:13** : I can do all things through Christ which strengtheneth me. **Psalm 27:12:** Deliver me not over unto the will of mine enemies: for false witnesses are risen up against me, and such as breathe out cruelty. **Psalm 35:19:** Let not them that are mine enemies wrongfully rejoice over me: neither let them wink with the eye that hate me without a cause. **Psalm 31:13-14:** For I have heard the slander of many: fear was on every side: while they took counsel together against me, they devised to take away my life. But I trusted in thee, O LOrd: I said, Thou art my God. **Isaiah 50:7:** For the Lord GOd will help me; therefore shall I not be confounded: therefore have I set my face like a flint, and I know that I shall not be ashamed.*

Praise Worship

 **PRAYER POINTS**

1. Oh Lord, reveal Your divine plan for my life, in the name of Jesus.
2. I break every circle of failure upon my life, in the name of Jesus.
3. I receive empowerment for speedy breakthroughs, in the name of Jesus.
4. Oh Lord, let the anointing of excellence fall on me, in the name of Jesus.
5. Every mark of rejection against my life, be wiped off by the blood of Jesus.
6. Oh Lord, purge my tongue by Your fire.
7. Every demonic power that wants to waste my labour and energy, be bound and be paralysed by the chains of God, in the name of Jesus.
8. Oh Lord, I ask for wisdom and knowledge to do my job right, in the name of Jesus.
9. I receive grace to be diligent in business, in the name of Jesus.
10. Oh Lord, anoint my handiwork for outstanding success, in the name of Jesus.

11. I excel above my colleagues 10 times like Daniel, in the name of Jesus.
12. I will find favour before my boss, in the name of Jesus.
13. Oh Lord, let the anointing to overcome fall upon me, in the name of Jesus.
14. I bind every spirit of fear, in the name of Jesus.
15. Oh Lord, let my request find favour before my boss, in the name of Jesus.
16. Every plan of the devil to put me to shame and ridicule, be cancelled by the fire of God, in the name of Jesus.
17. Oh Lord, make me a channel of blessings to those who work with me, in the name of Jesus.
18. Every satanic attempt to destroy my reputation, be frustrated, in the name of Jesus.
19. I bind every spirit of memory failure, in the name of Jesus.
20. I reject every curse of failure, in the name of Jesus.
21. Every power prolonging my breakthroughs, die, in the name of Jesus.
22. Every spirit of backwardness in my life, die, in the name of Jesus.
23. I reject snail and tortoise anointing, in the name of Jesus.
24. I refuse to labour in vain, in the name of Jesus.
25. Oh Lord, make me a proof producer, in the name of Jesus.
26. I bind and cancel all ungodly delay to the manifestation of my promotion, in the name of Jesus.
27. Father Lord, hasten Your word to perform miracles in every area of my life, in the name of Jesus.
28. Oh Lord, let my way be cleared to the top by Your hand of power, in the name of Jesus.
29. Every evil gang-up against my career, scatter by the fire of God, in the name of Jesus.
30. Father Lord, help me to offer profitable service, in the name of Jesus.
31. Any power hiding the key to my promotion, loose your hold and die, in the name of Jesus.

32. Holy Spirit, help me to identify and avoid evil business trap, in the name of Jesus.

33. I break the power of any sickness that will try to hinder me from achieving my vision, in the name of Jesus.

34. I receive grace to handle the ups and downs of my career, in the name of Jesus.

35. I receive abundant prosperity, in the name of Jesus.

36. I claim my divine promotion today, in the name of Jesus.

37. Every evil spoken against me where I work, die, in the name of Jesus.

38. I fire back every arrow of demotion fashioned against me, in the name of Jesus.

39. Every satanic principality at my workplace, be exposed and disgraced, in the name of Jesus.

40. Oh Lord, let all those who are sitting illegally on my benefits and promotions be unseated by fire, in the name of Jesus.

41. Oh Lord, let all those who are sitting and planning an illegal transfer for me from my place of blessing, be exposed and disgraced, in the name of Jesus.

42. Every hostile person and pretender hanging around me, be exposed and disgraced, in the name of Jesus.

43. Every ungodly schemes and devices of the wicked around me, be disappointed, in the name of Jesus.

44. All those who are watching me, seeking to accuse me wrongly, be embarrassed and be put to shame, in the name of Jesus.

45. Oh Lord, let every form of injustice against me in my place of work, be converted to divine promotion, in the name of Jesus.

46. I command every evil gang-up against me to scatter, in the name of Jesus.

47. Oh Lord, let all those who lift themselves in arrogance be humbled before me, in the name of Jesus.

48. Oh Lord, let my enemies begin to fight themselves, in the name of Jesus.

49. Oh Lord, let all those who take evil counsel together against me be disgraced, in the name of Jesus.

50. Every evil board meeting intended against me, be frustrated, in the name of Jesus.

51. Oh Lord, convert the wisdom of my antagonists to foolishness, in the name of Jesus.

52. Oh Lord, let the voice of the critics be silenced, in the name of Jesus.

53. Every wicked plot to distract me from achieving my goals, be exposed and frustrated, in the name of Jesus.

54. I receive boldness and strength to belittle mockery, slander and opposition in my workplace, in the name of Jesus.

55. Let God arise and let plotters of evil who hav risen against me scatter, in the name of Jesus.

56. Oh Lord, let every merchant of evil conspiring against me, be exposed and disgraced, in the name of Jesus.

57. Oh Lord, let all planning for my downfall and raising barriers, fall into their own trap, in the name of Jesus.

58. Oh Lord, accelerate my speed and cause me to overtake even my superiors, in the name of Jesus.

59. Oh Lord, let all my entitlements in my workplace locate me by fire, in the name of Jesus.

60. Every demonic intelligent operatives busy planning and working to scatter my career, be frustrated, in Jesus' name.

61. Every token and trap of liars against my career, be frustrated, in the name of Jesus.

62. Oh Lord, let Your glory overshadow my life, in the name of Jesus.

63. Oh Lord, order my steps and guide every move I make, in the name of Jesus.

64. Oh Lord, convert every ridicule in my life to miracles, in the name of Jesus.

65. Oh Lord, baptize me with the spirit of uncommon favour, in the name of Jesus.

66. Oh Lord, accelerate the timetable of my destiny, in the name of Jesus.

67. Every child of the devil occupying my position, somersault and die, in the name of Jesus.
68. Thank God for answers to your prayers.

CHAPTER FOUR

I MUST MANIFEST

I MUST MANIFEST

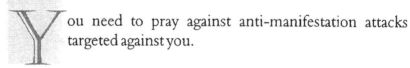

You need to pray against anti-manifestation attacks targeted against you.

1. When you discover that miracles, signs and wonders are scarce in your life, you must pursue a vigorous prayer programme.

2. When you discover that your prayers are bouncing back and testimonies are running away from you, you must take time to pray for a change that will completely put an end to such an un-pleasant situation.

3. If your life is void of glory and you lack the joy of testimonies, you need to pray.

4. If your star has been buried, you must declare war.

5. If you are denied of your portion you must pray like a wounded lion.

6. If your destiny has been buried in obscurity, you must pray until your glory sees the light of day.

7. If shame and failure have been hanging upon your head, you must pray fervently until the dark cloud clears.

Whatever has kept you from shinning like stars must be defeated. You must enter a season of manifestation. Your God must appear by fire and showcase His glory in your life.

To handle this prayer programme effectively you must take the following steps:

1. Locate the areas you desire changes in your life.
2. Make up your mind to cry for a change.
3. Pray with faith and aggression.
4. Decide to move to the next level.
5. Refuse to remain at the valley.
6. Pray until the powers holding tight to your blessings will experience hot coals of fire and drop them.
7. Pray for recovery and restoration.
8. Cry like blind Bartimaeus.
9. Pray until your testimonies come.
10. Cry unto God until your joy is full.
11. Pray away every form of hindrance.
12. Obtain your breakthroughs by faith.
13. Let your purpose be clear.
14. Do not rest until you possess your possessions.
15. Make use of the weapon of praise and worship.

Take these prayer points until your life becomes an avenue for signs and wonders. This is your season of manifestation. This is your hour of breakthrough. Pray and your blessings shall manifest by fire.

PRAYERS SECTION

Confession: 1 John 4:4: *Ye are of God, little children, and have overcome them: because greater is he that is in you, than he that is in the world.*

Praise Worship

 PRAYER POINTS

1. Father, I thank You for making me a star, in the name of Jesus.
2. Father, let Your divine favour locate me and lift me out of obscurity, in the name of Jesus.
3. Let every satanic embargo on my rising be broken, in the name of Jesus.
4. Every satanic chain keeping me from shining, break by fire, in the name of Jesus.
5. Every witchcraft hand placed on my star, wither, in the name of Jesus.
6. My star, arise and begin to shine, in the name of Jesus.
7. Let the resurrection power of our Lord Jesus Christ come upon my buried virtues, in the name of Jesus.
8. My destiny, hear the word of the living God: manifest by fire, in the name of Jesus.
9. Every evil veil cast upon my glory, be roasted, in the name of Jesus.
10. Every power of limitation, frustration and stagnation assigned against my destiny, die, in the name of Jesus.
11. Every satanic sanction upon my destiny, die, in the name of Jesus.
12. Where is the Lord God of Elijah? Arise and bring my destiny out of obscurity, in the name of Jesus.
13. Let the light of God shine on all my achievements for people to see, in the name of Jesus.
14. My portion shall not be transferred to another, in the name of Jesus.
15. Every strongman of obscurity in my life, die, in the name of Jesus.
16. Every handwriting of ordinances of bad luck assigned against my life, be wiped off by the blood of Jesus.

17. Every tree of bad luck planted against my life, be uprooted by fire, in the name of Jesus.

18. Every ancestral root of failure in my family line, be uprooted by fire, in the name of Jesus.

19. Every strongman of bad luck and failure assigned against my life, fall down and die, in the name of Jesus.

20. Every root of bad luck and failure in my life, dry up, in the name of Jesus.

21. I reject every inherited bad luck and failure, in the name of Jesus.

22. Every power keeping me away from my divine helpers, die, in the name of Jesus.

23. Every power blocking my opportunities, scatter, in the name of Jesus.

24. Every power assigned to be delaying my divine time and appointments, die, in the name of Jesus.

25. Every spirit of misfortune and failure, die, in the name of Jesus.

26. Every blindness to good opportunities, die, in the name of Jesus.

27. Every entrenched bad luck and failure, die, in the name of Jesus.

28. Every evil priest ministering failure against my life at any evil altar, fall down and die, in the name of Jesus.

29. Let my legs be ordained to carry me to my place of divine appointments, in the name of Jesus.

30. Good luck and blessings shall henceforth be my portion, in the name of Jesus.

31. Let rivers of favour and mercy flow into my destiny, in the name of Jesus.

32. Let favour and mercy continually be my companion, in the name of Jesus.

33. I shall not fail at the edge of my breakthroughs, in the name of Jesus.

34. I refuse to turn back at the edge of my success, in the name of Jesus.

CHAPTER FIVE

ARRESTING SLIPPERY BLESSINGS

ARRESTING SLIPPERY BLESSINGS

5

There is nothing as frustrating as being taken to the place of your blessing and discovering that your blessings are nowhere to be found. There is nothing as disheartening as getting to the edge of your breakthroughs and discovering that the breakthroughs have suddenly disappeared.

When expectations are denied, hopes are dashed, desires are not met and what you hope for never comes to pass, your heart will be discouraged and the urge to move forward will be completely gone.

You need to arrest the tide of slippery blessings. God does not want any of His children to grapple with slippery blessings. Unfortunately, heaven has released some blessings but demonic powers have made the recipients to catch nothing.

Peter and his partners went afishing, laboured throughout the night and caught nothing. They had nothing to show for their labours and persistent efforts

John 21:3 says:

> *Simon Peter saith unto them, I go a fishing. They say unto him, We also go with thee. They went forth, and entered into a ship immediately; and that night they caught nothing.*

The problem of slippery blessings have dribbled many and left them confused. The devil will not prevent you from making efforts, praying and expecting your blessings but he will stand at the gate of your breakthroughs and make sure that nothing comes to you.

Slippery blessings mean that there are no blessings at all. When you work and pray persistently and no blessings are on the horizon, it shows that the powers of slippery blessings are waging war against you.

The moment you discover that you can go through a whole season without a single testimony, there is a serious problem. You need this prayer programme when you have spread word concerning an intending blessings and the blessings never come.

It is a prayer programme you must handle with aggression if you happen to have been a victim of slippery blessings. It will help you if certain entitlements and benefits that could have been yours for a very long time are withdrawn for no justifiable reason.

This prayer programme will change your situation if you labour more than your contemporaries but what you reap is far below what you are entitled to. You need to arrest slippery blessings if you have sat down and you have discovered that your blessings are just not forthcoming even when you have anticipated their arrival.

This prayer programme will help you if you have prayed and fasted and there are no tangible results. This prayer programme is needed by those who have been told by their establishment that they are due for promotion but suddenly, the decisions are revoked. You need to arrest the mystery of slippery blessings if blessings have refused to show up even when you have sensed that the blessings were on the way.

You must arrest the tide of slippery blessings if you have discovered that it is an ancestral problem. You must pray fervently against this problem if you always end up obtaining half or part of what belongs to you. This prayer will come handy for those who are sweating profusely without any moment of rest or success.

You need these prayers if financial losses have been your constant experience. This prayer programme would change your situation if you have discovered that no matter how hard you have tried to come out of poverty, something comes up suddenly and drags you into the cage of poverty.

You need to pray aggressively if you have discovered that the curse of profitless hard work has been raging against your life, if you have discovered that witchcraft agents are sitting on your blessings.

To tackle the problem of slippery blessings, you must take the following steps:

1. Repent of every sin that has put slippery blessings in place.
2. Remove yourself from the umbrella of slippery blessings.
3. Pray for power to magnetise your blessings.
4. Revoke every covenant that has made you a perpetual victim of slippery blessings.
5. Go through personal deliverance.
6. Pray with aggression.
7. Claim God's promises.
8. Obtain your blessings by force.
9. Pray fervently until the yoke of slippery blessings is broken.

10. Declare that you shall not build and another inhabits, you shall not plant and another eats.

11. Declare that you shall eat the work of your hand.

Finally, this prayer programme will make a great difference in your life. Your situation will change and your blessings will locate you.

PRAYERS SECTION

Confession: **Isaiah 65:21-22:** *And they shall build houses, and inhabit them; and they shall plant vineyards, and eat the fruit of them. They shall not build, and another inhabit; they shall not plant, and another eat: for as the days of a tree are the days of my people, and mine elect shall long enjoy the work of their hands.*

Praise Worship

PRAYER POINTS

1. Lord Jesus, I thank You for Your programme for my life, in the name of Jesus.

2. Any sin in my life, blood of Jesus, cleanse and forgive me, in the name of Jesus.

3. O Lord, forgive me for every unfaithfulness in paying of tithes and offerings, in the name of Jesus.

4. Anything in my life that is cooperating with financial losses, die, in the name of Jesus.

5. Every curse and covenant of sleepy blessings, break by the power in the blood of Jesus.

6. Every anchor of financial losses in my life, break by fire, in the name of Jesus.

7. Every programme of slippery blessings, die, in the name of Jesus.

8. Every power within and around me behind losses in my life, be exposed and die, in the name of Jesus.

9. Every evil altar assigned against my blessings, catch fire, in the name of Jesus.

10. Every power of poverty of my father's/mother's house, my life is not your candidate, die, in the name of Jesus.

11. Every witchcraft coven assigned against my blessings, catch fire, in the name of Jesus.

12. Every ancestral spirit of poverty, loose your hold and die, in the name of Jesus.

13. Every evil altar ministering poverty into my life, catch fire, in the name of Jesus.

14. Every habitation of financial losses in my life, become desolate, in the name of Jesus.

15. Every power of captivity of my father's house, your time is up, fall down and die, in the name of Jesus.

16. Let the anointing of retention fall upon my life now, in the name of Jesus.

17. Every curse of profitless hard-work, break by fire, in the name of Jesus.

18. Every evil power behind sleepy blessings in my life, fall down and die, in the name of Jesus.

19. Every evil power assigned against my financial success, die, in the name of Jesus.

20. Let my destiny receive deliverance from all financial losses, in the name of Jesus.

21. You strongman of sleepy blessings, loose your hold and die, in the name of Jesus.

22. Every power repeating financial losses in my life, die, in the name of Jesus.

23. Witchcraft arrow of losses, go back to your sender, in the name of Jesus.

24. Every spirit of laziness and slothfulness, get out of my life, in the name of Jesus.

25. I repossess every good thing I've lost to the enemy, in the name of Jesus.

26. Henceforth, none of my blessings shall slip away, in the name of Jesus.
27. Thank God for answers to your prayers.

CHAPTER SIX

I SHALL SING MY SONG AND DANCE MY DANCE

I SHALL SING MY SONG AND DANCE MY DANCE

6

The devil hates to hear any sound of music in your camp. He does not want you to sing your song or dance your dance. But as far as God is concerned an unending rhythm of joyful songs should be found in your habitations at all times. God takes delight in giving you new songs on daily basis. He wants your joy to be so full that you will begin to dance joyfully.

It is therefore your responsibility to pray your way to breakthroughs. God wants you to sing for joy and celebrate your breakthrough through dancing. He is ever ready to put a new song in your mouth

Psalm 40:3 says:

> *And he hath put a new song in my mouth, even praise unto our God: many shall see it, and fear, and shall trust in the LORD.*

When God puts a new song in your mouth, praise will erupt from within. Then, you will sing unto Him a new song, and His praise from the end of the earth.

Isaiah 42:10 says:

> *As with a sword in my bones, mine enemies reproach me; while they say daily unto me, Where is thy God?*

The devil has continued to put the garment of mourning and sorrow upon people. For multitudes, there is no reason whatsoever to dance or celebrate. This situation must change. Whatever the devil has done to put your celebration on hold must be destroyed. All forms of evil barricades must be dismantled. Every enemy of your joy must be disgraced. However, you must pray until your nights of weeping come to an end and you are ushered into your season of singing and dancing. This particular prayer programme has been vomited by the Holy Ghost to lead you into breakthroughs that will make you sing and dance impulsively. You must cast aside all internal enemies of your joy. You must put away carnal roadblocks and self-constructed hindrances to your total joy.

These prayer points must not be handled half way. You must give yourself no rest until your joy is full and your cup of celebration begins to overflow. You need this prayer programme if you have gone through weeks, months and years without any testimony. You need the prayer points in this section if tears have flowed from your eyes ceaselessly and the sighing of the prisoner has been your lot for a very long time. You need to pray these prayers aggressively if you have become an object of ridicule. These prayers are of utmost importance if you want those who have mocked you to be forced to celebrate with you.

Beloved, these prayer points will give you access to sing the victor's song and dance the overcomer's dance. This is your season of rejoicing and celebrating the goodness of the Lord in the land of the living.

Psalms 118:17 says:

I shall not die, but live, and declare the works of the LORD.

 PRAYER SECTION

CONFESSIONS

Psalms 2:4: *He that sitteth in the heavens shall laugh: the Lord shall have them in derision.*

Psalms 40:3: *And he hath put a new song in my mouth, even praise unto our God: many shall see it, and fear, and shall trust in the Lord.*
Isaiah 42:10: *Behold, the Lord God will come with strong hand, and his arm shall rule for him: behold, his reward is with him, and his work before him.*

 # PRAYER POINTS

1. I shall laugh my enemies to scorn after the order of Elijah, in the name of Jesus.
2. This year, I shall sing my song and dance my dance, in the name of Jesus.
3. O God, arise and give me a turn-around miracle, in the name of Jesus.
4. Do something in my life, O Lord, that will make me to celebrate, in the name of Jesus.
5. O God, arise and open Your treasures unto me, in the name of Jesus.
6. O God, arise and give me open heavens, in the name of Jesus.
7. O Lord, make me a candidate of supernatural surprises, in the name of Jesus.
8. By fire, by force, O God, launch me into my next level, in the name of Jesus.
9. O God, arise and restore my past losses, in the name of Jesus.

10. Thou power of God, disgrace my detractors, in the name of Jesus.
11. Lord, contend with them that contend with me, in the name of Jesus.
12. Lord, let my generation celebrate me, in the name of Jesus.
13. Every arrow of mourning and sorrow, backfire, in the name of Jesus.
14. Lord, convert any pain in my life to gain, in the name of Jesus.
15. Oh Lord, give me my personal pentecost. Give me fire to fight, in the name of Jesus.
16. Lord, make me a blessing to my generation, in the name of Jesus.
17. I cancel tears and I cancel premature death, in the name of Jesus.
18. My Father, my Father, my Father, let people know that I am serving a living God, in the name of Jesus.
19. This year, I must not fail, in the name of Jesus.
20. My Father, deliver me from strange battles, in the name of Jesus.
21. My Father, cause this year to be my year of jubilee and rejoicing, in the name of Jesus.
22. O God, arise and fill my mouth with laughter, in the name of Jesus.
23. O God, arise and let my tears expire, in the name of Jesus.
24. O God, arise and let my shame expire, in the name of Jesus.
25. I receive uncommon wisdom to excel, in the name of Jesus.
26. My Father, accelerate my speed and close the gap between where I am and where I should be in life, in the name of Jesus.
27. Every power assigned to put off my light, receive confusion, in the name of Jesus.
28. Let the rainbow of glory appear in my situation, in the name of Jesus.

29. Every conspiracy against my life, lift away into the sea, in the name of Jesus.
30. Every captivity, arise and trouble my captivity, in the name of Jesus.
31. I recover all my known and unknown opportunities, in the name of Jesus.
32. I put on my dancing shoes. My sorrows are over, in the name of Jesus.
33. Open Your abundance unto me, O Lord, in the name of Jesus.
34. Sword of God, cast off every satanic attachment from my life, in the name of Jesus.
35. Darkness, break away from my life, in the name of Jesus.
36. Any mouth cursing me, be eaten by poison, in the name of Jesus

CHAPTER SEVEN

LET MY JORDAN DIVIDE

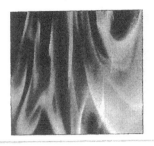

LET MY
JORDAN DIVIDE

(7)

There is a season in the life of everyone when a decisive change comes and there is a remarkable difference, between the past and the present. When you get to a point where going back is burdensome and moving forward is near impossible you need to pray until God changes the situation.

You need these prayers:

1. When you are at your wits end.
2. When you are overwhelmed by a dark cloud
3. When it appears as if your enemies are having a swell time mocking you.
4. When it appears as if you would soon drown.
5. When human help is nowhere in sight.
6. When a stubborn Jordan surrounds you.
7. When it appears as if there was no headway for your destiny.
8. When unrepentant enemies are mocking you.
9. When it becomes crystal clear that you are already

disconnected from the socket of your breakthroughs.

10. Until Jordan is divided supernaturally to bring God's will to pass in your life.

11. When you want to invoke the Lord God of Elijah to arise and divide your Jordan (2 Kings 2:14)

To pray these prayers effectively you must get to a point when you will not take no for an answer. You must also be ready to tackle the enemy head-on and settle for nothing less than the dividing of Jordan. You must be ready to shout with a loud voice saying, "Where is the Lord God of Elijah?

This prayer programme requires holy aggression. To carry it out successfully, you must be able to pray like a mad prophet.

I have a word of encouragement for you here: do not be tired. Pound the enemy to submission. These prayer points will make you to sweat. The more you are fervent in this prayer session the more positive manifestations you will experience. Nobody may know the degree of efforts you put into these prayer points, but when the results come people will be forced to declare that the God whom you serve is the God who answers by fire.

 PRAYER POINTS

Confessions **Psalm 68:4:** *Sing unto God, sing praises to his name: extol him that rideth upon the heavens by his name Jah, and rejoice before him.* **2 Kings 2:14:** *And he took the mantle of Elijah that fell from him, and smote the waters, and said, Where is the Lord God of Elijah? and when he also had smitten the waters, they parted hither and thither: and Elisha went over.*

Praise Worship

 **PRAYER POINTS**

1. Every power that needs to die for my testimony to manifest,

die, in the name of Jesus.

2. Every agenda of mocking powers for my life, backfire, in the name of Jesus.

3. By the power in the blood of Jesus, I receive miracles that will shock my friends and surprise my enemies, in the name of Jesus.

4. Dark authorities sponsoring continuous and repeated problems, scatter, in the name of Jesus.

5. By the power that divided the Red Sea, let my way open, in the name of Jesus.

6. By the power that stoned the head of Goliath, let my stubborn problems die, in the name of Jesus.

7. By the power that disgraced Senacherub, let evil covens gathered against me catch fire, in the name of Jesus.

8. By the power that divided the Jordan river, let my unusual breakthrough manifest, in the name of Jesus.

9. Every power mocking my prayers, receive double destruction, in the name of Jesus.

10. O God of Elijah, arise and make me a mysterious wonder, in the name of Jesus.

11. By the word of God which cannot be broken, I move into my next level, in the name of Jesus.

12. Every satanic priest ministering against my breakthroughs, be disgraced, in the name of Jesus.

13. My season of unusual laughter and victory dance, manifest, in the name of Jesus.

14. Whatever has tied down by destiny, break loose from my life, in the name of Jesus.

15. Witches toying with my destiny, be wiped off, in the name of Jesus.

16. O Lord, reshuffle my environment to favour me, in the name of Jesus.

17. I will be a champion and not a casualty, in the name of Jesus.

18. If I have been disconnected from my destiny, O God, arise and re-connect me, in the name of Jesus.

19. O Lord, whatever You have not positioned into my life, wipe them off, in the name of Jesus.
20. O God, dismantle the poison in my foundation, in the name of Jesus.
21. Circumstances affecting my success, bow, in the name of Jesus.
22. O God, arise and give me a strong reason to celebrate and laugh this year, in the name of Jesus.
23. The enemy shall weep concerning my life this year, in the name of Jesus.
24. My Father, show me unusual secrets of my next level, in the name of Jesus.
25. Every month of this year shall be a disappointment to the enemy, in the name of Jesus.
26. My Father, distract my enemies with problems that are bigger than them, in the name of Jesus.
27. O God, arise and invade my star and set it free, in the name of Jesus.
28. My adversaries, hear the word of the Lord,: "Carry your loads, in the name of Jesus."
29. Every serpent assigned to bite my destiny, die, in the name of Jesus.
30. O God, arise and fight for me in the day and in the night, in the valley and on the mountain, in the name of Jesus.
31. Every power assigned to scatter my resources, dry up, in the name of Jesus.
32. Every power assigned to suppress my elevation, die, in the name of Jesus.
33. Every satanic panel set up against me, scatter, in the name of Jesus.
34. Rod of the wicked attacking my progress, break, in the name of Jesus.
35. Delayed breakthroughs, delayed promotions, manifest by fire, in the name of Jesus.
36. I disarm all vagabond problems, in the name of Jesus.

37. I disgrace all discouraging powers, in the name of Jesus.
38. O God, arise and give my enemies leanness this year, in the name of Jesus.
39. My enemies will not rejoice over me this year, in the name of Jesus.
40. Sorrow and tears, I uproot you from my life by fire, in the name of Jesus.
41. Any power assigned to sink the boat of my salvation, die, in the name of Jesus.
42. My Father, deliver me from costly mistakes, in the name of Jesus.

CHAPTER EIGHT

BREAKING THE YOKE OF BAD LUCK

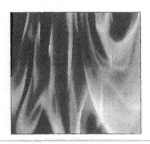

BREAKING THE YOKE OF BAD LUCK

8

One of the greatest problems that people are grappling with today can be attributed to the evil burden of bad luck. A lot of people struggle from dawn to dusk, yet they keep going in circles because the mystery of bad luck has programmed them to dwell in a negative realm in life. The yoke of bad luck is one of the manifestations of wicked programmes being activated by dark powers.

There is no way you can enjoy your life, experience. God's blessings and fulfill your destiny without dealing with the yoke of bad luck. To say that there is nothing like bad luck is to be simplistic. The Bible makes it crystal clear that a lot of people have been forced to place their heads under the yoke of bad luck.

Unfortunately, our ancestral past has made the mystery of the yoke of bad luck to flourish. Our ancestors erected a platforms that have made bad luck a common experience. It is, indeed, true that many have grown up in the dark places of the earth which have been described as the habitation of cruelty.

Whatever looks like the yoke of bad luck must break even if it has been put to place by enchantment, divination or incantations.

The Bible has declared that there is no enchantment against Jacob. When the yoke of bad luck is broken, there will be a new lease of life and vitality in you. God will make wars to cease. The bow, the spear and the chariot of bad luck will be consumed by the fire of the Holy Ghost

Psalms 46:8-9 says:

> *Come, behold the works of the LORD, what desolations he hath made in the earth. He maketh wars to cease unto the end of the earth; he breaketh the bow, and cutteth the spear in sunder; he burneth the chariot in the fire.*

When the yoke of bad luck is broken you will be able to declare **Psalms 16:6** says:

> *The lines are fallen unto me in pleasant places; yea, I have a goodly heritage.*

The yoke of bad luck is an invisible satanic burden. Once it is in place the victim will discover that nothing works. The prayer point below are divine solution to the bad luck dilemma.

Victims of bad luck experience favour famine. Blessings disappear mysteriously whenever it comes to the turn of those who are victims of bad luck. What has been available previously suddenly becomes unavailable.

Prayers for breaking the yoke of bad luck must be done with aggression. To deal with bad luck you need the weapon of holy violence. It is a yoke that must be broken with the force of aggressive prayers. Often times when bad luck has been in place for a long time you need to add deliverance prayers and combine fasting with prayer to break and grind the yoke to powder.

Breaking the yoke of bad luck prayers are needed by everyone in this environment. You will surely experience some manifestations as you take these prayer points.

Your enemies will either turn back or submit themselves to you. The uniqueness of this prayer programme resides in it is being an important aspect of Jehu prayers. When you pray fervently, problems that have been part of you for a long time will be dealt with. The powers of your father's house will let you go. Your heavens will open and demonic stumbling blocks will give way. Your testimonies will be awesome.

 PRAYER SECTION

Open your Bible to Psalms 1 and Psalms 46. Confess them out loud.

1. Thank the Lord for what He will do for you in this prayer programme.
2. Every satanic plan for my life, die, in the name of Jesus.
3. I use the token of the blood of Jesus to blot out all the hand-writings of ordinances of bad luck working against my life, in the name of Jesus.
4. Every crocodile power in my dreams, die, in the name of Jesus.
5. I violently uproot the tree of bad luck planted in my life by the enemy, in the name of Jesus.
6. I break every soul-tie with dead parents, in the name of Jesus.
7. Let the fire of God destroy the roots of bad luck in my life and family, in the name of Jesus.
8. I bind every spirit of Balaam working against my destiny, in the name of Jesus.
9. I bind and cast out of my life, every foul spirit of bad luck, in the name of Jesus.
10. I smash all demonic mirrors monitoring my life, in the name of Jesus.

11. Every strongman of bad luck attached to my life, fall down and die, in Jesus' name.
12. I shall not die young. I shall reach my full age, in the name of Jesus.
13. Let the blood of Jesus destroy the roots of bad luck in my life now, in Jesus' name.
14. I reject every demonic nickname, in the name of Jesus.
15. I renounce and reject all inherited or acquired spirits of bad luck, in Jesus' name.
16. My blood, be anointed with the power of the Holy Spirit, in the name of Jesus.
17. I receive total purification in the blood of Jesus from all the evil perfumes of bad luck, in the name of Jesus.
18. Every instrument of bewitchment, be roasted, in the name of Jesus.
19. You spirit of misfortune around me, receive the arrows of fire, in Jesus' name.
20. Every evil plant in my life, be uprooted, in the name of Jesus.
21. Father Lord, let the power of any entrenched bad luck be broken in my life today, in the name of Jesus.
22. I line up my life with my divine destiny, in the name of Jesus.
23. I sack and incapacitate all the satanic priests ministering at the altars of bad luck against my life, in Jesus' name.
24. All curses, spells, jinxes, bewitchment and enchantments of bad luck shall not prosper in my life, in Jesus' name.
25. Father Lord, open my eyes to know and see my opportunities, in the name of Jesus.
26. I will arise and shine, for my light has come and God's glory is risen upon me, in the name of Jesus.
27. Even if darkness and gross darkness cover the whole world, God's light and glory shall be seen upon me, in the name of Jesus.
28. Father Lord, in the name of Jesus, permit nobody to ever again say to me, "Ssorry, better luck next time."

29. Abraham did not miss his appointed time, I will not miss mine, too, in Jesus' name.
30. I command you legs of mine to carry me to the places of my blessing and progress, in the name of Jesus.
31. My head *(lay your right hand on your forehead)*, from now on, life shall be easy for you. You shall be desired, appreciated and rewarded, in the name of Jesus.
32. You dry bones of my destiny, come alive, in the name of Jesus.
33. I recover everything that I have lost to the spirit of bad luck, in the name of Jesus.
34. Lord, give no one the opportunity to sympathise with me this year, in Jesus' name.
35. I refuse to register and enrol in the school of misfortune, in the name of Jesus.
36. Like Daniel in Babylon, I receive the spirits of excellence, preference, faithfulness, diligence and errorless living, in the name of Jesus.
37. In the name of Jesus, I decree and command all my lost opportunities to return to me before the end of this year, in the name of Jesus.
38. O Lord, I thank You for answering my prayers.

CHAPTER NINE

VICTORIOUS LAUGHTER

VICTORIOUS LAUGHTER

9

There is a world of difference between sorrow and joy. If you have ever gone through a long season of sorrow mourning and despondency you will cherish the season of laughter and dancing. After battles come celebration. When you experience unchallengeable victory you are bound to burst into laughter and rejoicing.

When the enemy confronts you with battles from all fronts, it is your duty to fight aggressively until victory is yours and you are able to celebrate with uncommon joy. If you are surrounded by wicked enemies who pound and launch ferocious attacks at you from every direction, there is no way you can declare that your joy is full.

Victims of satanic attacks hardly laugh. Such people go about wearing long faces, a situation which leaves much to be desired. The situation will not change until you take the battle to the enemy and declare that enough is enough. There is no laughter without victory. There is no room for rejoicing until you achieve the conquest that will make the enemy to take a bow and submit unto you.

Psalms 66:3 says:

> *Say unto God, How terrible art thou in thy works! through the greatness of thy power shall thine enemies submit themselves unto thee.*

This prayer programme has been vomited by the Holy Ghost for those who want to celebrate victory over the powers that are mocking them. It is indeed true that he who laughs last laughs best. These prayer points will prove invaluable for those who shed tears day and night. It is a prayer programme that has been carved out for people who are desperate for a change. It is carved out for modern day Hannahs who are ready to pray their way to breakthroughs.

It portrays the spirit of Jacob when he declared, "Unless you bless me, I won't let you go." It is a prayer programme that will make you laugh and compel your enemy to cry. With this prayer programme God will wipe your tears, give you a new song and make you to burst into the type of laughter that will send confusion into the camp of the enemy. These prayer points will provoke heaven and sentence you to laughter 365 days of the year. I welcome you to your season of laughter. Your joy has come. Your celebration has started, your testimony shall proclaim the awesome power of the Almighty.

PRAYER SECTION

Confession: **Psalm 46:1-11:** *God is our refuge and strength, a very present help in trouble. Therefore will not we fear, though the earth be removed, and though the mountains be carried into the midst of the sea; Though the waters thereof roar and be troubled, though the mountains shake with the swelling thereof. Selah. There is a river, the streams whereof shall make glad the city of God, the holy place of the tabernacles of* *the most High. God is in the midst of her; she shall not be moved: God shall help her, and that right early. The heathen raged, the kingdoms were moved: he uttered his voice, the earth melted. The Lord of hosts is with us; the God of Jacob is our refuge. Come, behold the works of the Lord, what desolations he hath made in the earth. He maketh wars to cease unto the end of the earth; he breaketh the bow, and cutteth the spear in sunder; he burneth the chariot in the fire. Be still, and know that I am God: I will be exalted among the heathen, I will be exalted in the earth. The Lord of hosts is with us; the God of Jacob is our refuge. Selah.*

Praise Worship

 **PRAYER POINTS**

1. Thou power of God, disgrace my detractors, in the name of Jesus.
2. Lord, contend with them that contend with me, in the name of Jesus.
3. Lord, let my generation celebrate me, in the name of Jesus.
4. Every arrow of mourning and sorrow, backfire, in the name of Jesus.
5. Lord, convert any pain in my life to gain, in the name of Jesus.
6. Give me my personal pentecost, in Jesus' name.
7. Give me fire to fight, O Lord, in the name of Jesus.
8. I shall not die but live to declare the works of God, in the name of Jesus.
9. The numbers of my days shall be fulfilled, in the name of Jesus.
10. Every damaged organ in my body, be repaired by fire, in the name of Jesus.
11. My bones shall not be broken through accident, in the name of Jesus.
12. Every power that does not want to see me around, fall down and die, in the name of Jesus.

13. Any evil attached to my name against my blessings, be cut off and die, in the name of Jesus.

14. Let my name become poison in the mouth of my enemies, in the name of Jesus.

15. Anything attached to my name scarring opportunities away from me, die, in the name of Jesus.

16. Let the mention of my name bring favour into my life, in the name of Jesus.

17. My name, hear the word of the Lord: you will no longer scar opportunities away from me, in Jesus' name.

18. Every evil lot assigned against my blessings, die, in the name of Jesus.

19. Every stubborn evil altar priest, drink your own blood, in the name of Jesus.

20. I possess my possession stolen by the evil altar, in the name of Jesus.

21. I withdraw my name from every evil altar, in the name of Jesus.

22. I withdraw my blessings from every evil altar, in the name of Jesus.

23. I withdraw my breakthroughs from every evil altar, in the name of Jesus.

24. I break and loose myself from every inherited evil covenant of the earth, in the name of Jesus.

25. I break and loose myself from every inherited evil curse of the earth, in the name of Jesus.

26. I break and loose myself from every form of demonic bewitchment of the earth, in the name of Jesus.

27. I release myself from every evil domination and control from the earth, in the name of Jesus.

28. Let the blood of Jesus be transfused into my blood

29. O God, vex my stubborn oppressors in Your sore displeasure, in the name of Jesus.

30. O Lord, break my enemies with Your rod of iron, in Jesus' name.

31. O God, dash the power of stubborn pursuers in pieces like a potter's vessel, in the name of Jesus.

32. O God, arise with all Your weapons of war and fight my battle for me, in the name of Jesus.

33. O God, be my glory and the lifter of my head, in Jesus' name.

34. My Father, be a shield for me in every situation, in Jesus' name.

35. O God, hear my cry out of Your holy hill, in the name of Jesus.

36. I will not be afraid of 10,000 of people that have set themselves against me, in the name of Jesus.

WINNING THE MARRIAGE BATTLE

CHAPTER ONE

MY MARRIAGE, COME FORTH

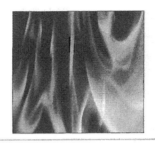

MY MARRIAGE, COME FORTH

1

Every situation in life is an entity. Like every situation in life, Marriage is an entity. It has an ear and can hear both negative and positive voices. If you allow situations in life to remain as they are, you will continue to go through unpleasant conditions. You can take control of the situation in your marriage through prayer and it can come alive and become what God wants it to be.

The force of prayer can be applied on your marriage and be made to conform with the divine image and purpose. But change will not occur unless you pray it into manifestation. All you need to do is to face your marital situation squarely and command it to come forth from the graveyard of oppression. The devil has swept many marriages into the valley. The only solution is to address your marriage the same way Jesus resurrected Lazarus when he was dead and stinking. When you command your marriage to come alive, the grave will give way and every dead cell in your marriage will receive life. A lot of marriages are dead and stinking, you need to pray if the following conditions describe your marriage.

1. Any marriage attacked by ancestral powers.
2. Any marriage besieged by witchcraft agents.
3. Any marriage characterized by a dead relationship.
4. Any marriage where there are frequent squabbles.
5. Any marriage in which the couple live like cat and rat.
6. Any marriage constantly under a siege.
7. Any marriage at the verge of hitting the rocks.
8. Any marriage characterised by incessant troubles through parental influence.
9. Any marriage filled with hatred and frustration.
10. Any marriage characterised by lack of divine honey that makes the family wholesome.
11. Any marriage filled with manifestation of curses.
12. Any marriage that experience mysterious fights day in day out
13. Any marriage that witnesses the success of the agenda of witchcraft.
14. Any marriage in which the couple have given up on each other.
15. Any marriage buried by household wickedness.

If these types of problems can be found in your marriage, you need to command it to come forth. You must pray that the divine agenda for your marriage will succeed. Your marriage must come forth. Every goodness of your marriage that has been buried must be exhumed. The health of your marriage cand be attained through this prayer programme. Pray until there is a remarkable change in your marriage.

PRAYER SECTION

Confessions: **Galatians 6:17:** *From henceforth let no man trouble me: for I bear in my body the marks of the Lord Jesus.* **Psalm 75:6:** *For promotion cometh neither from the east, nor from the west, nor from the* *south.* **Psalm 24:7-9:** *Lift up your heads, O ye gates; and be ye lift up, ye everlasting doors; and the King of glory shall come in. Who is this King of glory? The Lord strong and mighty, the Lord mighty in battle. Lift up your heads, O ye gates; even lift them up, ye everlasting doors; and the King of glory shall come in.* **Psalm 125:3:** *For the rod of the wicked shall not rest upon the lot of the righteous; lest the righteous put forth their hands unto iniquity.* **Eccles. 3:11:** *He hath made everything beautiful in his time: also he hath set the world in their heart, so that no man can find out the work that God maketh from the beginning to the end.* **Psalm 143:7:** *Hear me speedily, O Lord: my spirit faileth: hide not thy face from me, lest I be like unto them that go down into the pit.* **Jeremiah 1:12:** *Then said the Lord unto me, Thou hast well seen: for I will hasten my word to perform it.* **Isaiah 55:11:** *So shall my word be that goeth forth out of my mouth: it shall not return unto me void, but it shall accomplish that which I please, and it shall prosper in the thing whereto I sent it.* **2 Tim. 2:26:** *And that they may recover themselves out of the snare of the devil, who are taken captive by him at his will.* **Psalm 68:18:** *Thou hast ascended on high, thou hast led captivity captive: thou hast received gifts for men; yea, for the rebellious also, that the Lord God might dwell among them.* Galatians 3:13-14: *Christ hath redeemed us from the curse of the law, being made a curse for us: for it is written, Cursed is every one that hangeth on a tree: That the blessing of Abraham might come on the Gentiles through Jesus Christ; that we might receive the promise of the Spirit through faith.* **Col. 1:13:** *Who hath delivered us from the power of darkness, and hath translated us into the kingdom of his dear Son:* **Isaiah 49:25:** *But thus saith the Lord, Even the captives of the mighty shall be taken away, and the prey of the terrible shall be delivered: for I will contend with him that contendeth with thee, and I will save thy children.* **Eccles. 4:9-10:** *Two are better than one; because they have a good reward for their labour. For if they fall, the one will lift up his fellow: but woe to him that is alone when he falleth; for he hath not another to help him up.* **Genesis 2:23-24:** *And Adam said, This is now bone of my bones, and flesh of my flesh: she shall be called Woman, because she was taken out of Man. Therefore shall a man leave his father and his mother, and shall cleave unto his wife: and they shall be one flesh.* **Genesis 34:8:** *And Hamor communed with them, saying, The soul of my son Shechem* *longeth for your daughter: I pray you give her him to wife.* **Proverbs 21:1:** *The king's heart is in the hand of the Lord, as the rivers of water: he turneth it whithersoever he will.* **Rev. 3:7:** *And to the angel of the church in Philadelphia write; These things saith he that is holy, he that is true, he that hath the key of David, he that openeth, and no man shutteth; and shutteth, and no man openeth.*

Praise Worship

1. I command all demonic hindrance to my marriage to scatter, in the name of Jesus.
2. Oh Lord, let every demonic stronghold keeping my marriage in bondage release me and be destroyed, in the name of Jesus.
3. I bind every strongman holding my marriage captive, in the name of Jesus.
4. I break and loose myself from every spell of marital bondage and delay, in the name of Jesus.
5. I release myself from every conscious and unconscious covenant with the spirit of marital failure, in the name of Jesus.
6. Oh God, arise and let every enemy of my marital breakthrough be scattered, in the name of Jesus.
7. Oh Lord, baptize me with the spirit of favour, in the name of Jesus.
8. I release my marriage from the ditches of marriage destroyers, in the name of Jesus.
9. Oh Lord, let all marital hindrance be removed, in the name of Jesus.
10. I remove my name and my marriage partner from the book of marital failure, in the name of Jesus.
11. Holy Spirit, be my guide in choosing a life partner, in the name of Jesus.
12. I reject every spirit of marital frustration, in the name of Jesus.
13. Oh Lord, let my marriage become too hot to handle for

demonic agents, in the name of Jesus.

14. I release my marriage from the influence, control and domination of household wickedness, in Jesus' name.

15. Oh Lord, let every satanic angel diverting my marriage partner from me be paralysed, in the name of Jesus.

16. Oh Lord, let the joy of the enemy over my marital life be converted to sorrow, in the name of Jesus.

17. I bind every anti-marriage force, in the name of Jesus.

18. Oh Lord, let every spirit of demonic delay and marital hindrances be rendered impotent, in the name of Jesus.

19. I loose angels, to go and create breakthrough for my marriage, in the name of Jesus.

20. I receive the mandate to put to flight every enemy of my marital breakthrough, in the name of Jesus.

21. Oh Lord, help me to identify and deal with any weakness in me that can hinder my breakthroughs, in the name of Jesus.

22. You spirit of strife and anger, I bind and render you to naught in my life, in the name of Jesus.

23. You devil, take your legs away from my marital affairs, in the name of Jesus.

24. I bind and paralyse every spirit of error, in the name of Jesus.

25. I bind every spirit of bad luck, in the name of Jesus.

26. I bind every spirit of demonic postponement, in the name of Jesus.

27. I break all consequences of parental sins on my marital destiny, in the name of Jesus.

28. Every evil directed at my marriage, backfire, in the name of Jesus.

29. Oh Lord, make everything the enemy has says is impossible in my marriage possible, in the name of Jesus.

30. I release myself from the umbrella of any family marital captivity, in the name of Jesus.

31. I release myself from any inherited marital bondage, in the name of Jesus.

32. Every inherited demonic deposit working against my marital success, be flushed out by the blood of Jesus.

33. I break and loose myself from every collective marital evil covenant, in the name of Jesus.
34. Every marital foundational strongman attached to my life, die, in the name of Jesus.
35. Oh Lord, let any rod of the wicked rising up against my destiny, be rendered impotent for my sake, in the name of Jesus.
36. Every evil family tree working against my marriage, be uprooted by fire, in the name of Jesus.
37. Every ancestral problem passed down into my life, receive divine solution, in the name of Jesus.
38. Every marital curse of failure operating in my family, be broken by the blood of Jesus.
39. I pull down every demonic stronghold rising up against me, in the name of Jesus.
40. Every evil effect of polygamous background on my marriage, be cancelled by the blood of Jesus.
41. Oh Lord, help me to identify and deal with any recurring negative cycle responsible for my marital delay, in the name of Jesus.
42. I break every satanic cycle responsible for my marital delay, in the name of Jesus.
43. I release myself into my marital destiny, in the name of Jesus.
44. Every effect of parental curses upon my marriage, be cancelled by the blood of Jesus.
45. Every effect of demonic initiation upon my marital destiny, be cancelled by the blood of Jesus.
46. Every effect of demonic marriage upon my marital destiny, be cancelled by the blood of Jesus.
47. Every effect of demonic alteration of marital destiny upon my life, be cancelled by the blood of Jesus.
48. Every evil family river flowing into my life, dry up and die, in the name of Jesus.
49. I break myself free from every evil family marital pattern, in the name of Jesus.

50. I release myself from every evil marital bondage, in the name of Jesus.

51. Oh Lord, let every device of the enemy against my marital destiny be frustrated, in the name of Jesus.

52. Every anti-marriage spell and curse working against my destiny, be broken, in the name of Jesus.

53. Every bondage and bewitchment fashioned against my settling down in marriage, be broken, in Jesus' name.

54. Every force, scaring away my marriage partner, fall down and die, in the name of Jesus.

55. I break every yoke of marital failure, in the name of Jesus.

56. I paralyse the handiwork of household enemies and envious agent concerning my marital life, in the name of Jesus.

57. Every evil spirit wedding conducted consciously or unconsciously on my behalf, die, in the name of Jesus.

58. Oh Lord, let every enchantment, divination or incantation working against my settling down in marriage, die, in the name of Jesus.

59. Every demonic power hindering my marital breakthrough, be frustrated, in the name of Jesus.

60. I break every evil covenant working against my marital destiny, in the name of Jesus.

61. I destroy by fire every demonic instrument fashioned against my destiny, in the name of Jesus.

62. Every human agent hindering and working against my marriage, be exposed and die, in the name of Jesus.

63. All boasting powers delegated against my marriage, be silenced, in the name of Jesus.

64. I withdraw my marriage from the hands of the oppressors, in the name of Jesus.

65. I command all evil marks and labels in my life to be erased by the blood of Jesus.

66. Every power chasing away my divine helpers, die, in the name of Jesus.

67. Oh Lord, let heavenly fire ignite my marital life, in the name of Jesus.
68. Oh Lord, let the anointing for marital breakthrough fall powerfully on me, in the name of Jesus.
69. I reject every evil spiritual marriage contamination, in the name of Jesus.
70. Oh Lord, give me divine prescription to my marriage problems today, in the name of Jesus.
71. I receive power to overcome obstacles to my marital breakthroughs, in the name of Jesus.
72. Oh Lord, anoint my eyes to see divine vision, in the name of Jesus.
73. My marriage shall not be in struggle but in prosperity, in the name of Jesus.
74. I release myself from the spirit of bitterness, in the name of Jesus.
75. Thank God for answers to your prayers.

CHAPTER TWO

BREAKTHROUGH PRAYERS FOR SUPERNATURAL CONCEPTION

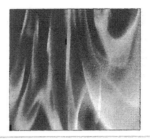

BREAKTHROUGH PRAYERS FOR SUPERNATURAL CONCEPTION

2

Children are God's heritage. When God puts supernatural conception in place, you are bound to carry your pregnancy full-term and experience the bliss of a joyful mother. Prayers for supernatural conception will grant you immunity. Your pregnancy cannot be tempered with. When a woman gets pregnant, it may not be hidden from friends and foes alike. Satanic agents are also able to detect pregnancies from its earliest stage. To keep enemies of your pregnancy at bay you must raise a prayer altar to insulate the baby in your womb. The mystery of supernatural conception must be understood. You can tap into the mystery of the Hebrew women when you pray aggressively. God becomes the Alpha and the Omega in your journey to safe delivery. Even before pregnancy takes place, you must pray for supernatural conception. Supernatural conception and you will be singled out from the crowd. When your colleagues complain of peculiar problems in pregnancy your case will be diffirent. When fellow women go through pain or first miscarriage your own pregnancy will be intact. When other women are subjected to all kinds of attacks during conception no power will touch you. When other women tell tales of woe, pain and agony yours will be testimonies galore.

When other children give birth to deformed children, yours will be a healthy bouncing baby. When others are played back and forth like football by witchcraft practitioners. God will simply issue a decree, concerning you saying; "Touch not my anointed" God will pour the oil of grace upon you during your season of pregnancy. Your health shall be sound and the power of the Holy Ghost shall overshadow the baby in your womb. The baby shall enjoy the constant flow of divine supply. Since yours is supernatural conception everything about your pregnancy will be supernatural. The power of the Most High will be made manifest in your conception. People far and near will declare that the finger of the Almighty is upon both the mother and the child. Additionally, when supernatural conception is in place there shall be supernatural supply of all the needs of the parents and the child.

You need not bother about the fears and troubles of those who go through hell. This prayer programme will separate the favoured from the ordinary pregnant woman. God is set to give you the blessings of supernatural conception.

PRAYER SECTION

Confession: Genesis 25:21; 33:5; Psalm 127:3; 1 Samuel 1:27: *And Isaac intreated the Lord for his wife, because she was barren: and the Lord was intreated of him, and Rebekah his wife conceived.* **Genesis 33:5**: *And they journeyed: and the terror of God was upon the cities that were round about them, and they did not pursue after the sons of Jacob.* **Ps 127:3**: *Lo, children are an heritage of the Lord: and the fruit of the womb is his reward.* **1 Samuel 1:27**: *For this child I prayed; and the Lord hath given me my petition which I asked of him.*

Praise Worship

1. Thanksgiving.
2. Select seven songs of praises to the Lord.
3. Oh God, arise and set the earthquake of deliverance into my womb, in the name of Jesus.
4. My womb, receive deliverance by fire, in the name of Jesus.
5. I reject every long-term or short-term barrenness, in the name of Jesus.
6. Every satanic deposit, contrary to child bearing, in my body and in the system of my husband, be flushed out, in the name of Jesus.
7. Every witchcraft padlock, used against my womb, catch fire, in the name of Jesus.
8. Holy Ghost fire, melt away any fibroid hindering conception, in the name of Jesus.
9. My Father locate the source of my problem and scatter it, in the name of Jesus.
10. By the blood of Jesus, I cancel every negative report against my conception, in the name of Jesus.
11. Any damage done to my womb, receive healing, in the name of Jesus.
12. Father, expose every secret responsible for delay in child bearing, in the name of Jesus.
13. Oh Lord, incubate my womb with Your fire, in the name of Jesus.
14. Every evil covenant that is working against my conception, be neutralized by the blood of Jesus.
15. Thou enemy from my mother/father's house responsible for child delay in my marriage, receive the judgement of fire, in the name of Jesus.
16. Thou enemy from in-laws home, responsible for delay in child bearing, be condemned by fire, in Jesus' name.
17. Every evil water, washing away my pregnancy, dry up, in the name of Jesus.

18. Every curse of barrenness in my lineage, I neutralise you, in the name of Jesus.
19. Anyone that needs to die for me to give birth to my own baby, fall down and die, in the name of Jesus.
20. Oh God of Hannah, Sarah and Elizabeth, visit me by fire, in the name of Jesus.
21. My womb, receive divine fertilisation this month, in the name of Jesus.
22. This month will not elude me, I receive grace to be pregnant, in the name of Jesus.
23. The Power that creates the heaven and the earth, create my children supernaturally, in the name of Jesus.
24. I refuse to waste money on conception again, in the name of Jesus.
25. Quality children, great children, shall surround my table, in the name of Jesus.
26. Oh Lord, give me miracle babies to the glory of Your name, in the name of Jesus.
27. Father, correct anything that is wrong with the reproduction organ of my husband, in the name of Jesus.
28. Every demon power energising miscarriage, loose your hold, in the name of Jesus.
29. Every unexplainable attack against my child bearing, backfire, in the name of Jesus.
30. Thank You, Lord, for everyone shall congratulate me, in the name of Jesus.

CHAPTER THREE

PROTECTION
OF CHILDREN

PROTECTION OF CHILDREN

③

The Bible places much premium on children. Their protection and preservation are of utmost importance to God. Right from the womb until God has made a provision to ensure that children are well protected from all harms and wicked attacks. Children are weak, during the age of innocence and are not able to pray for protection. They therefore need the adults to intercede for them.

Parents, pastors, children ministers and older members of the family should, from time to time, take the prayer points in this section. We should not wait until children are endangered or attacked. The axiom, "in the time of peace, prepare for war", makes a lot of sense. Do not wait until you sense danger, accident, health challenges or attacks that threaten the lives of children before you pray. It is the responsibility of every parent to stand in the gap and pray for their children.

Children are at risk in the following ways:

1.   Witchcraft attacks.
2.   Domestic accidents.
3.   The peril of being injured by domestic servants.
4.   The attack that comes from household wickedness.
5.   Childhood diseases.
6.   The proliferation of kidnappers.
7.   Infectious diseases.
8.   The threat of drinkers of blood and eaters of flesh.
9.   The danger of being injured by playmates.
10.   Wicked peer pressure.
11.   Obtaining dangerous items from mates and adults.
12.   The wickedness of envious neighbours.
13.   Attacks that come when children are asleep.
14.   Attacks during birth.
15.   Steakling the star during naming ceremony.
16.   Getting into trouble through innocent past times or leisure.
17.   Attacks during times in school.
18.   Food poisoning.

We have mentioned only few of the dangers which children are prone to. Parents, pastors and family members who love children must pray protective prayers for them. If the prayer points below are vigorously said, children will be spared lots of attacks. Take these prayer points aggressively and you may be saving the lives of precious children.

PRAYER SECTION

Confession: **Psalm 118:17; 56:13; 2Timothy 1:10:** *I shall not die, but live, and declare the works of the Lord.* **Psalm 56:13:** *For thou hast delivered my soul from death: wilt not thou deliver my feet from falling, that I may walk before God in the light of the living?* **2 Timothy 1:10:** *But is now made manifest by the appearing of our Saviour Jesus Christ, who hath abolished death, and hath brought life and immortality to light through the gospel:*

Praise Worship

1. Father, thank You for giving me wonderful children, in the name of Jesus.
2. Thank You, Lord, for making me a mother, in the name of Jesus.
3. I am a mother of living children, in the name of Jesus.
4. I hide the lives of my children, in the name of Jesus.
5. Jesus has tasted death for my children to stay alive, in the name of Jesus.
6. I insure the lives of my children with the blood of Jesus.
7. I thwart all the decisions and plans of the enemy against my children, in the name of Jesus.
8. Oh Lord, shield my children against evil attacks, in the name of Jesus.
9. I envelope my children with divine covering, in the name of Jesus.
10. I withdraw the name of my children from the book of death, in the name of Jesus.
11. Father, protect my children from kidnappers targeting them, in the name of Jesus.
12. Father, let Your fire consume every kidnappers targeting my children, in the name of Jesus.
13. I withdraw the names of my children from the book of kidnappers, in the name of Jesus.
14. Every evil gang-up against my children, scatter unto desolation, in the name of Jesus.
15. Oh Lord, deliver my children from the paw of the lion, in the name of Jesus.
16. My children, you will not answer the call of death, in the name of Jesus.
17. I insure the names of my children with the blood of Jesus.
18. *(Mention the name of your children and say:)* You will not go to the grave before me, in the name of Jesus.
19. Thou demon sending children to early grave, you will not locate any of my children, in the name of Jesus.

20. Father, deliver my children from any sickness that may want to claim their lives, in the name of Jesus.
21. Any portion in the body of my children that is infected with diseases, be cleansed by the blood of Jesus.
22. Every witch/wizard that wants to terminate the lives of my children, be roasted, in the name of Jesus.
23. Every harassment in the dream of my children, I stop you by fire, in the name of Jesus.
24. Every nightmare aimed at terminating the lives of my children, backfire, in the name of Jesus.
25. Arrows of untimely death fired into the lives of my children, backfire, in the name of Jesus.
26. Evil coffin constituted for any of my children, burry your maker, in the name of Jesus.
27. Arrows of slow death fired into the body of my children, be removed by the blood of Jesus.
28. Power of the grave, I render you impotent in the lives of my children, in the name of Jesus.
29. Any poison eaten by my children, be neutralised by the blood of Jesus.
30. Any sickness planted into the body of my children while they were sleeping, be flushed out by the blood of Jesus.
31. Every enemy from my father's/mother's home, that want to kill my children, kill yourself now, in the name of Jesus.
32. Holy Ghost fire, make the lives of my children untochable, in the name of Jesus.
33. My children's names, be incubated by fire, in the name of Jesus.
34. Any power that does not want me to enjoy my children at old age, die, in the name of Jesus.
35. I will not bury any of my children, in the name of Jesus.
36. Father, elongate the lives of my children, in the name of Jesus.
37. Oh Lord, swallow up death for the victory of my children, in the name of Jesus.

38. Power of rapid death, I transform you to rapid blessing for my children, in the name of Jesus.

39. Every incantation against my children, be converted to blessings, in the name of Jesus.

40. Father, deliver my children from the slaughter's slab, in the name of Jesus.

41. No secret cult will terminate the lives of my children, in the name of Jesus.

42. Every witch that wants to suck the blood of my children, suck your own blood, in the name of Jesus.

43. My children, you are anointed for the top, in the name of Jesus.

44. Oh death, my children are not your candidates, in the name of Jesus.

45. Angels of elevation, locate my children, in the name of Jesus.

46. My children, you will not walk in the path of destruction, in the name of Jesus.

47. Collective death, my children will not partake you, in the name of Jesus.

48. My children, you shall live to see your children's children, in the name of Jesus.

49. My children, you are alive to fulfil divine agenda, in the name of Jesus.

CHAPTER FOUR

MARITAL SANITATION

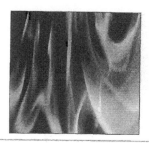

MARITAL SANITATION

4

This is a prayer programme that is vomited by the Holy Ghost to sanitise your marriage. Every problematic aspect of your marriage is carefully addressed. When you run the situation in your marriage through this marital sanitation prayers, your marriage can be salvaged, and the will of God will be done in your home. There is nothing that prayer cannot do. The problem is that most people neglect the weapon of prayer. You must go into this prayer session with faith in your heart. Every area addressed shall give birth to miracles. The sick areas of your marriage will receive the touch of divine healing. Problems that bother your mind will be solved. What has injected anxiety into your heart will no longer be a problem when you take these prayer points.

Prayers for marital sanitation is needed when:

1. When your marriage is threatened.
2. When you find it difficult to stay in your marital home.
3. When anti-marital arrows are at work.

4. When there is lack of favour in your marriage.
5. When marital unity is threatened.
6. When strange women are actively fighting against your home
7. When wicked powers are waging war against your home.
8. When evil advisers are trying to influence your home.
9. When there are visible hindrances between you and your spouse.
10. When your spouse is going astray.
11. When the spirit of deception is at work.
12. When mysterious powers are trying to turn your home upside-down.
13. When external influences are affecting your home.
14. When the spirit of instability is in charge of your home.
15. When your partner is affected by demonic blindness.
16. When your partner is under the spell of demonic manipulation.
17. When you have noticed that your relationship has been affected by curses and evil covenants.
18. When you want God to heal your relationship.

You need to muster all your spiritual energy as you take these prayer points.

PRAYER SECTION

Confession: **Psalm 65:2**: *O thou that hearest prayer, unto thee shall all flesh come.*

Praise Worship

1. Thank God because He is going to intervene in your marriage.
2. I destroy anything that is now going to stand between me and my prayers, in the name of Jesus.
3. Anointing to pray to the point of breakthroughs in my

marriage, fall upon me now, in the name of Jesus.

4. Lord Jesus, I invite You to come to my aid in every difficult situation in my marriage, in the name of Jesus.

5. All my matrimonial properties which the strange woman sat upon, I withdraw them all, in Jesus' name.

6. I withdraw the peace, harmony, unity, love and continuity between my husband and the strange woman, in Jesus' name.

7. Lord Jesus, let the strange and unholy love relationship between my husband and the strange woman die, in the name of Jesus.

8. I withdraw the favour of my husband from the strange woman, in the name of Jesus.

9. I stand against all the powers that push women out of their matrimonial homes, in Jesus' name.

10. All spiritual evil arrows presently in my marriage, fired from the strange woman, loose your grip upon my marriage and go back to your sender, in the name of Jesus.

11. Lord Jesus, wage war against every strange woman militating against my marriage, in Jesus' name.

12. I put hatred in the relationship between ....and ....., in the name of Jesus.

13. Angels of God, pollute the relationship between my husband and ...., in the name of Jesus.

14. Every strange woman militating against my marriage, receive the judgment of God, in the name of Jesus.

15. I nullify every judgment against me in my marriage, in the name of Jesus.

16. Let the hindrances to the manifestation of my restoration to my rightful home depart from me and my marriage, in the name of Jesus.

17. Thou Lion of Judah, consume every fake lion of the strange woman roaring against my marriage, in the name of Jesus.

18. Thunder fire of God, scatter to pieces the stronghold of the strange woman, in the name of Jesus.

husband and the strange woman, be rendered impotent and be roasted by the fire of God, in the name of Jesus.

20. Angels of the living God, brush off the love of _ _ _ from the heart of my husband, in the name of Jesus.

21. Lord Jesus, create a new heart in my husband's life, in the name of Jesus.

22. Every open door that the strange woman is using to gain ground in my husband's life and my home, receive the blood of Jesus and shut, in the name of Jesus.

23. God of new beginning, begin a new thing in my marital life, in the name of Jesus.

24. Blood of the Lamb, flow into the foundation of my marital life, in the name of Jesus.

25. Father Lord, let Your kingdom be established in my marriage, in the name of Jesus.

26. O Lord, put the walls of fire between my husband and the strange woman and let them be separated forever, in the name of Jesus.

27. Every evil veil covering the face of my husband, catch the fire of God and be consumed to ashes, in the name of Jesus.

28. Every trap of destruction fashioned against my husband by the strange woman, fail woefully, in Jesus' name.

29. Lord, I pray that.......will not find peace until he returns to his creator in repentance, in the name of Jesus.

30. I command the ways of all unfriendly friends confusing . . . to become dark and slippery, in the name of Jesus.

31. Let the angels of God arise and block the path of .... with thorns after the order of Balaam until ....runs back to the Saviour, in the name of Jesus.

32. Let all strange lovers begin to avoid.......as from today, in the name of Jesus.

33. Lord, ordain terrifying noises against all evil collaborators confusing......., in the name of Jesus.

34. O Lord, build a wall of hindrance around......so that he will be unable to carry out any ungodly activity, in the name of

Jesus.

35. Let all the good things that .   .   . is enjoying and hardening his heart to the truth be withdrawn, in Jesus' name.

36. Let . . . become sick and restless on tasting any alcohol or using any addictive material, in the name of Jesus.

37. I break every curse of the vagabond upon the life of . . . in the mighty name of Jesus.

38. Let the angels of the living God begin to pursue all strange lovers caging . . ., in the name of Jesus.

39. Lord, walk back to the foundation of my marriage and carry out the necessary surgical operation.

40. I bind every strongman militating against my home be frustrated, in the name of Jesus.

41. Let every gadget of marriage destruction in my home, in the name of Jesus.

42. Let every evil anti-marriage linkage with my parents be dashed to pieces, in the name of Jesus.

43. Every evil effect of external interferences in my marriage be completely neutralised, in the name of Jesus.

44. I paralyse every architect of conflict and hostility in my home, in the name of Jesus.

45. Let every evil power trying to re-draw my marriage map be put to shame, in the name of Jesus.

46. Let all extra-marital relationship with other "partners" collapse and die, in the name of Jesus.

47. I paralyse the activities of the following spirits (listed here under), and I command them to loose their hold upon......... , in the name of Jesus.
    - criticism- unreasonableness- accusation
    - arguing- intimidation- rejecting truth - P r i d e   S e l f - importance- Self-enteredness
    - Self-exaltation- Selfishness- Head-strong
    - Superiority- Intolerance- Cruelty
    - Reiteration- Impatience- Bitterness

- Anger- Hatred- Fighting
- Contention- Violence- Rebellion
- Deception- Restlessness- Withdrawal- Confusion-
Family molestation- Lust of eyes
- Lust of flesh- Dishonesty- Disrespect
- Personality disorders- Cursing-- Lying
- Inherited curses- Occult practices

48. Father, in the name of Jesus, give unto........, the spirits of wisdom and revelation in the knowledge of You.

49. Let every stronghold of the enemy barricading the mind of. . . from receiving the Lord be pulled down, in the name of Jesus.

50. Let all hindrances coming between the heart of ....and the gospel be melted away by the fire of the Holy Spirit.

51. In Jesus' name, I bind the strongman attached to the life of ...., keeping him from receiving Jesus Christ as his Lord and Saviour.

52. Lord, build a hedge of thorns around........, so that he turns to You, in Jesus' name.

53. In the name of Jesus, I break the curse placed on........, binding him from receiving the Lord.

54. You spirit of death and hell, release........, in the name of Jesus.

55. Every desire of the enemy on the soul of........will not prosper, in the name of Jesus.

56. I bind every spirit of mind blindness in the life of ...., in the name of Jesus.

57. Spirit of bondage, lukewarmness and perdition, release ......, in the name of Jesus.

58. I bind the strongman shielding ...., from receiving the gospel, in the name of Jesus.

59. Father, let spiritual blindness be erased from the life of......, in the name of Jesus.

60. I come against the powers of darkness blinding and holding.......back from receiving the gospel, in Jesus' name.

61. I command you spirit of the power of the air to loose your

hold on ....so that he will be free to accept Jesus as Lord and Saviour, in the name of Jesus.

62. I tear down and smash every stronghold of deception keeping.......... in the enemy's camp, in Jesus' name.

63. Let...........come from the kingdom of darkness and into the kingdom of light, in the name of Jesus.

64. Lord, let Your plan and purpose for the life of..........prevail.

65. By the blood of the Lord Jesus Christ, I loose..........from the bondage that the powers of darkness are putting on him/her, in Jesus' name.

66. By the blood of Jesus, I cancel and render null and void all commands issued by the powers of darkness in.......'s life, in Jesus' name.

67. I bind the god of this age and declare that he can longer blind ....in darkness, in the name of Jesus.

68. Father Lord, let Your power draw...........out of every trap, in the name of Jesus.

69. Let the powers of darkness be confounded and put to shame that seek after............in the name of Jesus.

70. Father Lord, grant..........opened eyes and ears, understanding heart and grace to be converted and healed, in the name of Jesus.

71. Lord, bring all of..........'s thoughts captive to the obedience of Christ.

72. Let the hedge of thorns be built around ....and let the hedge repel all the workers of darkness in his/her life, in Jesus' name.

73. Lord, grant...........conviction of sin with godly sorrow to repentance, in Jesus' name.

74. Thank God for answers to your prayer.

CHAPTER FIVE

BREAKTHROUGH PRAYERS FOR SUPERNATURAL CONCEPTION 1

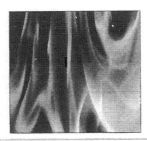

BREAKTHROUGH PRAYERS FOR SUPERNATURAL CONCEPTION 1

5

The issue of child bearing is so crucial that it must be addressed by every couple. The moment God decrees that you shall be fruitful in marriage, the kingdom of darkness has no right to tamper with His programme for you. Lots of casualties have been reported in recent times. During pregnancy all kinds of arrows are fired against women in their moment of weakness. The burden of carrying a child in the womb for a number of months is heavy enough, not to talk of when such a burden is compounded by demonic attacks coming from left, right and centre.

For some women, the problem of conception takes place right at the time they are supposed to become pregnant. But some powers have vowed that some women will not taste pregnancy. Hence, the moment some women get married the whole of hell is let loose and a demonic whirl-wind will continue to blow against those who are expectant. When such women visit hospitals they are told that nothing is wrong. Beloved, many people experience severe battles at the gate of conception.

Wicked spirits mount lofty roadblocks against conception. Immediately some women begin to see signs of pregnancy some wicked satanic soldiers invade their womb and there is turbulence until miscarriage is occasioned.

Those who are seeking the fruit of the womb should not take this battle for granted. Serious prayers must be said to cancel the satanic agenda against conception. Prayers must be continuous to ensure that there is nothing like miscarriage after conception. These prayers are needed by couples who are facing challenges in the area of fruitfulness. They are designed by the Holy Ghost against vicious cycle of constant miscarriage. If you have discovered that miscarriages are common in your lineage, you must say these prayers as a wounded lion. You need them to silence people who are asking: where is your God?

You need this prayer programme to silence every demonic tongue. You must pray your way to miraculous delivery. You must invoke the power of the Almighty and declare **Jeramiah 32:17 which says:**

> *Ah Lord GOD! behold, thou hast made the heaven and the earth by thy great power and stretched out arm, and there is nothing too hard for thee:*

PRAYER SECTIONS

Confession: **Luke 1:37:** *For with God nothing shall be impossible.* **Jeremiah 32:17**: *Ah Lord God! behold, thou hast made the heaven and the earth by thy great power and stretched out arm, and there is nothing too hard for thee:*

 **PRAYER POINTS**

1. Blood of Jesus, arise in Your bulldozing power and sanitise my reproductive organs, in the name of Jesus.

2. Holy Ghost fire, sanitise my..........for supernatural conception, in the name of Jesus.

3. O Lord, by the power that answereth Sarah and Hannah, visit my by fire, in the name of Jesus.

4. Creative power of God, repair any damage done to my reproductive structures, in the name of Jesus.

5. O God, arise and advertise Your creative power in my......., in the name of Jesus.

6. I pull down every stronghold of infertility, in the name of Jesus.

7. Every witchcraft power bewitching my.........., fall down and die, in the name of Jesus.

8. O Lord, by Your power which knows no impossibility, let my children manifest, in the name of Jesus.

9. This month shall not pass me by without blessings, in the name of Jesus.

10. My Father, bring forth signs and wonder in my life, in the name of Jesus.

11. I invite the power of God into every organ of my body, in the name of Jesus.

12. Healing power of God, flow into my........., in the name of Jesus.

13. I call forth my children from any captivity, in the name of Jesus.

14. Every clinical prophecy concerning my situation, be over-turned by fire, in the name of Jesus.

15. Where is the Lord God of Elijah, give me the miracle of supernatural conception, in the name of Jesus.

16. My Father, speak life and productiveness into my......., in the name of Jesus.

17. Every evil hand laid on my reproductive organs, catch fire, in the name of Jesus.

18. O God of deliverance, deliver me from infertility, in the name of Jesus,

19. I release my........., from the grip of evil plantations, in the

name of Jesus.

20. I reject every arrow assigned to torment my......, in the name of Jesus.

21. My glands, hormones and blood, receive the fire of deliverance, in the name of Jesus.

22. Every tree that the enemy has planted against my childbearing, be uprooted by fire, in the name of Jesus.

23. Every witchcraft decision on my child-bearing, be cancelled by fire, in the name of Jesus.

24. O God of fruitfulness, bring honey out of the rock for me, in the name of Jesus.

25. Any problem that came into my life through past sexual partners, receive solution, in the name of Jesus.

26. Any problem that came into my life through abortion, receive solution, in the name of Jesus.

27. Any problem that came into my life through the deposits of spirit husband/wife, be solved by fire, in the name of Jesus.

28. Any problem that came into my life through wrong surgery, be solved by fire, in the name of Jesus.

29. Any infertility deposits in my........, catch fire, in the name of Jesus.

30. Thou Great Physician, correct my body for supernatural conception, in the name of Jesus.

31. My body, reject every arrow of infertility, in the name of Jesus.

32. Every power assigned to embarrass me maritally, I kill you now, in the name of Jesus.

33. My Father, let me experience the glory power of Jehovah, in the name of Jesus.

34. Holy Ghost fire, incubate my...........for productivity, in the name of Jesus.

35. Any power stealing from my body, catch fire, in the name of Jesus.

36. Every glory that has departed from my life, return by fire, in the name of Jesus.

the name of Jesus.

38. I arise by fire and possess my possessions concerning child-bearing, in the name of Jesus.

39. My Father, bombard me with the anointing for fruitfulness, in the name of Jesus.

40. Holy Ghost fire, arise and burn away every anti-child-bearing infirmity, in the name of Jesus.

41. I speak destruction unto every mountain of infertility in my life, in the name of Jesus.

42. I speak death unto every mountain of infertility in my life, in the name of Jesus.

43. I speak paralysis unto every mountain of infertility in my life, in the name of Jesus.

44. I decree war against every mountain of infertility in my life, in the name of Jesus.

45. I curse every mountain of infertility to dry from its roots, in the name of Jesus.

46. I speak woe unto every mountain of infertility in my life, in the name of Jesus.

CHAPTER SIX

BREAKTHROUGH PRAYERS FOR SUPERNATURAL CONCEPTION 2

BREAKTHROUGH PRAYERS FOR SUPERNATURAL CONCEPTION 2

6

The issue of child bearing is so important in present day generation. The devil has afflicted many homes in the area of pregnancy and delivery. The weapon of prayer has proved to be invaluable in withstanding him. Hospitals have done quite a lot. Medical personel have assisted in no small way, but recent experiences have proved that the best way to tackle issues related to child bearing in the family is to do so spiritually. It is clear that the spiritual controls the physical. Whenever there are problems in the area of pregnancy and child bearing most of the time there are spiritual factors behind them.

Matthew 13:25 says:

> But while men slept, his enemy came and sowed tares among the wheat, and went his way.

Evil forces generally carry out their activities surreptitiously. They perfect their wicked plans when people are not vigilant. It is this hidden method that makes them to succeed. Whenever satanic agents finishes uprooting what has been planted, their victims begin to experience problems physically. The best way to tackle physical problems is to address their root spiritually. You must lay the axe at the root.

Matthew 3:10 says:

> And now also the axe is laid unto the root of the trees: therefore every tree which bringeth not forth good fruit is hewn down, and cast into the fire.

Once you tackle things from the spiritual realm everything will fall into line.

You need prayers for supernatural conception when:

1. You discover that strange things are happening to you.
2. You are going through your season of conception.
3. You are experiencing attacks.
4. People come to you physically or spiritually threatening that you will see trouble during conception and delivery.
5. Strange powers are fighting against your becoming a joyful mother.
6. You discover that most people who get married in your lineage find it difficult to get pregnant and experience safe delivery.
7. It becomes clear your season of pregnancy has become a season of incessant attacks.
8. The powers of your father's house are fighting tooth and nail to turn your joy to sorrow.
9. You have constant attacks in the dream during pregnancy and prior to delivery.
10. Medication has proved ineffective.
11. You sense that certain powers have waited for you in the area of child bearing.

These prayers must be said aggressively. You must not allow weakness to stop you from persistently praying. You must declare war against powers that have vowed that you will not carry your own baby. There must be fire in your prayers.

PRAYER SECTION

Confession: **Genesis 1:1-3:** *In the beginning God created the heaven and the earth. And the earth was without form, and void; and darkness was upon the face of the deep. And the Spirit of God moved upon the face of the waters. And God said, Let there be light: and there was light.* **John 1:1-3:** *In the beginning was the Word, and the Word was with God, and the Word was God. The same was in the beginning with God. All things were made by him; and without him was not any thing made that was made.* **Ezekiel 37:1-10:** *The hand of the Lord was upon me, and carried me out in the spirit of the Lord, and set me down in the midst of the valley which was full of bones, And caused me to pass by them round about: and, behold, there were very many in the open valley; and, lo, they were very dry. And he said unto me, Son of man, can these bones live? And I answered, O Lord God, thou knowest. Again he said unto me, Prophesy upon these bones, and say unto them, O ye dry bones, hear the word of the Lord. Thus saith the Lord God unto these bones; Behold, I will cause breath to enter into you, and ye shall live: And I will lay sinews upon you, and will bring up flesh upon you, and cover you with skin, and put breath in you, and ye shall live; and ye shall know that I am the Lord. So I prophesied as I was commanded: and as I prophesied, there was a noise, and behold a shaking, and the bones came together, bone to his bone. And when I beheld, lo, the sinews and the flesh came up upon them, and the skin covered them above: but there was no breath in them. Then said he unto me, Prophesy unto the wind, prophesy, son of man, and say to the wind, Thus saith the Lord God; Come from the four winds, O breath, and breathe upon these slain, that they may live. So I prophesied as he commanded me, and the breath came into them, and they lived, and stood up upon their feet, an exceeding great army.* **Philip. 3:10:** *That I may know him, and the power of his resurrection, and the fellowship of his sufferings, being made conformable unto his death.*

 **PRAYER POINTS**

1. O God that answereth by fire, open my gate of conception and pregnancy by fire, in the name of Jesus.
2. Every physical and spiritual hindrance to conception and child-bearing, clear away, in the name of Jesus.
3. Fire of God, purge my reproductive organ, in the name of Jesus.
4. Blood of Jesus, purge my reproductive organ, in the name of Jesus.
5. Every power assigned against my child-bearing, scatter, in the name of Jesus.
6. Yokes troubling my reproductive organs, break, in the name of Jesus.
7. By the power that made a way in the Red Sea, my Father, make a way for my child-bearing, in the name of Jesus.
8. Mandate of satan against my full-scale laughter, be buried, in the name of Jesus.
9. By the power of resurrection, let my conception manifest, in the name of Jesus.
10. Every wolf assigned to torment my child-bearing, die, in the name of Jesus.
11. Holy Ghost fire, purge my reproductive organs for supernatural child-bearing, in the name of Jesus.
12. Every agenda of barrenness for my life, I cancel you by the blood of Jesus.
13. O wind of resurrection, blow upon every organ of my body, in the name of Jesus.
14. Every dead organ in my body, come alive, in the name of Jesus.
15. I fire back every arrow of clinical prophecy, in the name of Jesus.
16. Blood of Jesus, send power into my womb, in the name of Jesus.
17. Holy Ghost fire, incubate my womb with Your resurrection power, in the name of Jesus.

18. Where is the Lord God of Elijah? Arise in Your resurrection power and incubate my life, in the name of Jesus.

19. Every arrow fired from the waters into my womb, backfire, in the name of Jesus.

20. Every strongman assigned to the gate of my womb, fall down and die, in the name of Jesus.

21. O God, arise and let my womb experience Your resurrection power, in the name of Jesus.

22. I decree life into my dead parts, in the name of Jesus.

23. I soak every organ of my body in the wonder working power of the blood of Jesus.

24. Power of God that breaketh yokes, break every yoke upon my womb, in the name of Jesus.

25. Every serpent and scorpion assigned against my womb, receive the fire of God and die, in the name of Jesus.

26. Angels of divine surgery, visit my womb, in the name of Jesus.

27. Every oppression assigned to make my womb fail, I crush you, in the name of Jesus.

28. Every witchcraft arrow fired against my womb, backfire, in the name of Jesus.

29. My womb shall not die but live to declare the works of God, in the name of Jesus.

30. I bind and cast out every spirit of Cain afflicting my womb, in the name of Jesus.

31. I bind and cast out every spirit of Goliath afflicting my womb, in the name of Jesus.

32. I bind and cast out every spirit of Pharaoh afflicting my womb, in the name of Jesus.

33. I bind and cast out every spirit of Herod afflicting my womb, in the name of Jesus.

34. I bind and cast out every spirit of Hamman afflicting my womb, in the name of Jesus.

35. Insects of death bitting my womb, die, in the name of Jesus.

36. Inherited serpent transferred into my womb, die, in the name of Jesus.

37. Holy Ghost fire, burn to ashes every satanic deposit in my womb, in the name of Jesus.
38. Every satanic rope tied around my womb, catch fire, in the name of Jesus.
39. I breathe in the fire of the Holy Ghost, and I breathe out every plantation of darkness, in the name of Jesus.
40. Every evil tree planted to render my womb powerless, be uprooted, in the name of Jesus.
41. Every curse issued against my womb, be broken by the power in the blood of Jesus.
42. Every arrow of mockery, shame and reproach fired against my womb, die, in the name of Jesus.
43. I drink the resurrection water from the Lord and I receive the resurrection power into my system, in the name of Jesus.

CHAPTER SEVEN

POWER TO DEFEAT MISCARRIAGE

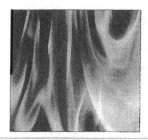

POWER TO DEFEAT MISCARRIAGE

(7)

od has established this prayer programme to put an end to the stigma of recurrent miscarriages. It is not good to take anything for granted. A single miscarriage is enough to provoke holy anger and make you to say, "Enough is enough." The enemy must not be allowed to have his way. He must not be permitted to negate the divine purpose for marriage, God's purpose has been made clear. Procreation or fruitfulness is the bonafide benefit of every child of God.

Genesis 1:28 says:

> *And God blessed them, and God said unto them, Be fruitful, and multiply, and replenish the earth, and subdue it: and have dominion over the fish of the sea, and over the fowl of the air, and over every living thing that moveth upon the earth.*

Whatever runs contrary to the divine injunction that declared "Be fruitful and multipl"y must be fought aggressively. Fruitlessness must be defeated. God's decree must be enforced. The fruit of your body must flourish. Even if the agenda of miscarriages is sponsored by dark powers, they must be defeated. A lot of couples have given in to defeat and discouragement, instead of defeating the agenda of dark powers. Beloved, miscarriage is an evil entity and is not God's will for your life. It will not bring glory to the Almighty. It will not make you sing your song and dance your dance. Neither can it make you to experience the manifestation of God's ability to deliver to the uttermost. You need to declare war against every power trying to frustrate you with miscarriages. Medical science, no doubt, makes efforts, but the greatest challenge to miscarriages is serious prayer programme that will locate the hiding place of the enemy and paralyse his weapon.

This prayer programme is for:

1. Those who are looking up to God for the fruit of the womb.
2. Families that are ridiculed by the enemy because of childlessness.
3. Couples that have gone in an out of hospitals without discovering the reason for constant miscarriages.
4. Women that are under spiritual attack.
5. Those who have experienced still births.
6. Victims of several abortions.
7. Womb that have miscarried several times.
8. Pregnant women who are threatened by spirit husbands
9. Those who have visited fetish priests or witchdoctors in the past.
10. Those who have experienced premature labour.
11. Women who suffer from fibroid.
12. Victims of ectopic pregnancy.
13. Women who have problematic wombs.
14. Those who are not able to get pregnant at all.

You need to carry out this prayer programme with holy aggression. You must defeat miscarriage. Your story must change. Your testimony must be heard.

PRAYER SECTION

Sources of Problem.

1. Marriage to unseen spouse.
2. Seeing yourself carrying children or someone collected your child in the dream.
3. Abortion committed in time past.
4. Appearances of palm oil, red pepper, or certain animals like goat, dog, cow, etc. in the dreams. These speak of evil dedication in the past and can hinder you from conceiving and delivering safely.
5. This spirit of error or mistake.
6. Mismanagement of the pregnancy by quack doctors.
7. Medical pollution.

Confessions: **Genesis 1:28**: *And God blessed them, and God said unto them, Be fruitful, and multiply, and replenish the earth, and subdue it: and have dominion over the fish of the sea, and over the fowl of the air, and over every living thing that moveth upon the earth.* **Exodus 23:26:** *There shall nothing cast their young, nor be barren, in thy land: the number of thy days I will fulfil.* **1 Samuel 2:4-6:** *The bows of the mighty men are broken, and they that stumbled are girded with strength. They that were full have hired out themselves for bread; and they that were hungry ceased: so that the barren hath born seven; and she that hath many children is waxed feeble. The Lord killeth, and maketh alive: he bringeth down to the grave, and bringeth up.* **Psalm 119:89:** *For ever, O Lord, thy word is settled in heaven.* **Eccles. 3:1:** *To every thing there is a season, and a time to every purpose under the heaven:* **Eccles. 3:14:** *I know that, whatsoever God doeth, it shall be for ever: nothing can be put to it, nor any thing taken from it: and God doeth it, that men should fear before him.* **Hosea 9:13-14:** *Ephraim, as I saw Tyrus, is planted in a pleasant place: but Ephraim shall bring forth his children to the murderer. Give them, O Lord: what wilt thou give? give them a miscarrying womb and dry breasts.* **Revelation 12:14-16:** *And to the woman were given two wings of a great eagle, that she might fly into the wilderness, into her* *place, where she is nourished for a time, and times, and half a time, from the face of the serpent. And the serpent cast out of his mouth water as a flood after the woman, that he might cause her to be carried away of the flood. And the earth helped the woman, and the earth opened her mouth, and swallowed up the flood which the dragon cast out of his mouth.*

PRAYER POINTS

1. I confess and repent of the sin of bloodshed I committed in my days of ignorance, in the name of Jesus.
2. Lord Jesus, wash away my sins of the past and their consequences, in the name of Jesus.
3. Lord Jesus, let sword depart from my marriage, in the name of Jesus.
4. O Lord, make ways for me where there is no way, in Jesus' name.
5. I break any covenant between me and spirit husbands or wives, in the name of Jesus.
6. Any of my clothes that the enemy has set aside to afflict my conception, be roasted, in Jesus' name.
7. Every bow of the mighty contending with my fruitfulness, break, break, break, in the name of Jesus.
8. Any decorations in my apartment that is bewitched, O Lord, reveal them to me, in the name of Jesus.
9. I destroy every evil stone or goat destroying my children in pregnancy, in the name of Jesus.
10. Any cloth the enemy is using to destroy my pregnancy, be roasted, in Jesus' name.
11. Let the strong east wind of the Lord blow against the Red Sea in my womb now, in the name of Jesus.
12. Every demonic instrument of operation set aside to abort my pregnancy, break to pieces, in the name of Jesus.
13. O Lord, fight against the destroyer working against my increase and fruitfulness, in the name of Jesus.
14. Every demonic doctor/nurse delegated by satan to destroy my pregnancy, inject yourself to death, in Jesus' name.

15. Let the blood of Jesus wash me and show me mercy, in the name of Jesus.

16. Every evil remote controlling gadget, being used to manipulate my pregnancy, be roasted by fire, in Jesus' name.

17. Thou Man of War, save me out of the hand of the wicked midwives, in the name of Jesus.

18. I render every weapon fashioned against my pregnancy impotent, in the name of Jesus.

19. O Lord, overthrow every Egyptian working against me in the midst of the sea, in the name of Jesus.

20. I close down every satanic broadcasting station fashioned against my pregnancy, in the name of Jesus.

21. I will see the great work of the Lord as I deliver my baby safely, in the name of Jesus.

22. I refuse to harbour any pregnancy killer in any department of my life, in the name of Jesus.

23. Every horse and the rider in my womb, family or office, be thrown into the sea of forgetfulness, in the name of Jesus.

24. I bind every spirit of error assigned against my pregnancy, in the name of Jesus.

25. O Lord, send Your light before me to drive miscarriages away from my womb and life, in the name of Jesus.

26. I bind the spirit of almost there; you will not operate in my life, in the name of Jesus.

27. I cast out every power casting out my children, in the name of Jesus.

28. I break every grip and hold of witchcraft over my pregnancy, in the name of Jesus.

29. From today, I shall not cast away my young, in the name of Jesus.

30. I paralyse every opposition to my pregnancy, in the name of Jesus.

31. I will fulfil the number of the days of this pregnancy, in the name of Jesus.
32. Any member of my family reporting my pregnancy to the evil ones, receive the slap of the angels of God, in Jesus' name.
33. I shall not cast out my pregnancy before delivery, in the name of Jesus.
34. Every territorial demon working against my marriage, receive the thunder fire of God, in the name of Jesus.
35. Every spirit of still-birth and threatened abortion, be consumed by fire, in the name of Jesus.
36. I nullify every satanic threat against my pregnancy, in the name of Jesus.
37. I shall not bring forth to murderers, in the name of Jesus.
38. Every power/spirit, visiting me at night or in the dream to terminate my pregnancy, fall down and die, in the name of Jesus.
39. Every power of murderers, be shattered, in the name of Jesus.
40. I nullify every evil influence of satanic visitation upon my pregnancy, in the name of Jesus.
41. O Lord, deliver me from the womb that miscarries, in the name of Jesus.
42. Let the plug of my womb receive the power of the Holy Spirit to carry my pregnancy to the point of delivery, in the name of Jesus.
43. Let every violence of miscarriages stop permanently, in the name of Jesus.
44. I reject every manifestation of fever during my pregnancy, in the name of Jesus.
45. Every evil power appearing through a dog, a man or a woman, be destroyed by fire, in the name of Jesus.
46. I reject every satanic stress during my pregnancy, in the

name of Jesus.

47. You evil children causing abortion, die, in the name of Jesus. I am loosed from your oppression, in the name of Jesus.

48. I decree death of spirit husband or spirit wife killing my children, in the name of Jesus.

49. O earth, help me to conquer the power of miscarriages, in the name of Jesus.

50. O Lord, give me wings of a great eagle to escape from miscarriages, in the name of Jesus.

51. O Lord, give me a man-child, in the name of Jesus.

52. I declare that I am fruitful and I will bring forth in peace, in the name of Jesus.

53. I overcome miscarriages by the power of the Lord, in the name of Jesus.

54. My Father, cover me with Your shield and put me under Your banner, in the name of Jesus.

55. Every power that has swallowed my children, vomit them now, in the name of Jesus.

56. Let every foundation of miscarriages receive the judgement of God, in the name of Jesus.

57. I command fibroid to drop off my womb, in the name of Jesus.

58. Let every low sperm count be converted to full sperm count, in the name of Jesus.

59. Throughout the period of the pregnancy, I shall not be stressed, in the name of Jesus.

60. I receive angelic ministration, in the name of Jesus.

61. Let my body be strong to labour, in the name of Jesus.

62. O Lord, send Your heavenly nurse to minister to me throughout the period of this pregnancy, in the name of Jesus.

63. I shall bring forth a normal child to the glory of God, in the

name of Jesus.

64. O Lord, deliver me from the spirit of error and mistake, in the name of Jesus.

65. I judge the hold of mismanagement via wrong medical advise or wrong medication, in the name of Jesus.

66. Cervix, be closed up, let there be no contraction of dilation before the nine months period, in the name of Jesus.

67. I receive power from on high to bring forth, in the name of Jesus.

68. I break the horn of the wicked exercising evil against me, in the name of Jesus.

69. Holy Spirit, envelope me and overshadow me throughout the period of this pregnancy, in the name of Jesus.

70. I will not labour in vain, neither will I bring forth for trouble, in the name of Jesus.

71. As I build, I will inhabit and as I plant, I shall eat, in the name of Jesus.

72. I and the children that God has given me are for signs and wonders, in the name of Jesus.

73. Thank God for answers to your prayers.

CHAPTER EIGHT

CRUSHING MISCARRIAGES

8

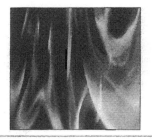

CRUSHING MISCARRIAGES

8

God's perfect will is fruitfulness. The fruit of the womb is His generous gifts to all families. He wants you to be fruitful. His command at the beginning is that we should be fruitful, multiply and populate the earth. When He blesses a couple with the fruit of the womb, the enemy of fruitfulness will attempt programming miscarriages. But the good news is that there is a divine legislation against miscarriages that are sponsored by the kingdom of darkness.

God's decree is in **Exodus 23:26**:

> *There shall nothing cast their young, nor be barren, in thy land: the number of thy days I will fulfil.*

What God has programmed is that right from conception to the time of delivery nothing should temper with or terminate the seed that has been planted by His hand. Any form of miscarriage runs contrary to God's agenda for your life.

The truth is that when there is a conflict between God's

programme and demonic machinations, the divine programme will prevail against God's decree. It has been settled eternally that the gates of hell shall not prevail. Miscarriage is one of the manifestations of fruitlessness. The best thing to do is to begin to pray against it.

Prevention, they say, is better than cure. Do not wait for the enemy to attack your pregnancy. Focus your attention on security and immunity. Pray prayers that will incubate your womb with the fire of the Holy Ghost. You must declare loud and clear that miscarriage is not your lot.

You must crush miscarriage before you are crushed or devastated by it. You must learn how to identify early symptoms of miscarriage.

You must spot the locations from where attacks on your pregnancy are coming. You must become so prayerful as to deflect the arrows of miscarriage. When as a pregnant woman you have dreams of things like palm-oil or blood, there is trouble. When you have dreams of theft of your seed, it may be an indication that the devil wants to cause miscarriage or probably terminate your pregnancy. When you dream of certain personalities rough-handling you fighting against you or you may be in for miscarriage.

When you dream of someone appearing to to you threatening that you will not be safely delivered of your pregnancy it may be a serious threat. When you dream of being pursued by masquerade or fetish priests, you may risk an impending miscarriage. To keep dark agents away from your pregnancy you need to muster all your spiritual energy and say no to miscarriage or untimely death. This prayer must be said violently, continuously and prophetically. God is set to cancel the agenda of miscarriages in your family.

PRAYERS SECTION

Confessions: Genesis 1:28: *And God blessed them, and God said unto them, Be fruitful, and multiply, and replenish the earth, and subdue it: and have dominion over the fish of the sea, and over the fowl of the air, and over every living thing that moveth upon the earth.* **1 Samuel 2:4-6:** *The bows of the mighty men are broken, and they that stumbled are girded with strength. They that were full have hired out themselves for bread; and they that were hungry ceased: so that the barren hath born seven; and she that hath many children is waxed feeble. The Lord killeth, and maketh alive: he bringeth down to the grave, and bringeth up.* **Exodus 23:26:** *There shall nothing cast their young, nor be barren, in thy land: the number of thy days I will fulfil.* **Revelation 12:14-16:** *And to the woman were given two wings of a great eagle, that she might fly into the wilderness, into her place, where she is nourished for a time, and times, and half a time, from the face of the serpent. And the serpent cast out of his mouth water as a flood after the woman, that he might cause her to be carried away of the flood. And the earth helped the woman, and the earth opened her mouth, and swallowed up the flood which the dragon cast out of his mouth.* **Psalm 119:89:** *For ever, O Lord, thy word is settled in heaven.*

Praise Worship

 **PRAYER POINTS**

1. Thank the Lord because He is faithful to His words.
2. I apply the blood of Jesus upon my life.
3. Any covenant between me and spirit husband/wife, break, by the power in the blood of Jesus.
4. Every bow of the mighty assigned against my fruitfulness, die, in the name of Jesus.
5. Every evil stone assigned to be killing my children from the womb, die, in the name of Jesus.
6. O God, arise and let Your wind blow off every satanic Red Sea assigned against my life, in the name of Jesus.

7. Every destroyer working against my fruitfulness, scatter, in the name of Jesus.

8. Every wicked midwife assigned against my delivery, die, in the name of Jesus.

9. The great hand of the Lord shall be upon me for safely delivery of my children, in the name of Jesus.

10. Every satanic horse and his rider within and around me, working against my fruitfulness, die, in the name of Jesus.

11. Let the light of God send every darkness in my womb away, in the name of Jesus.

12. Every power assigned to be casting out my children, scatter and die, in the name of Jesus.

13. I decree by the decree of heaven, that henceforth I shall not cast my young, in the name of Jesus.

14. Every force of the Egyptians working against my fruitfulness, scatter by fire, in the name of Jesus.

15. The numbers of the days of my pregnancy shall be fulfilled, in the name of Jesus.

16. My pregnancy shall not be cast out before delivery, in the name of Jesus.

17. Every spirit of still-birth assigned against my pregnancy, die, in the name of Jesus.

18. Every spirit of threatened abortion assigned against my pregnancy, die, in the name of Jesus.

19. In the name of the Lord of hosts, I shall not bring forth to murderers, in the name of Jesus.

20. Every power of spiritual murderers assigned against my pregnancy, die, in the name of Jesus.

21. O God, arise and let my womb be delivered from the power of miscarriage, in the name of Jesus.

22. Every rage of the power of miscarriage, assigned against my pregnancy, be silenced by the power in the blood of Jesus.

23. Every satanic projection in my dreams against my pregnancy, die, in the name of Jesus.

24. Every satanic child assigned to be aborting my pregnancy, your time is up, die, in the name of Jesus.

25. By fire, by thunder, I release myself from the grip and hold of evil child, in the name of Jesus.

26. You spirit husband/wife killing my physical children, loose your hold and die, in the name of Jesus.

27. O earth, o earth, o earth, hear the word of the Lord, swallow up every power assigned to be aborting my pregnancy, in the name of Jesus.

28. Every foundation of miscarriage in my life, be uprooted by fire, in the name of Jesus.

29. Every horn of the wicked waiting to exercise evil against my delivery, die, in the name of Jesus.

30. Every evil growth in my womb, dry up by fire, in the name of Jesus.

31. Every problem of low sperm count, receive solution by fire, in the name of Jesus.

32. By the power in the blood of Jesus, I am delivered from the power of miscarriage, in the name of Jesus.

33. O Lord, give me a man-child, in the name of Jesus.

34. I am fruitful and I shall bring forth in peace, in the name of Jesus.

35. Every power that has swallowed my children, vomit them by fire, in the name of Jesus.

36. Any stress that will bring miscarriage to me during my pregnancy, die, in the name of Jesus.

37. My body, receive strength to deliver, in the name of Jesus.

38. Let heavenly midwife, nurse and doctor be assigned to minister to me, in the name of Jesus.

39. Every spirit of error and mistake, I bind you, in the name of Jesus.

40. Issue of wrong medication shall not be my lot, in the name of Jesus.

41. You my cervix, you shall not contract or dilate before my time of delivery, in the name of Jesus.

42. Holy Ghost fire, envelope and overshadow me throughout the period of my pregnancy, in the name of Jesus.

43. The children that God has given me and I are for signs and wonders, in the name of Jesus.

O GOD OF POSSIBILITIES, ARISE

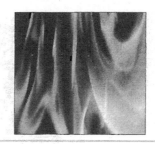

O GOD OF POSSIBILITIES, ARISE

9

There is a season in the life of everyone for asking the God of possibilities to arise. This is a time to pray for uncommon manifestations of divine signs and wonders. Why should a child of God go through life without occurrence of miracles, signs and wonders. Why should those who are called by the name of the Lord spend their lives without experiencing the types of miracles that were very common in the lives of our Pentecostal fathers.

It is God's desire to overshadow and inundated His children with supernatural blessings and miracles. However, for this to happen we are required to pray and ask God to arise and manifest His power.

Ezekiel 36:37 says:

> *Thus saith the Lord GOD; I will yet for this be enquired of by the house of Israel, to do it for them; I will increase them with men like a flock.*

When you ask God to arise, miracles will flow unhindered. When you knock at heaven's door, God will arise and scatter the enemies of your breakthroughs, impossibilities will become possible and hindrances will be dismantled. Problems will be converted to testimonies, hopelessness will disappear and your story will change. The manner with which you handle this prayer programme will determine the way heaven will attend to your situation. There is a mystery behind this prayer programme. When you ask the God of possibilities to arise, no power will be able to erect any stumbling block that will barricade you from possessing your possessions.

Beloved, the type of prayer that will make God to arise must be fervent, persistent and backed up by the power of the Holy Ghost. When the God of possibilities arise doors will open on their own accord, power will change hands and God will demonstrate the fullness of His power in every department of your life.

Do you want a change of situation? Then let your prayers move God to intervene in your situation. Cry passionately before the throne of mercy. Raise a voice against wicked powers in the kingdom of darkness that have bombarded your life with raging impossibilities.

This is your opportunity to prove that although certain things are impossible with men, all things are possible with God.

Matthew 19:26 says:

> *But Jesus beheld them, and said unto them, With men this is impossible; but with God all things are possible*

Your prayers must be aggressive. Your faith must be strong and your plea must be persistent. This is the prayer programme you have been waiting for to move out of the dungeon of impossibility into the realm of divine possibilities. As you pray these prayers like a wounded lion, God shall roar and your miracles shall flow from heaven.

PRAYER SECTION

Confessions: **Philippians 4:13:** *I can do all things through Christ which strengtheneth me.* **Luke 1:37:** *For with God nothing shall be impossible.* **Matthew 19:26:** *But Jesus beheld them, and said unto them, With men this is impossible; but with God all things are possible.*

 PRAYER POINTS

1. I and the children that God has given me are for signs and wonders, in the name of Jesus.
2. Father, let signs and wonders be my lot, in the name of Jesus.
3. Every obstacle in my life, give way to miracles, in the name of Jesus.
4. Every frustration in my life, become a bridge to my miracles, in the name of Jesus. .
5. I hold the blood of Jesus against demonic delay of my miracles.
6. I decree by fire and thunder that I shall not die before the manifestation of my miracles, in Jesus' name.
7. You miracle hijackers, release my miracles now by fire, in the name of Jesus.
8. Thank the Lord because this year is your year of dumbfounding miracles.
9. O God, arise and speak healing and creative miracles into my life, in the name of Jesus.
10. My organs, receive creative miracles, in the name of Jesus.
11. My Father, arise by Your signs and wonders and visit my life, in the name of Jesus.
12. Like the rising of the sun, O God of wonders, arise in my life, in the name of Jesus.
13. O God of sign and wonders, You are the heavenly Surgeon,

touch me by Your power, in the name of Jesus.

14. Let the wonder-working power of God be released on my situation for signs and wonders, in the name of Jesus.

15. Let signs and wonders appear in my life, in the name of Jesus.

16. Holy Ghost fire, visit me with Your signs and wonders, in the name of Jesus.

17. I decree by fire and thunder that I shall not die before the manifestation of my miracles, in Jesus' name.

18. Oh God, arise and hear me in the day of trouble, in the name of Jesus.

19. Oh Lord, I run into Your name that is a strong tower, in the name of Jesus.

20. Oh Lord, let all my stubborn problems be buried, in the name of Jesus.

21. I shall not die because of my problems, in the name of Jesus.

22. I shall not be disgraced because of my problems, in the name of Jesus.

23. Let the fire of God begin to attack all miracle hijackers assigned against my life, in the name of Jesus.

24. God has made me a product of His possibility and no good thing shall be impossible for me, in the name of Jesus.

25. Every curse and covenant of impossibility over my life, break, in the name of Jesus.

26. Thou Goliath of impossibility in my life, die, in the name of Jesus.

27. I shall not die undiscovered, in the name of Jesus.

28. I shall not die unused and unsung, in the name of Jesus.

29. I shall not die uncelebrated and unmissed, in the name of Jesus.

30. I shall not die unfruitful and unfulfilled, in the name of Jesus.

31. Every good thing the enemy has swallowed in my life, be vomited, in the name of Jesus.

32. Oh God, arise and send me help from the sanctuary and

strengthen me out of Zion, in Jesus' name.

33. Let my rescue and deliverance be announced from heaven, in the name of Jesus.

34. Before I finished praying these prayers, oh Lord, let Your angels move into action on my behalf, in Jesus' name.

35. Every prince of Persia and all territorial spirits around me that are hindering the manifestation of God's miracle in my life, scatter, in the name of Jesus.

36. I bind and cast out of my vicinity, all prayer and miracle blockers, in the name of Jesus.

37. You miracle hijackers, release my miracles now by fire, in the name of Jesus.

38. Every satanic umbrella preventing the heavenly showers of blessings from falling on me, catch fire, in the name of Jesus.

39. Oh God, arise and let my heavens open right now, in the name of Jesus.

40. I shall not give up, because I have believed to see the goodness of the Lord in the land of the living, in the name of Jesus.

41. O Lord, let my soul be prevented from death, my eyes from tears and my feet from falling, in Jesus' name.

42. People will hear my testimonies and glorify the name of God in my life, in the name of Jesus.

43. My Father, let Your divine intervention in my life bring souls to the kingdom of God, in the name of Jesus.

44. I use the blood of Jesus to fight and defeat every spirit of impossibility in my life, in the name of Jesus.

45. I release myself from the collective captivity of impossibility, in the name of Jesus.

46. Every seed, root and tentacles of impossibility in my life, die, in the name of Jesus.

47. I withdraw my name and all about my life from the altar of impossibility, in the name of Jesus.

48. I refuse to swim in the ocean of impossibility, in the name of Jesus.

49. Every King Uzziah making it impossible for me to see the glory of God, die, in the name of Jesus.

50. The wind of impossibility shall not blow in my direction, in the name of Jesus.

51. You river of impossibility flowing near and around me, dry up now, in the name of Jesus.

52. I receive the strength of the Lord to leap over the wall of impossibility, in the name of Jesus.

53. Every Red Sea of impossibility, part, in the name of Jesus.

54. You angels of possibility and success, begin to minister unto me, in the name of Jesus.

55. With God on my side, no good thing shall be impossible for me, in the name of Jesus.

56. I will reach my goals before my enemies will know what is happening, in the name of Jesus.

57. I shall fulfill my destiny, whether the enemy likes it or not, in the name of Jesus.

58. My steps shall be ordered by the Lord to fulfill my destiny, in the name of Jesus.

59. Let my disgrace be turned into grace, in the name of Jesus.

60. Let the dry bones of my destiny, come alive, in the name of Jesus.

61. Henceforth, I embark on a journey into destiny accomplishments in all ramifications, in the name of Jesus.

62. I cut off the spiritual umbilical cord through which evil flows into my destiny, in the name of Jesus.

63. No evil words from the sun, the moon and the stars will prosper in my life, in the name of Jesus.

64. Every evil word and chanting from prayer mats, evil forests, sacred trees, road junctions, marine environment and occult prayer houses, be silenced, in the name of Jesus.

65. Father, I thank You for a change in my situation, in the name of Jesus.

CHAPTER TEN

BREAKTHROUGH PRAYERS FOR SUPERNATURAL CONCEPTION 3

BREAKTHROUGH PRAYERS FOR SUPERNATURAL CONCEPTION 3

10

The prayer points in this section are unique. This programme has been vomited by the Holy Ghost to break the backbone of childlessness. It will take you to the realm of supernatural conception, change your story to glory and make the impossible possible. The essence of the programme is to help you connect yourself with breakthroughs in the area of child-bearing. When you experience supernatural conception you will frustrate the agenda of the dark kingdom. Your conception and child-bearing will daze your enemies, confound the scotters and make everyone around you come to terms with the fact that when God is at work, no one can stop Him.

As far as the devil is concerned, everything has been done to prevent you from singing your song, and putting on your dancing shoes as a joyful mother or a fulfilled father. If the devil has perfected his wicked plan, you need breakthroughs prayers to turn the evil tide. With the mystery of supernatural conception, your journey to the realm of child-bearing will become a successful one.

Supernatural conception is God's programme that has been designed to turn barren women to joyful mothers.

Psalms 113:9 says:

> *He maketh the barren woman to keep house, and to be a joyful mother of children. Praise ye the LORD.*

These prayers will make the Holy Ghost to incubate your pregnancy. Right from the beginning to the end you will experience special divine protection. Miscarriages, bareness, still-births and inability to become pregnant will not be your lot. No matter how long you have suffered the stigma of childlessness, God will put an end to your gloom.

The breakthrough prayers in this section will put in place the overwhelming presence of the Holy Spirit. God will overshadow you and your conception will remain a wonderful experience.

Whatever has been responsible for the challenges you have gone through, God will arise on your behalf and the Holy Ghost shall overshadow you and the divine seed placed in your womb shall leap for joy.

When you handle the prayer points below aggressively, the strangers shall be frightened and be ejected from their hidden places. You shall defeat all the powers that have defeated you. God has decided to do a new thing. However, you must be ready to pray like never before. These breakthrough prayers will lead you into the amazing miracles of supernatural conception. Power will change hands, and you will conceive and give birth to children supernaturally. Let the anointing of Jehu come upon you. This is a battle you must fight and win.

PRAYER SECTION

Confession: **Isaiah 43:19:** *Behold, I will do a new thing; now it shall spring forth; shall ye not know it? I will even make a way in the wilderness, and rivers in the desert.*

Psalms 113:9: *He maketh the barren woman to keep house, and to be a joyful mother of children. Praise ye the Lord.*

Aggressive Praise and Worship

 PRAYER POINTS

1. Any dark, conscious or unconscious covenant made by parents for child-bearing that is now affecting me, be cancelled by the power in the blood of Jesus.
2. I renounce any conscious and unconscious relationship between me and spirit marriage, in the name of Jesus.
3. Every property of the queen of the coast in my life, be roasted by fire, in the name of Jesus.
4. Every demonic deposit in my womb, catch fire, in the name of Jesus.
5. Every demonic snake planted in my reproductive organs, catch fire, in the name of Jesus.
6. Every demonic rope tying my reproductive organs, catch fire, in the name of Jesus.
7. Every evil power assigned to be hindering conception, fall down and die, in the name of Jesus.
8. Every demonic vessel in the waters collecting my husband's sperm, catch fire, in the name of Jesus.
9. Every demonic food from the waters in my body, melt away by the blood of Jesus.
10. Every witchcraft coven harboring my womb, release it and catch fire, in the name of Jesus.
11. Every satanic sacrifice to marine powers against my child-bearing, die, in the name of Jesus.

12. Every satanic bird assigned against my marriage, fall down and die, in the name of Jesus.
13. Every witchcraft fire assigned against my body, die, in the name of Jesus.
14. Every pot of affliction assigned against my reproductive organs, catch fire, in the name of Jesus.
15. Every collaboration of witchcraft powers and water spirits against my child-bearing, scatter, in Jesus' name.
16. Every evil tree assigned against my children, be uprooted by fire and die, in the name of Jesus.
17. Every ancestral power assigned against my child-bearing, receive the wrath of God and die, in the name of Jesus.
18. Every ancestral evil dedication that is affecting my child-bearing, die, in the name of Jesus.
19. Every covenant made on my behalf to be worshiping idols of my father's house, break by the blood of Jesus.
20. Every evil power in my environment assigned against my child-bearing, die, in the name of Jesus.
21. Every evil altar assigned against my life from my place of birth, catch fire, in the name of Jesus.
22. Every environmental witchcraft assigned against child-bearing in my environment, scatter, in the name of Jesus.
23. Any witchcraft burial done with human being where I live and is affecting my child-bearing, die, in the name of Jesus.
24. I call for my children to begin to come forth by the power in the blood of Jesus.
25. Any household wickedness fashioned against my child-bearing, scatter, in the name of Jesus.
26. Let the blood of my children that any evil power has drunk become poison in its belly, in the name of Jesus.
27. Any satanic altar harboring my wedding pictures, catch fire, in the name of Jesus.
28. Anything taken from my body and used against my child-bearing, die, in the name of Jesus.
29. Every weapon used in tying my baby, catch fire, in the name

30. I fire back every arrow of death assigned against my child-bearing, in the name of Jesus.
31. Any power using my menstruation against my life, die, in the name of Jesus.
32. I reject demonic manipulation of my menstruation, in the name of Jesus.
33. Every demonic growth in my womb, be cut off, in the name of Jesus.
34. Every power assigned to use the delay in child-bearing to break my marriage, loose your hold and die, in the name of Jesus.
35. Any strange object in my body hindering child-bearing, die, in the name of Jesus.
36. Every spirit of miscarriage or still-birth, I cast you out, in the name of Jesus.
37. Any evil hand assigned to touch my baby, be cut off, in the name of Jesus.
38. I shall not die but live to give birth and to nurse my children, in the name of Jesus.

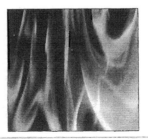

77 PRAYERS TO BRING HONEY INTO YOUR MARRIAGE

(11)

God specialises in turning worse conditions to pleasant ones. He takes delight in turning hopeless situations around and He has a passion for the family. With His supernatural power He is able to take you as you are, bring His supernatural ability to bear and turn your worse condition into raw material for a glorious condition. If there is one realm where God delights in making this possible, it is in the realm of marriage.

Beloved, there is enough honey in heaven to make every marriage to become delightful and glorious. God can turn the bitterness in your marriage into sweet honey. No matter how many dark spots there are in your marriage, God is ready to build His divine rays of sunlight and make your home heaven on earth. When there is no honey in your marriage, you finances will nose-dive, joy will jump out of the window, peace will become elusive and fulfillment will be difficult to come by. Families that lack honey in their home suffer friction, needs will not be met and satisfaction will be scanty. You need to pray that your marriage will experience days of heaven on earth. There will be abundant honey in your home.

Deuteronomy 11:21 says:

> *That your days may be multiplied, and the days of your children, in the land which the LORD sware unto your fathers to give them, as the days of heaven upon the earth.*

Numbers 14:8 says:

> *If the LORD delight in us, then he will bring us into this land, and give it us; a land which floweth with milk and honey.*

You need these prayers if there is no peace in your life. You need them if your marriage is on the verge of collapse. They are divine life line for rescuing ailing marriages.

PRAYER SECTION

Confession: **Matthew 15:13:** *But he answered and said, Every plant, which my heavenly Father hath not planted, shall be rooted up.* **Deuteronomy 11:21:** *That your days may be multiplied, and the days of your children, in the land which the Lord sware unto your fathers to give them, as the days of heaven upon the earth.* **Numbers 14:8:** *The Lord is longsuffering, and of great mercy, forgiving iniquity and transgression, and by no means clearing the guilty, visiting the iniquity of the fathers upon the children unto the third and fourth generation.*

Praise Worship

 PRAYER POINTS

1. Lord, uproot what You have not planted in my marital life today, in the name of Jesus.
2. Every power caging my marriage, loose your hold, in the name of Jesus.

3. I break every curse of unstable marriage, in the name of Jesus.
4. I break every curse of barrenness in marriage, in the name of Jesus.
5. I break every curse of hardship in marriage, in the name of Jesus.
6. I divorce every spirit wife/husband, in the name of Jesus.
7. Anything done for me while I was young and affecting my marriage, be nullified, in the name of Jesus.
8. Every evil-soul tie of the past affecting my marriage, I break you by the blood of Jesus.
9. Blood of Jesus, nullify every demonic transaction affecting my marriage, in the name of Jesus.
10. I nullify every covenant of multiple marriages, in the name of Jesus.
11. Let the glory of my marriage begin to manifest now, in the name of Jesus.
12. Lord, release all heavenly blessings upon my marriage now, in the name of Jesus.
13. Let me and my wife/husband know God the more and never be disconnected from the Almighty, in the name of Jesus.
14. O God, let Your protection from evil and attacks of the enemies be upon me and my wife/husband, in the name of Jesus.
15. Let the wisdom of God to take good and godly decisions come upon me and my wife/husband, in the name of Jesus.
16. O Lord, let not the attention of my husband/wife be shifted from me, in the name of Jesus.
17. I stand against every spirit of poverty and claim supernatural supply, in the name of Jesus.
18. Let me and my wife/husband receive help from God to always take good action and to react in the fear of God, in the name of Jesus.
19. Let our faith be established in the Lord and let not the spirit of fear overwhelm us, in the name of Jesus.

20. I come against every spirit of pride, anger, oversleeping, laziness, procrastination, unforgiveness, stinginess, carelessness, malice and nagging in my life, in the name of Jesus.

21. Father, let the sexual desire and fantasies of my wife/husband always be toward me and not any other woman/man, in the name of Jesus.

22. I bind the spirit of lust and immorality, in the name of Jesus.

23. Let the spirit of joy always overwhelm the spirit, soul and body of my wife/husband, in the name of Jesus.

24. Father, let Your power of protection be upon our children. Give us money, wisdom to take care of them.

25. Let Your power visit them and make them great in life, in the name of Jesus.

26. Let utterance and the unction of the Lord fall upon my wife/husband to deliver the word of God with power and boldness, in the name of Jesus.

27. Let my wife/husband always associate with godly people that will make her/him better in her/his calling, in the name of Jesus.

28. O God, keep me and my wife/husband to build a blissful marriage and to raise godly children, in the name of Jesus.

29. I release the blood of Jesus to the foundations of my marriage, in the name of Jesus.

30. Let the blood of Jesus destroy every negative traditional marriage rites and covenants, in the name of Jesus.

31. I severe and separate myself and my family from every ancestral, generational, family and personal curses working against my marriage and home, in the name of Jesus.

32. Let every curse working against my marriage and home be broken, in the name of Jesus.

33. I reject and reverse every evil covenant working against my life, marriage and home, in the name of Jesus.

34. I reject and reverse every curse of separation/divorce or instability in marriage, in the name of Jesus.

35. O Lord, I renounce every self imposed curse and pronouncement over my life and marriage, in the name of Jesus.

36. Let all that are contending against my marriage and home fall down and die, in the name of Jesus.

37. Let every gathering and programming against my marriage and matrimonial home break by fire, in the name of Jesus.

38. I command you spirit of asunder to loose my marriage now and go, in the name of Jesus.

39. O Lord, heal my marriage and home from every satanic attack, in the name of Jesus.

40. I roast by fire every hand of evil working against my life, marriage and home, in the name of Jesus.

41. O Lord, let every arrow sent to scatter and destroy my marriage and home return to the senders, in the name of Jesus.

42. I roast by fire every evil planting in my home and marriage, in the name of Jesus.

43. I scatter by fire all evil advisers and influence against my marriage and home, in the name of Jesus.

44. O Lord, let all those working against my marriage and home go into exile now, in the name of Jesus.

45. I reject and reverse all that God has not ordained for my life, marriage, home, husband/wife and children, in the name of Jesus.

46. Every evil seed sown to scatter my marriage, die now, in the name of Jesus.

47. I destroy every witchcraft operation against my life and marriage, in the name of Jesus.

48. I command all evil vultures working against my marriage to die, in the name of Jesus.

49. I release the flow of God's love in my wife's/husband's heart for me, in the name of Jesus.

50. O Lord, bind my wife's/husband's and I together with the Holy Ghost, in the name of Jesus.

51. I release the thunder and fire of God against all evil altars and priests working against my marriage, home, and children, in the name of Jesus.

52. I evacuate by fire every human agent and unwanted guests operating in my matrimonial home, in the name of Jesus.

53. I evacuate by fire every spiritual agent operating in my matrimonial home, in the name of Jesus.

54. Every spirit of death released against my spouse, my children and me, return to your senders, in the name of Jesus.

55. I cleanse my matrimonial home and bed with the blood of Jesus.

56. I circle my home with the blood of Jesus and fire of the Holy Ghost and declare it an evil-free zone, in the name of Jesus.

57. I release confusion into the camp of my enemies, in the name of Jesus.

58. You evil authority in my family and home, fall down and die, in the name of Jesus.

59. Every problem in my marriage and home resisting solution, be consumed now by fire, in the name of Jesus.

60. I am a stone set in Zion for the rising and falling of many in the name of Jesus.

61. Let all that rise up against my marriage and home fall for my sake, in the name of Jesus.

62. Holy Ghost fire, revive my marriage to the glory of God, in the name of Jesus.

63. O Lord, let Your peace reign in my marriage, in the name of Jesus.

64. O Lord, let every garment of sorrow that the devil and his agents have designed against my marriage be destroyed, in the name of Jesus.

65. O Lord, of upliftment, uplift us to your glory, in the name of Jesus.

66. My marriage shall be a good example to others, in the name of Jesus.

67. I shall not be a problem to my own family, in the name of Jesus.

68. O Lord, bless me in abundance so that I will be able to meet up with my responsibilities, in the name of Jesus.

69. O Lord, let there be peace between me and my wife and my entire household, in the name of Jesus.

70. O Lord of direction, direct my steps, in the name of Jesus.

71. With the blood of Jesus, I destroy every spirit of evil habits that I am used to, in the name of Jesus.

72. I come against every spirit of misunderstanding between me and my husband, in the name of Jesus.

73. With the blood of Jesus I come against every spirit husband and spirit wife fighting against my marriage, in the name of Jesus.

74. O Lord, I present my children into Your able hands, bless them, in the name of Jesus

75. O Lord, let my children be a good example to others, in the name of Jesus.

76. O Lord, let Your peace and joy reign mightily in my family, in the name of Jesus.

77. O Lord, increase the love between me and my wife/husband, in the name of Jesus.

78. My household will be blessed to the glory of God, in the name of Jesus.

79. My children and I shall be for signs and wonders, in the name of Jesus.

80. Thank God for answers to your prayers.

SECTION 4

BREAKING
THE CHAINS

CHAPTER ONE

DEALING WITH HIDDEN BONDAGE

1

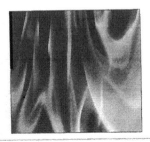

DEALING WITH HIDDEN BONDAGE

(1)

When bondage is concealed, it is quite difficult to deal with it. Whenever the devil wants to perpetuate bondage; he hides it. A lot of people are grappling with secret bondage. There are many ways of dealing with bondage. The nature of a particular bondage determines the method of dealing with it. General methods may not do. You must know how to deal with every form of hidden bondage.

Applying the right method at the right time to specific bondage patterns will enable you to deal with hidden satanic bondage. The power of the Holy Spirit is able to deal with any type of bondage. The Holy Spirit will locate evil strangers and frighten them out of their hidden places.

Psalm 18:45 says:

> *The strangers shall fade away, and be afraid out of their close places.*

When the battle is taken up with uncommon aggression, powers that keep people under bondage secretly will lose their victims. It is unfortunate that a lot of people claim that they are not under any kind of bondage. The truth is that the worst type of bondage is the bondage that is not detected.

Blind victims of terrible bondage often claim that they are not under the bondage of any power. The more you are not able to locate areas of bondage in your life, the more you allow the devil to dig into your life and conceal terrible bondages. The devil knows that the moment you are able to admit and locate your areas of bondage, you are on your way out of the cage. You must therefore seek knowledge at all costs.

Beloved, there is no harm in praying against bondage. Even if you pray and there is no bondage to deal with you would not have lost anything.

However, if there are hidden places of bondage in your life and you refuse to pray it will be disastrous. The greatest weapon you can use is that of the fire of the Holy Ghost. When you address your foundation by invoking the fire of the Holy Ghost you will locate hidden bondages and deal with them decisively. Besides setting your life on fire through fervent prayers, you can make use of the weapon of continuous bombardment. Some powers may not jump out of their hiding places until they are pounded continuously.

This prayer programme is needed when:

1. You discover that general prayers are not working.
2. Mysterious things are happening in your life.
3. The devil succeeds each time he attacks you.
4. Ancestral problems are legion in your life.
5. The spirit of error is at work.
6. Evil patterns are visible.
7. Satanic agents have consistently made you their targets.

To handle these prayer points you must do the following:

1. Fight ignorance.
2. Be ready to pray until your life becomes too hot for the enemy to handle.
3. Let the fire of the Holy Ghost burn on the altar of your life.
4. Take these prayer points with Holy aggression, be ready to spend enough time on these prayer points until you secure your release.
5. Do not settle for anything less than your total deliverance.

 PRAYER POINTS

Confession: **Isaiah 49:25:** *But thus saith the Lord, Even the captives of the mighty shall be taken away, and the prey of the terrible shall be delivered: for I will contend with him that contendeth with thee, and I will save thy children.*

Praise Worship

 PRAYER POINTS

1. Lord, I thank You for the blood of Jesus Christ which cleanses from all sins.
2. I soak myself in the blood of Jesus Christ.
3. I release myself from any inherited bondage, in the name of Jesus.
4. I release myself from the grip of any failure and bad luck transferred into my life from the womb, in Jesus' name.
5. I destroy completely every dark covenant made on my behalf, in the name of Jesus.
6. I break and loose myself from every inherited evil family curse, in the name of Jesus.
7. I vomit every concoction I have been fed with as a child, in the name of Jesus.
8. I plead the blood of Jesus Christ against all witchcraft spirits

manipulating my life, in the name of Jesus.

9. I destroy the rod of the wicked with Holy Ghost fire, in the name of Jesus.

10. I cancel the consequences of any evil local name, nickname or ancestral name attached to my person, in the name of Jesus.

11. I uproot all evil plants from my life, in the name of Jesus.

12. I release my spirit, soul and body from every evil domination and control, in the name of Jesus.

13. I smash and remove completely all the gates of hell shutting out my blessings, in the name of Jesus.

14. I come against all evil designs against my life, family, children, husband/wife, in the name of Jesus.

15. I destroy all demonic incisions, in the name of Jesus.

16. I divorce myself from all demonic marriages in dreams and trances, in the name of Jesus.

17. I cleanse myself from all inherited infirmities and sicknesses, in the name of Jesus.

18. I cleanse myself from all demonic pollution of my mind, in the name of Jesus.

19. I chase out all spirits of anxiety, worry and impatience, in the name of Jesus.

20. I send Holy Ghost fire to the camp of witches and wizards. I scatter their conspiracies, in the name of Jesus.

21. I destroy all evil thoughts and imaginations against me, in the name of Jesus.

22. I frustrate the spirit of loneliness, in the name of Jesus.

23. I bind every spirit intimidating me, in the name of Jesus.

24. Let God arise and let all the enemies of my breakthroughs scatter, in the name of Jesus.

25. I snatch all the keys to my success and multiple breakthroughs in the hands of my enemies, in the name of Jesus.

26. Let the light of the gospel shine on every black spot of my life, in the name of Jesus.

27. I break my covenants with familiar spirits, in the name of Jesus.
28. I break my covenants with false and fake prophets, in the name of Jesus.
29. I break my covenants with occultic spirits, in the name of Jesus.
30. I bind every spirit of Balaam, in the name of Jesus.
31. I reject the spirit of heaviness and dizziness, in the name of Jesus.
32. I bind the spirit of confusion and fear, in the name of Jesus.
33. I shall not die but live. I reject the spirit of death, in the name of Jesus.
34. I reject the spirit of false accusation, in the name of Jesus.
35. I smash all demonic mirrors to pieces, in the name of Jesus.
36. My destiny, become excellent, in the name of Jesus.
37. I defeat the spirit of hatred, in the name of Jesus.
38. Poverty is not for me, I am for prosperity, success and blessings, in the name of Jesus.
39. I refuse to die young, I shall reach my full age, in the name of Jesus.
40. I reject the spirit of anger, in the name of Jesus.
41. I reject the spirit of envy and jealousy, in the name of Jesus.
42. I reject the spirit of the fear of man, in the name of Jesus.
43. I destroy all demonic names and nicknames given to me right from my mother's womb, in the name of Jesus.
44. Demons cannot drink my blood, for it is anointed with the power of the Holy Spirit, in the name of Jesus.
45. I attack the attackers of my blessings, in the name of Jesus.
46. I conquer the spirit of death, in the name of Jesus.
47. I vomit all demonic concoctions, in the name of Jesus.
48. All demonic incisions or marks on my body, be wiped off by the blood of Jesus.
49. I destroy all sacrifices made on my behalf, in the name of Jesus.
50. Let all those collaborating with evil forces against me be roasted by the fire of God, in the name of Jesus.

51. Every instrument of bewitchment set in motion against me, be roasted, in the name of Jesus.
52. Any dark power trying to attack me to get promotion, fall down and die, in the name of Jesus.
53. I dethrone all the foreign kings and queens reigning over my life, in the name of Jesus.
54. I overthrow the authority of the powers of darkness, in the name of Jesus.
55. I pull down every tree not planted by my Father in heaven, in the name of Jesus.
56. Let my name be removed from the lists and books of failures, backwardness and poverty, in the name of Jesus.
57. Let God's wisdom to take right decisions fall upon me, in the name of Jesus.

CHAPTER TWO

DIVINE MEDICATION

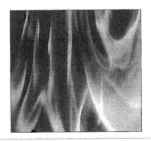

DIVINE
MEDICATION
②

This prayer programme will grant you the keys of the mystery of divine healing. It has been declared in the Scripture that God's word is a mighty instrument of healing and health. Therefore, prayer points concerning divine medication will work wonders in your body.

This prayer programme will take you to the theatre of heaven where you will go through a life-changing spiritual treatment. No matter how long you have languished or suffered certain diseases or ailments, when God comes to the scene and gives you a single dose of His divine medication, the result would be awesome.

The best way to handle anything is to take it back to the manufacturer. When handled by the manufacturer everything would be normalised. If you have tried certain prescriptions and you are far from enjoying total health, you need divine medication. God is the Creator of every organ in your body and He alone knows how the organs would function perfectly and your entire body would be wholesome. Human efforts would remain imperfect but when God takes over, His healing virtue would flow through your system and whatever is in the state of disintegration, pain or malfunctioning would receive divine touch and normalcy would return.

A lot of people have not known how to reap all the benefits that can be found in divine medication. One single injection from the Almighty would fill every gap in your body, restore every spent energy, energise every tired nerve, heal any ailing part and restore health in your body. Divine medication is all you need.

There is no injection that can be compared with prayers into your blood streams. When you are fervent in prayers the effect would be visible in your body. Those who pray until their systems are charged by the fire of the Holy Ghost enjoy soundness of health. These prayer points will invite heavenly surgeons into your body to perform divine operations.

The purpose of divine medication is to stimulate the flow of divine healing into your body. When you receive the healing touch of the Almighty, long-standing diseases will vanish, incurable ailments will die, recurrent diseases will be sent packing. A great deal of awesome power resides in divine medication. This prayer programme will take you to the divine hospital where the best medical facilities can be found.

You need these prayer points:

1. You want to enjoy divine health.
2. When you want to kill every germ of sickness.
3. When you want to put an end to constant attacks on your health.
4. When your entire body needs general overhauling.
5. When you need your blood to be sanitised.
6. When there are strange diseases in your body.
7. When there are stubborn health problems that have defied

medication.

8. When you are sick and tired of being sick.
9. When you have discovered that your poor health condition can be traced to unseen powers.
10. When you are tired of expending huge financial resources on your poor health.
11. When you need the type of divine touch that will completely transform your health and change your status from a sickler to someone whose health is sound.
12. When you want to be a symbol of divine health.
13. When you want to take a single pill that would heal a number of diseases.
14. When you want to enjoy your health.
15. When you want to defeat the arrow of untimely death
16. When the enemy has subjected your body to a habitation of poor health.
17. When you want to have access to the best health facility that can be found here on earth.
18. When you want God to bless you with the miracle of divine health
19. When you want to enjoy the benefit of redemption in the area of health

These prayers must be handled fervently, persistently and thoroughly. You must get rid of anything that would not allow divine medication to function in your body. You must charge your foundation by fire. Finally, you must allow God to keep you in His divine theatre until you are completely healed. The healing virtue of God has been made available. Total healing is yours. Pray until the benefits of divine healing are enjoyed and experienced by you.

PRAYERS SECTION

Confession: **Exodus 15:26:** *And said, If thou wilt diligently hearken to the voice of the Lord thy God, and wilt do that which is right in his* *sight, and wilt give ear to his commandments, and keep all his statutes, I will put none of these diseases upon thee, which I have brought upon the Egyptians: for I am the Lord that healeth thee.* **Isaiah 53:5:** *But he was wounded for our transgressions, he was bruised for our iniquities: the chastisement of our peace was upon him; and with his stripes we are healed.*

Praise Worship

 # PRAYER POINTS

1. Every organ of my body, cooperate with the blood of Jesus.
2. Revival power, resurrection power, rejuvenating power, come upon every organ of my body, in the name of Jesus.
3. Any organ of my body that has lost its function, resume your functions now, in the name of Jesus.
4. Blood of Jesus, speak life into my head, my heart, my liver, my kidney, my bladder, my womb, etc, in the name of Jesus.
5. I reject every evil clinical prophecy, in the name of Jesus.
6. I pull down every satanic bewitchment upon any organ of my body, in the name of Jesus.
7. Every pronouncement of man about my health that is contrary to my life, I cancel it by the blood of Jesus.
8. By the word of God through which all things were created, let my life experience divine power, in the name of Jesus.
9. Holy Ghost fire, renew my strength, in the name of Jesus.
10. Blood of Jesus, renew my strength, in the name of Jesus.
11. My Father, make me a mysterious wonder, in the name of Jesus.
12. Where is the Lord God of Elijah? Arise and reorganise my organ for uncommon testimonies, in the name of Jesus.
13. Every power speaking death and malfunctioning into any organ of my body, die, in the name of Jesus.
14. I receive fresh energy, fresh fire, fresh power into every organ of my body, in the name of Jesus.

15. Father, dispatch Your heavenly surgeons to work upon my life, and maken the impossible possible, in the name of Jesus.

16. By the power of the God of Elijah, let uncommon breakthroughs manifest in my life, in the name of Jesus.

17. Let the Prince of Peace speak peace unto every storm in my life, in the name of Jesus.

18. O God arise with Your healing power and visit me, in the name of Jesus.

19. Every altar of affliction of sickness, catch fire, in the name of Jesus.

20. Any curse or covenant, aiding sickness in my life, be broken by the power in the blood of Jesus.

21. Any sickness on my body, be shaken off by fire, in the name of Jesus.

22. Every mountain of sickness, be rolled away by fire, in the name of Jesus.

23. I drink the blood of Jesus and I command the roots of sicknesses in my life to dry up, in the name of Jesus.

24. Every plantation of sickness in my body, catch fire, in the name of Jesus.

25. Every agent of sickness in my body, come out and die, in the name of Jesus.

26. Let my body be redeemed from the power of sickness and diseases, in the name of Jesus.

27. Let the power of death and hell behind any sickness in my body, loose its hold and die, in the name of Jesus.

28. I shall not die but live to declare the works of God, in the name of Jesus.

29. Every water of affliction of sickness flowing into my life, be cut off, in the name of Jesus.

30. Any evil association against my health, scatter, in the name of Jesus.

31. Any evil weapon fashioned against my health, die, in the name of Jesus.

32. Every fire of sickness tormenting my life, East wind, blow them away, in the name of Jesus.
33. Let the fire of Holy Ghost melt away sicknesses in my body, in the name of Jesus.
34. Every power of sickness and diseases in my body, die by fire, in the name of Jesus.
35. Every witchcraft caldron cooking my health, catch fire, in the name of Jesus.
36. Let my light break forth and my health spring forth speedily, in the name of Jesus.
37. I bear in my body the mark of the blood of Jesus. Therefore, let sickness flee away from my habitation, in the name of Jesus.
38. Every witchcraft ordinance written against my health, die, in the name of Jesus.

CHAPTER THREE

HEALING CAPSULE

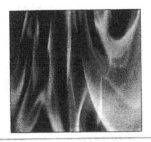

HEALING CAPSULE

3

There are lots of healing benefits to obtain from God's spiritual hospital. He has provided all manner of potent healing capsules to make you enjoy divine healing and health. He has given us the prayer points in this programme as capsules that will fight germs, deflect arrows that are shot to make us sick. Every prayer point here can be likened to a very powerful capsule. It will lay a very powerful axe at the root of infirmities that are threatening your health and wellbeing. The efficiency of prayer will be discovered as you take these prayer points.

Healing capsule prayers are useful when:

1. You want to attack sickness from the root.
2. When you want to enjoy divine healing.
3. When you want God's healing virtue to flow through your system.
4. When you want to put an end to all types of psychosomatic diseases.

5. When you want to deal with ailments that are sponsored by witchcraft.
6. When you want to deal with recurrent diseases.
7. When you want to enjoy robust health.
8. When you want to obtain healing for sickness that has defied medication.
9. When you want to enjoy consistent sound health.
10. When you want to experience instantaneous and constant healing.
11. When you desire your testimony to be full in the area of good health.

To experience healing and resounding health you need:

1. Faith in the power of prayer.
2. You need a full close of the healing capsule.
3. You must avoid any internal mechanism that will counter the healing capsule.
4. You need to pray with such an aggression that will frighten every hidden stranger out of their hidden place.
5. You must settle for nothing less than full and comprehensive healing.

As you pray, expect a miracle. The Ancient of Days has declared, "I am the Lord that healeth thee! Healing and health are yours, in the name of Jesus.

PRAYERS SECTION

Confession: **Exodus 15:26:** *And said, If thou wilt diligently hearken to the voice of the Lord thy God, and wilt do that which is right in his sight, and wilt give ear to his commandments, and keep all his statutes, I will put none of these diseases upon thee, which I have brought upon the Egyptians: for I am the Lord that healeth thee.* **Isaiah 53:5:** *But he was wounded for our transgressions, he was bruised for our iniquities: the chastisement of our peace was upon him; and with his stripes we are healed.*

🖐 PRAYERS POINTS

1. Thank You Father for the benefits and provision of the blood of Jesus.
2. I sprinkle the blood of Jesus upon my body - from the top of my head to the soles of my feet.
3. I paralyse with the blood of Jesus, all satanic oppressors delegated against me, in Jesus' name.
4. I curse every work of darkness in my life to dry to the roots by the blood of Jesus.
5. I defeat, paralyse and erase ....(pick from the under listed), by the blood of Jesus.
6. I overcome every spirit of infirmity by the blood of the Lamb.
7. No spirit, power or personality shall be able to put any sickness on me because I am redeemed by the blood of the Lamb.
8. Let the blood of Jesus speak peace unto every organ in my body.
9. Every root of infirmities in my life, dry up, in the name of Jesus.
10. Every citadel of sickness in my life, catch fire, in the name of Jesus.
11. I reject every evil clinical prophecy, in the name of Jesus.
12. Every power speaking death and malfunctioning into any organ of my body, die, in the name of Jesus.
13. O God, arise with Your healing power and visit me, in the name of Jesus.
14. Any curse or covenant aiding sickness in my life, be broken by the power in the blood of Jesus.
15. I drink the blood of Jesus and I command the roots of sicknesses in my life to dry up, in the name of Jesus.
16. Let my body be redeemed from the power of sickness and diseases, in the name of Jesus.
17. Any evil association against my health, scatter, in the name

of Jesus.

18. Every witchcraft caldron cooking my health, catch fire, in the name of Jesus.

19. Every witchcraft ordinance written against my health, die, in the name of Jesus.

20. Thank God for your healing.

CHAPTER FIVE

BREAKING INTERNAL CHAINS

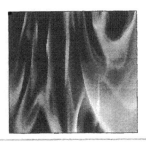

DIVINE INTERNAL SURGERY

4

ealing and health are gifts from the Almighty. There is nothing as permanent as divine healing or divine health. When God heals, He heals permanently. As far as heaven is concerned, there is nothing like an incurable disease. God is ready to go to the root of any sickness and wipe it out completely. Jesus' death on the cross of Calvary has fully paid for our healing. Every stripe He received and the blood that oozed out of his body have sealed our healing. You only need to appropriate what God has finished. When Jesus declared "It is finished", reference was made to our total healing and health. Whatever is the source of any sickness plaguing your body, the healing virtue has cancelled it.

God has given you an access to the greatest hospital in the universe. It is the hospital where The Great Physician is the resident doctor. There is no disease He cannot cure, there is no operation he cannot perform, there is no infirmity he cannot cancel. He is able to put an end to any kind of health problem. Jesus is your Great Physician. The price He paid at Calvary has given you free access to healing and health.

This prayer programme takes you to the root of every sickness or infirmity. The prayer points will lay the axe at the root of every recurrent health problem. Every prayer points is a drug that has been divinely empowered to fish out and kill any bacteria in your body. When you make use of these prayer points you automatically receive immunity that will make every hidden stranger to be frightened and jump out of your body. This prayer programme takes you to the operating theatre of the Holy Ghost where doctor Jesus will heal you totally and freely.

Divine internal surgery is about to take place in your body. Known and unknown curses or diseases will be addressed. You will be injected with divine vitamins and antibiotics which, charged with the fire of the Holy Ghost, will grant you a clean bill of health. This prayer programme is needed by:

1. Those who have been declared incurable by hospitals.
2. Those who are grappling with terminal diseases.
3. Those whose medical science has failed to diagnose what is wrong with them.
4. Those whose health problems are traceable to spiritual attacks.
5. Those whose problems have brought fear into their hearts.

You must pray fervently until you feel in your body a new surge of healing and health.

PRAYER SECTION

Confession: **Isaiah 53:5-6**: *But he was wounded for our transgressions, he was bruised for our iniquities: the chastisement of our peace was upon him; and with his stripes we are healed. All we like sheep have gone astray; we have turned every one to his own way; and the Lord hath laid on him the iniquity of us all.*

Song:

The Great Physician now is here. Hear the footsteps of Jesus

He has broken all the fetters. He touched me

 # PRAYER POINTS

1. Organs of my body, hear the word of the Lord: reject the voice of the grave, in the name of Jesus.
2. Thou cleansing power in the blood of Jesus, sanitiSe my body, in the name of Jesus.
3. Thou Great Physician, send surgeons from heaven to work on me now, in the name of Jesus.
4. Agenda of infirmity for my life, die, in the name of Jesus.
5. Operating theatre of God, arise, admit me and work on me now, in the name of Jesus.
6. Damage done to my body by infirmities, be repaired by fire, in the name of Jesus.
7. Divine antibiotics, divine medication, bombard my body by fire, in the name of Jesus.
8. I withdraw every conscious and unconscious co-operation with any internal disorder, in the name of Jesus.
9. Any power stealing my healing virtues, come out and die, in the name of Jesus.
10. Anointing that breaks the yoke, break every internal yoke and chains, in the name of Jesus.
11. Healing virtues from the King of kings, and the Lord of lords, saturate my body now, in the name of Jesus.
12. O Lord, save me and I shall be saved. Heal me and I shall be healed, in the name of Jesus.
13. O God of possibilities, make me whole, in the name of Jesus.
14. Let my body be electrified with the healing power of God, in the name of Jesus.
15. My Father, shake me loose from every grip of sickness, in

the name of Jesus.

16. I shall not die but live to declare the works of God, in the name of Jesus.

17. Thou creative power of God, mobilise Your resources into my life, in the name of Jesus.

18. Rain of healing waters from above, soak every organ in my body, in the name of Jesus.

19. Spirit of Goliath, spirit of Herod, spirit of Pharaoh, release my body, in the name of Jesus.

20. Physical and spiritual poisons, come out of my body now, in the name of Jesus.

21. I cough our and vomit any plantation of darkness in my body, in the name of Jesus.

22. Every internal affliction and oppression in my body, die, in the name of Jesus.

23. Agents of disruption in my body, come out and die, in the name of Jesus.

24. My Father, let Your angelic surgeons visit every part of my life, in the name of Jesus.

25. Yoke breaker, Jesus Christ, break my yoke now, in the name of Jesus.

26. My body, hear the word of the Lord, receive divine repair, in the name of Jesus.

CHAPTER FIVE

BREAKING INTERNAL CHAINS

BREAKING INTERNAL CHAINS

5

Most of life's problems can be traced to the existence of stubborn chains that are tying people down. Those who are tied down in the spiritual realm will always go through intractable and protracted problems. Chain-like problems are generally difficult to handle. It is quite easy to deal with physical and noticeable chains, but hidden internal chains are the worst type of chains to deal with.

Internal chains come from within and are often self-crafted. They often prepare tough platforms for external chains. When the foundation is laid by internal chains, such problems will rope layers of chains round the life of the victim. It is indeed true that the internal thief that beckons the external thief to come in and rob. To deal with external chains you must first address internal chains.

The moment you are done with internal chains, the external ones will break. Chains are instruments of oppression, constructed to put humanity in bondage. However, I have good news for you. Jesus is the bondage breaker. The first place to start with is within. No matter how many times you go through deliverance, bondage will remain part and parcel of you as long as you nurture and habour internal chains.

The shortest route to the realm of freedom is the route of dealing with internal chains. Internal chains may not appear lofty but the truth is that they are stubborn. When you thoroughly examine the manifestations of internal chains you will discover that a lot of people go about with invisible internal chains. You need to break the internal chains that you are struggling with. They are secret sins and bad habits. You need to break internal chains when you are responsible for putting external chains in place, when you experience failure at the edge of miracles, when you find yourself building with one hand and destroying with another, when you find it difficult to remove self-imposed barriers, when you are struggling with compulsive negative habits, when you discover that little termites are busy consuming what you have spent years to achieve.

You need to break internal chains when you suddenly discover that there are internal agents that are aiding and abetting satanic external aggression, when you discover that what works for others is not working for you. You should fight the enemies to a standstill and give up every property of his in your possession.

PRAYERS SECTION

Confessions: **Luke 13:12:** *And when Jesus saw her, he called her to him, and said unto her, Woman, thou art loosed from thine infirmity.* **Acts 10:38:** *How God anointed Jesus of Nazareth with the Holy Ghost and with power: who went about doing good, and healing all that were oppressed of the devil; for God was with him.*

Praise Worship

 **PRAYER POINTS**

1. Thank the Lord because He is the bondage breaker and the Great Physician.
2. Oh God, arise and inject the blood of Jesus into my blood stream, in the name of Jesus.
3. Holy Ghost fire, purge every defilement away from my life, in the name of Jesus.
4. Anything planted in my body to oppress me, come out now, in the name of Jesus.
5. Any curse operating upon any organ of my body, break, in the name of Jesus.
6. Every authority assigned to torment me, expire, in the name of Jesus.
7. Every programme of affliction for my body and destiny, expire, in the name of Jesus.
8. Anything I've eaten or swallowed that is chaining me inside, I vomit you by fire, in the name of Jesus.
9. Blood of Jesus, Holy Ghost fire, sanitise my body, soul and spirit, in the name of Jesus.
10. Every wicked handwriting operating in my body organs, be wiped off by the blood of Jesus.
11. My body, hear the word of the Lord: reject every arrow of darkness, in the name of Jesus.
12. Any tree that the Father has not planted inside my body, be uprooted by fire, in the name of Jesus.
13. Voice of the Almighty, speak wholeness into every department of my life, in the name of Jesus.
14. Divine power of creativity and repair, operate in my life now, in the name of Jesus.
15. My Father, cause every instrument of affliction in my body to expire, in the name of Jesus.
16. Any evil hand laid upon any organ of my body, wither, in the name of Jesus.

17. I reject totally any bewitchment of any organ of my body, in the name of Jesus.
18. My Father, carry out on me divine surgery that will move my life forward, in the name of Jesus.
19. Any power cooking my spirit man in a caldron, fall down and die, in the name of Jesus.
20. Every internal yoke assigned against me, break, in the name of Jesus.
21. Satanic summons of my spirit man in a crystal ball or a dark mirror, backfire, in the name of Jesus.
22. Every evil hand fashioned to manipulate my life, catch fire, in the name of Jesus.
23. Every evil load in any part of my body, go back to your senders, in the name of Jesus.
24. Where is the Lord God of Elijah? Arise and kill every poison in my body, in the name of Jesus.
25. Every hidden infirmity and silent sickness, die, in the name of Jesus.
26. Every rage of the enemy assigned to send me backward, break, in the name of Jesus.
27. Every dark incantation uttered against my wholeness, backfire, in the name of Jesus.
28. You eaters of flesh and drinkers of blood assigned against me, eat your flesh and drink your blood, in the name of Jesus.
29. Rain of affliction assigned to trouble my life, carry your warfare back to the enemy, in the name of Jesus.
30. Every evil mountain confronting my body, I cast you into the sea, in the name of Jesus.
31. Any power circulating my name for evil, carry your load, in the name of Jesus.
32. Every internal chain suffocating my life, break, in the name of Jesus.
33. By the power that breaks the gates of brass and cuts the bars of iron asunder, let all my spiritual chains break, in the name of Jesus.

34. Any power organised to disorganise me, I bury you alive, in the name of Jesus.
35. Thank the Lord for answering your prayers.

CHAPTER SIX

HOLY PURGING

6

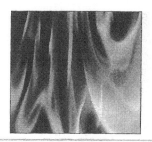

HOLY PURGING

6

Make these confessions boldly and loudly:

Matthew 3:10: *And now also the axe is laid unto the root of the trees: therefore every tree which bringeth not forth good fruit is hewn down, and cast into the fire. Every tree that bringeth not forth good fruit is hewn down, and cast into the fire.* **Galatians 3:13-14:** *Christ hath redeemed us from the curse of the law, being made a curse for us: for it is written, Cursed is every one that hangeth on a tree: That the blessing of Abraham might come on the Gentiles through Jesus Christ; that we might receive the promise of the Spirit through faith.* **2 Timothy 4:18:** *And the Lord shall deliver me from every evil work, and will preserve me unto his heavenly kingdom: to whom be glory for ever and ever. Amen.* **Colossians 1:13:** *Who hath delivered us from the power of darkness, and hath translated us into the kingdom of his dear Son.* **Colossians 2:15:** *And having spoiled principalities and powers, he made a shew of them openly, triumphing over them in it.* **Psalm 56:9:** *When I cry unto thee, then shall mine enemies turn back: this I know; for God is for me.* **Malachai 4:2:** *But unto you that fear my name shall the Sun of righteousness arise with healing in his wings; and ye shall go forth, and* *grow up as calves of the stall.* **Col 2:14-15:** *Blotting out the handwriting of ordinances that was against us, which was contrary to us, and took it out of the way, nailing it to his cross; And having spoiled principalities and powers, he made a shew of them openly, triumphing over them in it.* **Matthew 8:17:** *That it might be fulfilled which was spoken by Esaias the prophet, saying, Himself took our infirmities, and bare our sicknesses.* **Romans 16:20:** *And the God of peace shall bruise Satan under your feet shortly. The grace of our Lord Jesus Christ be with you. Amen.* **I John 3:8b:** *For this purpose the Son of God was manifested, that he might destroy the works of the devil.* **2 Timothy 4:18:** *And the Lord shall deliver me from every evil work, and will preserve me unto his heavenly kingdom: to whom be glory for ever and ever. Amen.*

Jesus is Lord over my spirit, soul and body, for the word of God tells me that at the name of Jesus every knee shall bow. I can do all things through Christ who strengthens me. The Lord is my shepherd, I shall not want. Jesus has delivered me from the powers of darkness and has translated me into His kingdom. In Jesus I have redemption and forgiveness of sins through His shed blood. Jesus has blotted out the handwriting of ordinances that was against me which was contrary to me, and took it out of the way, nailing it to His cross. I am the body of Christ. I am redeemed from the curse of the law because Jesus bore my physical and spiritual diseases in His body. I have the mind of Christ and I hold the thoughts, feelings and purposes of His heart.

 **PRAYER SECTION**

Praise Worship

 **PRAYER POINTS**

1. Thank God for HIS mighty power to save to the uttermost for power to deliver from any form of bondage.
2. Confess your sins and those of your ancestors, especially

those sins linked to evil powers and idolatry.

3. I cover myself with the blood of Jesus.

4. I apply the blood of Jesus on my spirit, soul, body and my womb.

5. I release myself from any inherited bondage and limitations in the name of Jesus.

6. O Lord, send Your axe of fire to the foundation of my life and destroy every evil plantation.

7. Let the blood of Jesus flush out from my system every inherited satanic deposit in the name of Jesus.

8. I release myself from the grip of any problem transferred into my life from the womb in the name of Jesus.

9. Let the blood of Jesus and the fire of the Holy Ghost cleanse every organ in my body in the name of Jesus.

10. I break and loose myself from every inherited evil covenant, in the name of Jesus.

11. I break and loose myself from every inherited evil curse, in the name of Jesus.

12. I vomit every evil consumption that I have been fed with as a child, in the name of Jesus.

13. I command all foundational strongmen attached to my life to be paralysed, in the name of Jesus.

14. Let any rod of the wicked rising up against my family line be rendered impotence for my sake, in the name of Jesus.

15. I cancel the consequences of any evil local name attached to my person, in the name of Jesus.

16. *(Pray aggressively against the following evil foundations:)* You (*pick the under listed one by one*), loose your hold over my life and be purged out of my foundation, in the name of Jesus.
    - Destructive effect of polygamy- Evil physical design- Unscriptural manners of conception- Parental Curses Envious rivalry-Demonic blood transfusion-Evil dedication- Demonic alteration of destiny- Demonic incisions- Demonic marriage - Dream pollution- E v i l laying on of hands

- Demonic sacrifice- Fellowship with family idols
- Fellowship with local idols
- Fellowship with demonic consultants
- Wrong exposure to sex- Exposure to evil diviner
- Demonic initiations- Inherited infirmity

17. You evil foundational plantations, come out of my life with all your roots, in the name of Jesus.
18. I break and loose myself from every form of demonic bewitchment, in the name of Jesus.
19. I release myself from every evil domination and control, in the name of Jesus.
20. Let the blood of Jesus be transfused into my blood vessel.
21. Let every gate opened to the enemy by my foundation be closed forever with the blood of Jesus.
22. Lord Jesus, walk back into every second of my life and deliver me where I need deliverance, heal me where I need healing, transform me where I need transformation.
23. Let the power in the blood of Jesus separate me from the sins of my ancestors.
24. Let the blood of Jesus remove any unprogressive label from every aspect of my life.
25. O Lord, create in me a clean heart by Your power.
26. O Lord, renew a right spirit within me.
27. O Lord, teach me to die to self.
28. O Lord, ignite my calling with Your fire.
29. O Lord, anoint me to pray without ceasing.
30. O Lord, establish me as a holy person unto You.
31. O Lord, restore my spiritual eyes and ears, in the name of Jesus.
32. O Lord, let the anointing to excel in my spiritual and physical life fall on me.
33. O Lord, produce in me the power of self-control and gentleness.
34. O Lord, let the anointing of the Holy Spirit break every yoke of backwardness in my life.

35. Holy Ghost, breathe on me now, in the name of Jesus.
36. Holy Ghost fire, ignite me to the glory of God.
37. Let every rebellion flee from my heart, in the name of Jesus.
38. I command every spiritual contamination in my life to receive cleansing by the blood of Jesus.
39. Let the brush of the Lord scrub out every dirtiness in my spiritual pipe, in the name of Jesus.
40. Every rusted spiritual pipe in my life, receive wholeness, in the name of Jesus.
41. I command every power eating up my spiritual pipe to be roasted, in the name of Jesus.
42. I renounce any evil dedication placed upon my life, in the name of Jesus.
43. I break every evil edict and ordination, in the name of Jesus.
44. O Lord, cleanse all the soiled parts of my life, in Jesus' name.
45. O Lord, deliver me from every foundational Pharaoh, in Jesus' name..
46. O Lord, heal every wounded part of my life, in Jesus' name.
47. O Lord, bend every evil rigidity in my life, in Jesus' name.
48. O Lord, re-align every satanic straying in my life, in Jesus' name.
49. O Lord, let the fire of the Holy Spirit warm every satanic freezing in my life, in the name of Jesus.
50. O Lord, give me a life that kills death, in Jesus' name.
51. O Lord, kindle in me the fire of charity, in the name of Jesus.
52. O Lord, glue me together where I am opposed to myself, in Jesus' name.
53. O Lord, enrich me with Your gifts, in Jesus' name.
54. O Lord, quicken me and increase my desire of the things of heaven, in Jesus' name.
55. By Your rulership, O Lord, let the lust of the flesh in my life die, in the name of Jesus.
56. Lord Jesus, increase daily in my life, in Jesus' name.

57. Lord Jesus, maintain Your gifts in my life, in Jesus' name.

58. O Lord, refine and purge my life by Your fire, in Jesus' name.

59. Holy Spirit, inflame and fire my heart, in the name of Jesus.

60. Holy Ghost fire, begin to burn away every power of the bond woman in me, in the name of Jesus.

61. O Lord, make me ready to go wherever You send me.

62. Lord Jesus, never let me shut You out.

63. Lord Jesus, work freely in me and through me.

64. Let the fire of God saturate my womb, in the name of Jesus.

65. Let every design against my life be completely nullified, in the name of Jesus.

66. Let all evil labels fashioned by the camp of the enemy against my life be rubbed off by the blood of Jesus.

67. Sing the song HOLY GHOST FIRE, FIRE FALL ON ME with full concentration and in faith.

68. I vomit every satanic deposit in my life, in the mighty name of Jesus. *(Prime the expulsion of these things by coughing slightly. Refuse to swallow any saliva coming out from the mouth)*

69. I break myself loose from the bondage of stagnancy, in the mighty name of Jesus.

70. Lord, destroy with Your fire anything that makes Your promise to fail upon my life, no matter the origin, in Jesus' name.

71. Let the blood, the fire and the living water of the Most High God wash my system clean from:-
    - Unprofitable growth in my womb
    - Evil plantation -Evil deposits from spirit husband- Impurities acquired from parental contamination- Evil spiritual consumption- Hidden sicknesses
    - Remote control mechanisms
    - Physical and spiritual incisions
    - Satanic poisons
    - Evil stamps, labels and links.

72. Let every area of my life become too hot for any evil to inhabit, in the name of Jesus.

73. Evil growth in my life, be uprooted, in the name of Jesus.

74. Let my body reject every evil habitation, in the mighty name of our Lord Jesus Christ.

75. O Lord, reverse all evil arrangements attracted consciously or unconsciously to my life, in Jesus' name.

76. I reject all evil manipulations and manipulators, in the mighty name of Jesus.

77. I break the power of the occult, witchcraft and familiar spirits over my life, in the name of Jesus.

78. I deliver and pass out any satanic deposit in my intestine, in the name of Jesus.

79. I deliver and pass out any satanic deposit in my reproductive organs, in the name of Jesus.

80. I deliver and pass out any satanic deposit in my womb, in the name of Jesus.

81. In the name of Jesus, I declare before all the forces of darkness that "Jesus Christ is Lord over every department of My Life."

82. You foreign hand laid on my womb, release me, in the name of Jesus.

83. In the name of Jesus, I renounce, break and loose myself from all:
    - demonic holds - psychic powers
    - bonds of physical illness - bondage

84. In the name of Jesus, I break and loose myself from all evil curses, chains, spells, jinxes, bewitchments, witchcraft or sorcery which may have been put upon me.

85. Let a creative miracle take place in my womb and reproductive system, in the name of Jesus.

86. Father, I ask You, in the name of Jesus Christ, to send out Your angels to unearth and break all evil storage vessels fashioned against me

87. I loose myself from every evil influence, dark spirit and satanic bondage, in Jesus' name.

88. I confess and declare that my body is the temple of the Holy Spirit, redeemed, cleansed and sanctified by the blood of

Jesus Christ, in Jesus' name.

89. I bind, plunder and render to naught every strongman assigned to my womb, reproductive system and marital life, in the name of Jesus.

90. God who quickens the dead, quicken my womb and reproductive system, in the name of Jesus.

91. I release myself from the hold of spirits of sterility, infertility and fear, in the name of Jesus.

92. All spirits rooted in fornication, come out of my life with all your roots, in the mighty name of our Lord Jesus.

93. All spirits rooted in sexual perversion, come out of my life with all your roots, in the mighty name of our Lord Jesus.

94. All spirits rooted in spirit husband/wife come out of my life with all your roots, in the mighty name of our Lord Jesus.

95. All spirits rooted in masturbation, come out of my life with all your roots, in the mighty name of our Lord Jesus.

96. All spirits rooted in guilt, come out of my life with all your roots, in the mighty name of our Lord Jesus.

97. All spirits rooted in pornography, come out of my life with all your roots, in the mighty name of our Lord Jesus.

98. O God, arise and set me free from every problem that is higher than me, in the name of Jesus.

99. Sing this song: "There is power mighty in the blood."

100. Thank the Lord for your healing and deliverance.

PRAYER SECTION

Praise Worship

 # PRAYER POINTS

1. Thank God for HIS mighty power to save to the uttermost for power to deliver from any form of bondage.

2. Confess your sins and those of your ancestors, especially those sins linked to evil powers and idolatry.

3. I cover myself with the blood of Jesus.

4. I apply the blood of Jesus on my spirit, soul, body and my womb.

5. I release myself from any inherited bondage and limitations in the name of Jesus.

6. O Lord, send Your axe of fire to the foundation of my life and destroy every evil plantation.

7. Let the blood of Jesus flush out from my system every inherited satanic deposit in the name of Jesus.

8. I release myself from the grip of any problem transferred into my life from the womb in the name of Jesus.

9. Let the blood of Jesus and the fire of the Holy Ghost cleanse every organ in my body in the name of Jesus.

10. I break and loose myself from every inherited evil covenant, in the name of Jesus.

11. I break and loose myself from every inherited evil curse, in the name of Jesus.

12. I vomit every evil consumption that I have been fed with as a child, in the name of Jesus.

13. I command all foundational strongmen attached to my life to be paralysed, in the name of Jesus.

14. Let any rod of the wicked rising up against my family line be rendered impotence for my sake, in the name of Jesus.

15. I cancel the consequences of any evil local name attached to my person, in the name of Jesus.

16. *(Pray aggressively against the following evil foundations:)* You (*pick the under listed one by one*), loose your hold over my life and be purged out of my foundation, in the name of Jesus.
    - Destructive effect of polygamy- Evil physical design - Unscriptural manners of conception- Parental Curses- Envious rivalry- Demonic blood transfusion - Evil dedication- Demonic alteration of destiny - Demonic incisions- Demonic marriage - Dream pollution- Evil laying on of hands - Demonic sacrifice- Fellowship with family idols - Fellowship with local idols - Fellowship with demonic consultants - Wrong exposure to sex

Exposure to evil diviner - Demonic initiations- Inherited infirmity

17. You evil foundational plantations, come out of my life with all your roots, in the name of Jesus.
18. I break and loose myself from every form of demonic bewitchment, in the name of Jesus.
19. I release myself from every evil domination and control, in the name of Jesus.
20. Let the blood of Jesus be transfused into my blood vessel.
21. Let every gate opened to the enemy by my foundation be closed forever with the blood of Jesus.
22. Lord Jesus, walk back into every second of my life and deliver me where I need deliverance, heal me where I need healing, transform me where I need transformation.
23. Let the power in the blood of Jesus separate me from the sins of my ancestors.
24. Let the blood of Jesus remove any unprogressive label from every aspect of my life.
25. O Lord, create in me a clean heart by Your power.
26. O Lord, renew a right spirit within me.
27. O Lord, teach me to die to self.
28. O Lord, ignite my calling with Your fire.
29. O Lord, anoint me to pray without ceasing.
30. O Lord, establish me as a holy person unto You.
31. O Lord, restore my spiritual eyes and ears, in the name of Jesus.
32. O Lord, let the anointing to excel in my spiritual and physical life fall on me.
33. O Lord, produce in me the power of self-control and gentleness.
34. O Lord, let the anointing of the Holy Spirit break every yoke of backwardness in my life.
35. Holy Ghost, breathe on me now, in the name of Jesus.
36. Holy Ghost fire, ignite me to the glory of God.
37. Let every rebellion flee from my heart, in the name of Jesus.
38. I command every spiritual contamination in my life to

receive cleansing by the blood of Jesus.

39. Let the brush of the Lord scrub out every dirtiness in my spiritual pipe, in the name of Jesus.

40. Every rusted spiritual pipe in my life, receive wholeness, in the name of Jesus.

41. I command every power eating up my spiritual pipe to be roasted, in the name of Jesus.

42. I renounce any evil dedication placed upon my life, in the name of Jesus.

43. I break every evil edict and ordination, in the name of Jesus.

44. O Lord, cleanse all the soiled parts of my life, in Jesus' name.

45. O Lord, deliver me from every foundational Pharaoh, in Jesus' name..

46. O Lord, heal every wounded part of my life, in Jesus' name.

47. O Lord, bend every evil rigidity in my life, in Jesus' name.

48. O Lord, re-align every satanic straying in my life, in Jesus' name.

49. O Lord, let the fire of the Holy Spirit warm every satanic freezing in my life, in the name of Jesus.

50. O Lord, give me a life that kills death, in Jesus' name.

51. O Lord, kindle in me the fire of charity, in the name of Jesus.

52. O Lord, glue me together where I am opposed to myself, in Jesus' name.

53. O Lord, enrich me with Your gifts, in Jesus' name.

54. O Lord, quicken me and increase my desire of the things of heaven, in Jesus' name.

55. By Your rulership, O Lord, let the lust of the flesh in my life die, in the name of Jesus.

56. Lord Jesus, increase daily in my life, in Jesus' name.

57. Lord Jesus, maintain Your gifts in my life, in Jesus' name.

58. O Lord, refine and purge my life by Your fire, in Jesus' name.

59. Holy Spirit, inflame and fire my heart, in the name of Jesus.

60. Holy Ghost fire, begin to burn away every power of the

bond woman in me, in the name of Jesus.

61. O Lord, make me ready to go wherever You send me.
62. Lord Jesus, never let me shut You out.
63. Lord Jesus, work freely in me and through me.
64. Let the fire of God saturate my womb, in the name of Jesus.
65. Let every design against my life be completely nullified, in the name of Jesus.
66. Let all evil labels fashioned by the camp of the enemy against my life be rubbed off by the blood of Jesus.
67. Sing the song HOLY GHOST FIRE, FIRE FALL ON ME with full concentration and in faith.
68. I vomit every satanic deposit in my life, in the mighty name of Jesus. *(Prime the expulsion of these things by coughing slightly. Refuse to swallow any saliva coming out from the mouth)*
69. I break myself loose from the bondage of stagnancy, in the mighty name of Jesus.
70. Lord, destroy with Your fire anything that makes Your promise to fail upon my life, no matter the origin, in Jesus' name.
71. Let the blood, the fire and the living water of the Most High God wash my system clean from:-
    - Unprofitable growth in my womb
    - Evil plantation -Evil deposits from spirit husband
    - Impurities acquired from parental contamination
    - Evil spiritual consumption
    - Hidden sicknesses
    - Remote control mechanisms
    - Physical and spiritual incisions
    - Satanic poisons
    - Evil stamps, labels and links.
72. Let every area of my life become too hot for any evil to inhabit, in the name of Jesus.
73. Evil growth in my life, be uprooted, in the name of Jesus.
74. Let my body reject every evil habitation, in the mighty name of our Lord Jesus Christ.

75. O Lord, reverse all evil arrangements attracted consciously or unconsciously to my life, in Jesus' name.

76. I reject all evil manipulations and manipulators, in the mighty name of Jesus.

77. I break the power of the occult, witchcraft and familiar spirits over my life, in the name of Jesus.

78. I deliver and pass out any satanic deposit in my intestine, in the name of Jesus.

79. I deliver and pass out any satanic deposit in my reproductive organs, in the name of Jesus.

80. I deliver and pass out any satanic deposit in my womb, in the name of Jesus.

81. In the name of Jesus, I declare before all the forces of darkness that "Jesus Christ is Lord over every department of My Life."

82. You foreign hand laid on my womb, release me, in the name of Jesus.

83. In the name of Jesus, I renounce, break and loose myself from all:
    - demonic holds - psychic powers
    - bonds of physical illness - bondage

84. In the name of Jesus, I break and loose myself from all evil curses, chains, spells, jinxes, bewitchments, witchcraft or sorcery which may have been put upon me.

85. Let a creative miracle take place in my womb and reproductive system, in the name of Jesus.

86. Father, I ask You, in the name of Jesus Christ, to send out Your angels to unearth and break all evil storage vessels fashioned against me

87. I loose myself from every evil influence, dark spirit and satanic bondage, in Jesus' name.

88. I confess and declare that my body is the temple of the Holy Spirit, redeemed, cleansed and sanctified by the blood of Jesus Christ, in Jesus' name.

89. I bind, plunder and render to naught every strongman

assigned to my womb, reproductive system and marital life, in the name of Jesus.

90. God who quickens the dead, quicken my womb and reproductive system, in the name of Jesus.

91. I release myself from the hold of spirits of sterility, infertility and fear, in the name of Jesus.

92. All spirits rooted in fornication, come out of my life with all your roots, in the mighty name of our Lord Jesus.

93. All spirits rooted in sexual perversion, come out of my life with all your roots, in the mighty name of our Lord Jesus.

94. All spirits rooted in spirit husband/wife come out of my life with all your roots, in the mighty name of our Lord Jesus.

95. All spirits rooted in masturbation, come out of my life with all your roots, in the mighty name of our Lord Jesus.

96. All spirits rooted in guilt, come out of my life with all your roots, in the mighty name of our Lord Jesus.

97. All spirits rooted in pornography, come out of my life with all your roots, in the mighty name of our Lord Jesus.

98. O God, arise and set me free from every problem that is higher than me, in the name of Jesus.

99. Sing this song: "There is power mighty in the blood."

100. Thank the Lord for your healing and deliverance.

PRAYER SECTION

Praise Worship

 PRAYER POINTS

1. Thank God for HIS mighty power to save to the uttermost for power to deliver from any form of bondage.

2. Confess your sins and those of your ancestors, especially those sins linked to evil powers and idolatry.

3. I cover myself with the blood of Jesus.

4. I apply the blood of Jesus on my spirit, soul, body and my womb.

5. I release myself from any inherited bondage and limitations in the name of Jesus.

6. O Lord, send Your axe of fire to the foundation of my life and destroy every evil plantation.

7. Let the blood of Jesus flush out from my system every inherited satanic deposit in the name of Jesus.

8. I release myself from the grip of any problem transferred into my life from the womb in the name of Jesus.

9. Let the blood of Jesus and the fire of the Holy Ghost cleanse every organ in my body in the name of Jesus.

10. I break and loose myself from every inherited evil covenant, in the name of Jesus.

11. I break and loose myself from every inherited evil curse, in the name of Jesus.

12. I vomit every evil consumption that I have been fed with as a child, in the name of Jesus.

13. I command all foundational strongmen attached to my life to be paralysed, in the name of Jesus.

14. Let any rod of the wicked rising up against my family line be rendered impotence for my sake, in the name of Jesus.

15. I cancel the consequences of any evil local name attached to my person, in the name of Jesus.

16. *(Pray aggressively against the following evil foundations:)* You *(pick the under listed one by one)*, loose your hold over my life and be purged out of my foundation, in the name of Jesus.
    - Destructive effect of polygamy- Evil physical design
    - Unscriptural manners of conception- Parental Curses-
    Envious rivalry- Demonic blood transfusion
    - Evil dedication- Demonic alteration of destiny   -
    Demonic incisions- Demonic marriage   -
    Dream pollution- Evil laying on of hands
    - Demonic sacrifice- Fellowship with family idols
    - Fellowship with local idols
    - Fellowship with demonic consultants
    - Wrong exposure to sex- Exposure to evil diviner
    - Demonic initiations- Inherited infirmity

17. You evil foundational plantations, come out of my life with all your roots, in the name of Jesus.

18. I break and loose myself from every form of demonic bewitchment, in the name of Jesus.

19. I release myself from every evil domination and control, in the name of Jesus.

20. Let the blood of Jesus be transfused into my blood vessel.

21. Let every gate opened to the enemy by my foundation be closed forever with the blood of Jesus.

22. Lord Jesus, walk back into every second of my life and deliver me where I need deliverance, heal me where I need healing, transform me where I need transformation.

23. Let the power in the blood of Jesus separate me from the sins of my ancestors.

24. Let the blood of Jesus remove any unprogressive label from every aspect of my life.

25. O Lord, create in me a clean heart by Your power.

26. O Lord, renew a right spirit within me.

27. O Lord, teach me to die to self.

28. O Lord, ignite my calling with Your fire.

29. O Lord, anoint me to pray without ceasing.

30. O Lord, establish me as a holy person unto You.

31. O Lord, restore my spiritual eyes and ears, in the name of Jesus.

32. O Lord, let the anointing to excel in my spiritual and physical life fall on me.

33. O Lord, produce in me the power of self-control and gentleness.

34. O Lord, let the anointing of the Holy Spirit break every yoke of backwardness in my life.

35. Holy Ghost, breathe on me now, in the name of Jesus.

36. Holy Ghost fire, ignite me to the glory of God.

37. Let every rebellion flee from my heart, in the name of Jesus.

38. I command every spiritual contamination in my life to receive cleansing by the blood of Jesus.

39. Let the brush of the Lord scrub out every dirtiness in my spiritual pipe, in the name of Jesus.

40. Every rusted spiritual pipe in my life, receive wholeness, in the name of Jesus.

41. I command every power eating up my spiritual pipe to be roasted, in the name of Jesus.

42. I renounce any evil dedication placed upon my life, in the name of Jesus.

43. I break every evil edict and ordination, in the name of Jesus.

44. O Lord, cleanse all the soiled parts of my life, in Jesus' name.

45. O Lord, deliver me from every foundational Pharaoh, in Jesus' name..

46. O Lord, heal every wounded part of my life, in Jesus' name.

47. O Lord, bend every evil rigidity in my life, in Jesus' name.

48. O Lord, re-align every satanic straying in my life, in Jesus' name.

49. O Lord, let the fire of the Holy Spirit warm every satanic freezing in my life, in the name of Jesus.

50. O Lord, give me a life that kills death, in Jesus' name.

51. O Lord, kindle in me the fire of charity, in the name of Jesus.

52. O Lord, glue me together where I am opposed to myself, in Jesus' name.

53. O Lord, enrich me with Your gifts, in Jesus' name.

54. O Lord, quicken me and increase my desire of the things of heaven, in Jesus' name.

55. By Your rulership, O Lord, let the lust of the flesh in my life die, in the name of Jesus.

56. Lord Jesus, increase daily in my life, in Jesus' name.

57. Lord Jesus, maintain Your gifts in my life, in Jesus' name.

58. O Lord, refine and purge my life by Your fire, in Jesus' name.

59. Holy Spirit, inflame and fire my heart, in the name of Jesus.

60. Holy Ghost fire, begin to burn away every power of the bond woman in me, in the name of Jesus.

61. O Lord, make me ready to go wherever You send me.

62. Lord Jesus, never let me shut You out.

63. Lord Jesus, work freely in me and through me.

64. Let the fire of God saturate my womb, in the name of Jesus.

65. Let every design against my life be completely nullified, in the name of Jesus.

66. Let all evil labels fashioned by the camp of the enemy against my life be rubbed off by the blood of Jesus.

67. Sing the song HOLY GHOST FIRE, FIRE FALL ON ME with full concentration and in faith.

68. I vomit every satanic deposit in my life, in the mighty name of Jesus. *(Prime the expulsion of these things by coughing slightly. Refuse to swallow any saliva coming out from the mouth)*

69. I break myself loose from the bondage of stagnancy, in the mighty name of Jesus.

70. Lord, destroy with Your fire anything that makes Your promise to fail upon my life, no matter the origin, in Jesus' name.

71. Let the blood, the fire and the living water of the Most High God wash my system clean from:-
    - Unprofitable growth in my womb
    - Evil plantation -Evil deposits from spirit husband-
    Impurities acquired from parental contamination- E v i l
    spiritual consumption- Hidden sicknesses
    - Remote control mechanisms
    - Physical and spiritual incisions
    - Satanic poisons
    - Evil stamps, labels and links.

72. Let every area of my life become too hot for any evil to inhabit, in the name of Jesus.

73. Evil growth in my life, be uprooted, in the name of Jesus.

74. Let my body reject every evil habitation, in the mighty name of our Lord Jesus Christ.

75. O Lord, reverse all evil arrangements attracted consciously or unconsciously to my life, in Jesus' name.

76. I reject all evil manipulations and manipulators, in the mighty name of Jesus.

77. I break the power of the occult, witchcraft and familiar spirits over my life, in the name of Jesus.

78. I deliver and pass out any satanic deposit in my intestine, in the name of Jesus.

79. I deliver and pass out any satanic deposit in my reproductive organs, in the name of Jesus.

80. I deliver and pass out any satanic deposit in my womb, in the name of Jesus.

81. In the name of Jesus, I declare before all the forces of darkness that "Jesus Christ is Lord over every department of My Life."

82. You foreign hand laid on my womb, release me, in the name of Jesus.

83. In the name of Jesus, I renounce, break and loose myself from all:
    - demonic holds - psychic powers
    - bonds of physical illness - bondage

4. In the name of Jesus, I break and loose myself from all evil curses, chains, spells, jinxes, bewitchments, witchcraft or sorcery which may have been put upon me.

85. Let a creative miracle take place in my womb and reproductive system, in the name of Jesus.

86. Father, I ask You, in the name of Jesus Christ, to send out Your angels to unearth and break all evil storage vessels fashioned against me

87. I loose myself from every evil influence, dark spirit and satanic bondage, in Jesus' name.

88. I confess and declare that my body is the temple of the Holy Spirit, redeemed, cleansed and sanctified by the blood of Jesus Christ, in Jesus' name.

89. I bind, plunder and render to naught every strongman assigned to my womb, reproductive system and marital life, in the name of Jesus.

90. God who quickens the dead, quicken my womb and reproductive system, in the name of Jesus.

91. I release myself from the hold of spirits of sterility, infertility and fear, in the name of Jesus.

92. All spirits rooted in fornication, come out of my life with all your roots, in the mighty name of our Lord Jesus.

93. All spirits rooted in sexual perversion, come out of my life with all your roots, in the mighty name of our Lord Jesus.

94. All spirits rooted in spirit husband/wife come out of my life with all your roots, in the mighty name of our Lord Jesus.

95. All spirits rooted in masturbation, come out of my life with all your roots, in the mighty name of our Lord Jesus.

96. All spirits rooted in guilt, come out of my life with all your roots, in the mighty name of our Lord Jesus.

97. All spirits rooted in pornography, come out of my life with all your roots, in the mighty name of our Lord Jesus.

98. O God, arise and set me free from every problem that is higher than me, in the name of Jesus.

99. Sing this song: "There is power mighty in the blood."

100. Thank the Lord for your healing and deliverance.

WINNING FOUNDATIONAL WARS

CHAPTER ONE

POWER AGAINST ANCESTRAL POWERS

POWER AGAINST ANCESTRAL POWERS

1

The battle against ancestral powers is a battle that must be fought decisively. Ancestral powers are powers that will not easily release their victims. They derive their strength from a deep knowledge of your family history and thrive on covenants and pledges made by your ancestors. They ensure that their victims are held tight. They bind generations, even unborn children are not beyond their grip. The powers of your father's house and the powers of your mother's house operate with uncommon aggression. Unless you deal with them you may not be able to live your life freely. Their mystery is deep. Whenever foundational covenants are in place there will be manifestations in the lives of members of the lineage at home and abroad.

A lot of people are tied by ancestral padlocks. The fact that idol worship is found in your foundation explains why you are grappling with ancestral bondage. Family idols that existed several years ago still receive their dues in this modern generation. Even when they have been discarded or abandoned, their influence and manifestations are still great. These powers have stolen the virtues of several family members.

You need to take this prayer programme seriously, especially if:

1. Your ancestors were idol worshipers.
2. Your grandparents were fetish priests.
3. Your parents and grandparents were devotees of fetish shrines.
4. Your ancestors were involved with demonic rituals.
5. Your grandparents fought intra-tribal wars.
6. Your ancestors obtained their children from idols.
7. The power of your father's house has been troubling you.
8. Yours parents or grandparents secretly worshipped idols or got involved in fetish practices on your behalf.
9. Your family name has something to do with idol worship.
10. Your family praise names are demonic.
11. Fetish powers have played active roles in your foundation.
12. There are foundational curses in your background.
13. Your ancestors made covenants by pledging their children.
14. You happen to come from a riverine area.
15. You experience mysterious hindrances.
16. You notice an evil pattern in your ancestral line.
17. There are traces of dedication to family idols.
18. There is chronic poverty in your lineage.
19. There are deep mysteries in your family line.
20. Your place of birth or village has remained backward.

These and other symptoms show that you must break ancestral yokes. You must release yourself from any form of umbrella bondage, or the yoke of collective captivity. You need complete deliverance. If you add fasting to your prayers it will be very effective. Do not allow any bondage to remain in place. Pray until you are totally free.

PRAYERS SECTION

Confession: Psalm 68:1: *Let God arise, let his enemies be scattered: let them also that hate him flee before him.*

Praise Worship

 PRAYER POINTS

1. Thou power of deliverance, fall upon me now, in the name of Jesus.
2. Blood of Jesus, purge my foundation.
3. Every foundational curse in my life, break, in the name of Jesus.
4. Every foundational covenant in my life, break, in the name of Jesus.
5. Every foundational bondage in my life, break, in the name of Jesus.
6. Every foundational arrester, be arrested, in the name of Jesus.
7. Every darkness planted in my foundation, scatter, in the name of Jesus.
8. Every serpent in my foundation, die, in the name of Jesus.
9. Every scorpion in my foundation, die, in the name of Jesus.
10. Let God arise and let all foundational witchcraft scatter, in the name of Jesus.
11. Every seed of witchcraft in my foundation, die, in the name of Jesus.
12. Every foundation of confusion in my life, die, in the name of Jesus.
13. Holy Spirit, shake down every foundational stronghold, in the name of Jesus.
14. Every foundational familiar spirit, I bind you and cast you out, in the name of Jesus.
15. Every foundational marine power, bow, in the name of Jesus.

16. Every seed of poverty in my foundation, die, in the name of Jesus.

17. Every foundational padlock, break, in the name of Jesus.

18. I repent from all ancestral idol worship, in the name of Jesus.

19. Every idol of my father's house, loose your hold over my life, in the name of Jesus.

20. Every strongman of the idol of my father's house, die, in the name of Jesus.

21. I silence the evil cry of any idol fashioned against me, in the name of Jesus.

22. All consequences of ancestral idol worship upon my life, I wipe you off by the blood of Jesus.

23. Holy Ghost fire, burn down all spiritual shrines of my father's house, in the name of Jesus.

24. Oppression agenda of my family idol, die, in the name of Jesus.

25. Every blood speaking against my generational line, be silenced by the blood of Jesus.

26. Every idol power speaking against my destiny, scatter, in the name of Jesus.

27. I break all ancestral covenants with any idol power, in the name of Jesus.

28. Every bitter water flowing in my family from any idol, dry up, in the name of Jesus.

29. Any rope tying my family line to any family idol, break, in the name of Jesus.

30. Every landlord spirit troubling my destiny, be paralysed, in the name of Jesus.

31. Every outflow of satanic family name, die, in the name of Jesus.

32. I recover every benefit stolen by idol powers, in the name of Jesus.

33. Where is the God of Elijah? Arise, disgrace every family idol, in the name of Jesus.

34. Every satanic priest ministering in my family line, be retrenched, in the name of Jesus.
35. Arrows of affliction originating from idolatry, loose your hold, in the name of Jesus.
36. Every influence of idol worship in my life, die, in the name of Jesus.
37. Every network of idol power in my place of birth, scatter, in the name of Jesus.
38. Every satanic dedication that speaks against me, be dismantled by the power in the blood of Jesus.
39. I vomit every food with idolatrous influence that I have eaten, in the name of Jesus.
40. Let the stone of hindrance constructed by family idols be rolled away, in the name of Jesus.
41. The voice of foundational idols will never speak again, in the name of Jesus.
42. Every strongman assigned by the idols of my father's house against my life, die, in the name of Jesus.
43. Every satanic promissory note issued on my behalf by my ancestors, be reversed, in the name of Jesus.
44. Garments of opposition designed by ancestral idols, roast, in the name of Jesus.
45. My glory buried by family idols, come alive by fire, in the name of Jesus.
46. Thou power of strange gods legislating against my destiny, scatter, in the name of Jesus.
47. Idols of my place of birth, I break your chain, in the name of Jesus.
48. Every problem attached to my family name, be neutralised, in the name of Jesus.
49. Every power searching the oracle to know my progress, die, in the name of Jesus.
50. Family idols, receive the consuming fire of God, in the name of Jesus.
51. I release myself from any bondage present in my family line, in the name of Jesus.

52. Any evil pattern laid by my ancestors, break, in the name of Jesus.

53. No enchantment shall hold me captive, in the name of Jesus.

54. I break the pattern of darkness that locked me up, in the name of Jesus.

55. I release my life from the yoke of my village, in the name of Jesus.

56. Every curse that came to me through the sins of my ancestors, break by the blood of Jesus.

57. Every ancestral transmission of affliction, break and die, in the name of Jesus.

58. Every ancestral transmission of failure, break and die, in the name of Jesus.

59. Every ancestral transmission of backsliding, break and die, in the name of Jesus.

60. Every ancestral transmission of poverty, break and die, in the name of Jesus.

61. Every ancestral transmission of untimely death, break and die, in the name of Jesus.

62. Every ancestral transmission of disease and infirmity, break and die, in the name of Jesus.

63. Every ancestral transmission of bad luck, break and die, in the name of Jesus.

CHAPTER TWO

ATTACKING SATANIC WAREHOUSE

ATTACKING SATANIC WAREHOUSE

2

Satanic warehouse is the place where wicked weapons of the dark kingdom are kept. More importantly, it is the place where the confiscated blessings of God's children are hidden. In the physical realm the Customs Department seize contrabands and goods for reasons best known to them. The cost of confiscated items: vehicles, gadgets and machinery, etc. that can be found in the warehouse meant for keeping such items will run into billions of Naira.

On the other hand, if God would open your eyes to see what has been confiscated and kept in the satanic warehouse you will be shocked. The wicked satanic warehouse contains confiscated husbands, wives, children, certificates, breakthroughs, promotions, scholarships, overseas travels, contracts, landed properties, houses, appointments, grants, academic success, glorious opportunities, peace, joy, etc.

As long as what belongs to you has been kept in the satanic warehouse, you cannot enjoy the blessings. The satanic warehouse is a wicked abode. It can be described as a habitation of cruelty. There are lots of people who have been destined to possess their possessions, but have been wickedly robbed by terrible powers. You must not allow the enemy to swallow what belongs to you.

If your property has been rotting away in satanic warehouse, now is the time to declare war against the satanic strongholds that have vowed that you will not enjoy what belongs to you. Do not allow the enemy to have his way. You must take the battle to his gates. You must invade the satanic warehouse and free what belongs to you. You cannot afford to go to the grave without enjoying what heaven has freely given to you. Powers that have passed your blessings to other hands and eventually locked them up in a fortified wicked warehouse must be challenged and forced to restore what they have stolen.

You need this prayer programme when:

1. Your benefits are denied.
2. Your blessings are seized.
3. Your virtues are stolen.
4. You have experienced the mystery of incomplete projects.
5. You have discovered that you have not been able to posses your possessions.
6. You have achieved nothing in spite of your numerous talents.
7. You have become beggarly instead of being a generous giver.
8. You are struggling with shame and misery.
9. You are constantly a victim of armed robbers.
10. You are not able to receive good when you have paid for them.
11. You constantly have dreams of seeing your properties locked up.
12. Benefits and rights for what belongs to you are given to

those who do not deserve them.

13. Wicked powers have sat on your blessings.
14. You labour like an elephant but reap like an ant.

Beloved, you must declare "enough is enough". You must target your prayers against the satanic warehouse and pray until you recover your confiscated blessings.

PRAYERS SECTION

Confession: **Psalm 68:1**: *Let God arise, let his enemies be scattered: let them also that hate him flee before him.*

Praise Worship

 PRAYER POINTS

1. I receive power from above to break through the troops of the enemy, in the name of Jesus.
2. I receive power from above to recover all my stolen virtues, in the name of Jesus.
3. Let there be release of all my confiscated blessings, in the name of Jesus.
4. Every power that has swallowed my blessings, vomit them by fire, in the name of Jesus.
5. Let my blessings become too hot for the enemy to handle, in the name of Jesus.
6. Let the angels of God visit the camp of my enemy and recover all my long-awaited blessings for me, in the name of Jesus.
7. I refuse to be a victim of failure, in the name of Jesus.
8. I refuse to be a victim of limitation, in the name of Jesus.
9. Let all my delayed blessings come forth by fire, in the name of Jesus.
10. After the order of King David, I pursue all my enemies, in the name of Jesus.

11. After the order of King David, I overtake all my enemies, in the name of Jesus.

12. After the order of King David, I recover all my stolen blessings, in the name of Jesus.

13. Let the blood of Jesus and the wall of fire surround my recovered blessings, in the name of Jesus.

14. Let every area through which the enemy is stealing from me be blocked by the blood of Jesus.

15. Let the angels of God arrest every thief of blessings assigned against my life, in the name of Jesus.

16. I shall not misuse my recovered blessings, in the name of Jesus.

17. Every power assigned to be stealing from me, die, in the name of Jesus.

18. Any evil power harbouring my blessings in any coven, scatter, in the name of Jesus.

19. Any coven assigned against my blessings, catch fire, in the name of Jesus.

20. Every satanic watch night keeping the enemy's warehouse, be arrested and die, in the name of Jesus.

21. I recover by fire every good thing ever stolen from me, in the name of Jesus.

22. Spiritual weakness and spiritual sickness afflicting my life, die, in the name of Jesus.

23. Every internal power drinking the blood of spiritual power in my life, die, in the name of Jesus.

24. Every arrow fired into my spiritual life, backfire, in the name of Jesus.

25. Serpents and scorpions of powerlessness, die, in the name of Jesus.

26. Power that cannot be insulted by any power o f darkness, fall upon me, in the name of Jesus.

27. My life, arise by fire and defeat your defeat, in the name of Jesus.

28. Holy Ghost fire, empower my life, in the name of Jesus.

29. I receive power to trample upon the dragon of powerlessness, in the name of Jesus.
30. O God, arise and inject Your fire into my bones, in the name of Jesus.
31. O God, arise and inject Your power into my blood, in the name of Jesus.
32. Blindness, deafness and tiredness in the spirit realm, die, in the name of Jesus.
33. Dominion power, fall upon me now, in the name of Jesus.
34. I crush every agent of backsliding, in the name of Jesus.

CHAPTER THREE

GO FORWARD BY FIRE

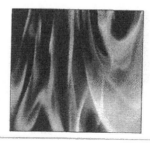

GO FORWARD BY FIRE

3

CONFESSIONS: Deuteronomy 28:13: *And the LORD shall make thee the head, and not the tail; and thou shalt be above only, and thou shalt not be beneath; if that thou hearken unto the commandments of the LORD thy God, which I command thee this day, to observe and to do them.* **Proverbs 21:1**: *The king's heart is in the hand of the LORD, as the rivers of water: he turneth it whithersoever he will.* **1 Samuel 17:45-46**: *Then said David to the Philistine, Thou comest to me with a sword, and with a spear, and with a shield: but I come to thee in the name of the LORD of hosts, the God of the armies of Israel, whom thou hast defied. This day will the LORD deliver thee into mine hand; and I will smite thee, and take thine head from thee; and I will give the carcases of the host of the Philistines this day unto the fowls of the air, and to the wild beasts of the earth; that all the earth may know that there is a God in Israel.* **Deuteronomy 33:25-27**: *Thy shoes shall be iron and brass; and as thy days, so shall thy strength be. There is none like unto the God of Jeshurun, who rideth upon the heaven in thy help, and in his excellency on the sky. The eternal God is thy refuge, and underneath are the everlasting arms: and he shall thrust out the enemy from before thee; and shall say, Destroy them.* **Jeremiah 1:19** :*And they shall fight against* *thee; but they shall not prevail against thee; for I am with thee, saith the LORD, to deliver thee.* **Nahum 1:7-8**: *The LORD is good, a strong hold in the day of trouble; and he knoweth them that trust in him. But with an overrunning flood he will make an utter end of the place thereof, and darkness shall pursue his enemies.* **Psalm 75:6**: *For promotion cometh neither from the east, nor from the west, nor from the south.* **Psalm 113:5,7-8**: *Who is like unto the LORD our God, who dwelleth on high, He raiseth up the poor out of the dust, and lifteth the needy out of the dunghill; That he may set him with princes, even with the princes of his people.* **Philipians 4:13,19**: *I can do all things through Christ which strengtheneth me. But my God shall supply all your need according to his riches in glory by Christ Jesus.* **Galatians 6:17**: *From henceforth let no man trouble me: for I bear in my body the marks of the Lord Jesus.*

- ❖ In the name of Jesus Christ, as I confess of the word of God into my life, I believe and I receive the power in the word into my spirit, into my soul ad into my body, in the name of Jesus Christ Amen.

- ❖ In my mouth is the power of life and death. I speak life unto myself and I speak destruction unto all my enemies and all unto their weapons against me, in Jesus, name .

- ❖ With my heart I believe unto righteousness and with my mouth confession is made unto salvation, in Jesus' name.

- ❖ The name of Jesus is my authority over all the powers of darkness including satan, in Jesus' name .

- ❖ As I make this confession, I command that at the name of Jesus Christ every knee should bow, of all things in heaven, all things in earth and all things under the earth, in Jesus' name .

- ❖ As I speak the word of God right now, I send it to run swiftly and become operational, to manifest and fulfill the purpose for which I send it, in Jesus' name .

- ❖ Right not, I command the word to go forth, in Jesus' name.

- ❖ I am a child of God. I believe in the Father, I believe in the Son and I believe in the Holy Ghost, in Jesus' name.

- ❖ I believe that Jesus Christ came in the flesh and laid down His life, and shed His blood for me on the cross of Calvary, in Jesus' name.
- ❖ I believe that Jesus has defeated satan, and delivered me from this present evil world and satan, in Jesus' name.
- ❖ I have accepted Jesus Christ as my personal Saviour and I belong to Him. I am a new creature. Old things are passed away. My old life is done away with. I am now living a new life, The life I now live is in Christ Jesus. Jesus Christ has paid the price for me with His blood and set me free. Satan and all his demons have no more power or dominion over my life, in Jesus' name.
- ❖ Jesus has set me free indeed, and I am free indeed, in Jesus' name .
- ❖ Jesus has delivered me from all the powers of darkness, from principalities, powers, dominions and all the forces of darkness, in the name of Jesus Christ.
- ❖ The devil has no more dominion over me, in Jesus' name.
- ❖ I submit myself into the mighty hand of God and I command satan and all his demons to vacate, release me and flee from me right now, in the name of Jesus Christ.
- ❖ In the name of Jesus Christ, there is no condemnation for those who are in Christ Jesus. There is no condemnation for me for I am in Christ Jesus, in Jesus' name.
- ❖ The Spirit of life in Christ Jesus that dwells on the inside of me has delivered me from satan and from the law of sin and death, in Jesus' name.
- ❖ In the authority of the name of Jesus Christ, I break, damage, destroy and command to be uprooted right now all covenants, agreements, statements, names and requests of any kind, promises of any kind and all links of any type made with the kingdom of darkness, including everything that the enemy is holding against me. I break them, cast them down, cancel and reject all of them, in Jesus' name.
- ❖ I damage any association with the kingdom of darkness held

knowingly. or unknowingly, whether in my sleep or when I was awake. I dissociate myself and separate myself from all of them, in the name of Jesus Christ.

❖ In the name of Jesus Christ, I command right now total destruction of all yokes, burdens, fears, oppressions and terrors of the enemy against me. I reject and cancel them, in Jesus' name.

❖ I command total destruction of all enchantments, witchcraft, divinations, spells, curses, ordinances and hand writings made by the enemy against me, a child of God, in the name of Jesus Christ.

❖ I declare that all the devilish acts of the enemy in my life are erased and finished, in Jesus' name.

❖ Right now, I cut all the links with the kingdom of darkness, in Jesus' name.

❖ All the works of the enemy against me are now damaged, wiped away and forgotten forever, in the name of Jesus Christ.

❖ Jesus Christ has set me free from all the captivity of satan and all his demons, in Jesus' name.

❖ When Jesus Christ ascended, He led captivity captive. He has broken down the gates of brass, cut asunder the bars of iron and delivered me from all the imprisonments of the devil, in Jesus' name.

❖ Jesus has broken down and scattered all the powers of the enemy against me, in Jesus' name .

❖ All powers in heaven and on earth are given unto me by Christ Jesus. In the authority of His name. I have the keys to the kingdom of heaven. Whatsoever I loose on earth is loosed in heaven. Right now, in Jesus' name, I loose myself from every imprisonment of the devil and his followers, in Jesus' name.

❖ Whatsoever I bind on earth is bound in heaven. Right now I bind and I put a stop to all the numerous activities of the devil made against me, in Jesus' name.

- ❖ I ask for the vengeance of the Lord upon all my enemies: for vengeance is the Lord's. The Lord shall repay.
- ❖ I send the wrath of God to pour like water upon all my enemies, in Jesus' name. I conquer and lock them up, for God is for me and no one can rise up or be against me, in Jesus' name.
- ❖ Jesus Christ is the fighter of all my battles and all the attacks that my enemies have made against me, in Jesus' name.
- ❖ I do not trust in my own arrow, I do not trust in my own sword and I do not fight for myself. It is not by might, nor by power, but by the Spirit of the Lord, in the name of Jesus Christ.
- ❖ I hand over all my battles to the Lord Jesus Christ. He fights for me and I hold my peace, in Jesus' name.
- ❖ I am an overcomer through the name of Jesus Christ. I am victorious in all circumstances and situations, in the name of Jesus.
- ❖ I do not need to fight in this battle or any other battle. I stand still, put my trust in God and shall see His salvation, in the name of Jesus Christ. Jesus Christ has defeated all my enemies. They are brought down and fallen under my feet, in Jesus' name. Right now, I crush them all to the ground and I command them to lick up the dust of the earth under my feet.
- ❖ God has equipped me and made me a danger and a terror to all my enemies, in Jesus' name. The Lord has sent the fear and dread of me upon all my enemies. The report or information of me shall cause them to fear, tremble and be in anguish, in Jesus' name.
- ❖ I am a soldier for Christ and I am wearing the whole armour of God, in the name of Jesus Christ.
- ❖ The armour of God gives me power over the principalities, against powers, against rulers of darkness of this world, against spiritual wickedness, against all the powers of darkness and even against satan himself, in Jesus' name. .

- ❖ I am God's power house. His power resides inside of me and is manifesting on the outside of me, in Jesus name.

- ❖ The glory of God is as a covering round about me, in Jesus' name. At the presence of God in my life, I command the wicked to perish before me; I command the wicked to perish and melt away like wax in the fire, in the name of Jesus. None shall be able to stand before me all the days of my life, in Jesus' name.

- ❖ I am built up in Christ Jesus. As Jesus is so I am on the face of this earth, in the name of Jesus Christ.

- ❖ I am a container for the fire of the Holy Ghost and the power of God resides inside me, in Jesus' name.

- ❖ As I speak the word of God, I send it to go forth as fuel of unquenchable fire to burn all my enemies to ashes, in the name of Jesus.

- ❖ I receive the fire of God to encircle me and protect me from all my enemies, in Jesus' name.

- ❖ I am fire-proof to all the enemies' fire and weapons of war against me , in Jesus' name.

- ❖ I am a danger to the whole kingdom of darkness I am as a live wire. Anyone that touches or tries to touch me shall be electrocuted, in Jesus' name.

- ❖ The word of God says, "Never touch or try to harm a child of God." I am the apple of God's eye. Anyone that intends or plots evil against me, God shall destroy, in Jesus' name.

- ❖ I am redeemed by the blood of Jesus Christ that was shed for me on the cross of Calvary. Right now, I take of the blood I use it to set a boundary round about me, in Jesus' name.

- ❖ I receive the blood of Jesus Christ upon me and upon my house where I live, in Jesus' name.

- ❖ When the enemy sees the blood, he will passover. The destroyers will not be able to enter the house because of the blood of Jesus Christ. If my enemies seek me, they shall not be able to find me, for my life is hidden in the blood of

Jesus, in Jesus' name.

❖ I know who I am in Christ; I am a royal priesthood, I am a holy nation I am a chosen generation and I am a peculiar person delivered from the kingdom of darkness into the marvellous light of Christ Jesus, in Jesus' name.

❖ I know who I am in Christ, in Jesus name. All demons, even satan, are subject to me, in Jesus' name. I push down all my enemies and they cannot hurt me, in Jesus' name.

❖ As I make this confession, I send mighty destruction to scatter, destroy and break in pieces every gathering or association of my enemies against me, in Jesus' name. No plot, device or counsel of the wicked against me shall stand, and every tongue that shall rise up against me in judgement, I condemn, in Jesus' name.

❖ Jesus Christ saves me from all those that rise up against me, in Jesus' name, Jesus is my defender, He is my Rock, my Deliverer, my Strength, my Fortress and my High Tower, in Jesus' name.

❖ No weapon that is formed against me shall prosper, in Jesus' name.

❖ If the enemy comes against me, the Spirit of the Lord will lift up a standard against he and he cannot pass through, in Jesus' name.

❖ The Lord Jesus Christ has set a bound round about me. There is a strong hedge of protection round about me, a powerful hedge that all the demons in hell, including satan, can never cross to reach me, in Jesus' name.

❖ I am a child of God. I am dwelling in the secret place of the Most High God. I am protected and covered under the shadow of the wings of Jehovah, in Jesus' name.

❖ The word of God is the power of God, and the entrance of the word of God into my life has brought His light into my life and darkness cannot comprehend it, in Jesus' name. I send forth this light in me as a twoedged sword to destroy the kingdom of darkness, in Jesus' name.

❖ The word of God is quick and powerful in my mouth. God has put the power of His word in my mouth, in Jesus' name. I trust in the word of God. It stands sure when I speak it and it will accomplish the purpose for which I have spoken it, in Jesus' name.

❖ Right now, I send the word of God as a missile to destroy principalities, powers, thrones, rulers of darkness and all wicked spirits, in Jesus' name.

❖ I receive the word of God as a shield and covering over my life, in Jesus' name.

❖ My God is the God that answers by fire. He has fully armed me with His fire for the destruction of all my enemies, including satan, in Jesus' name.

❖ My body is the temple of the Holy Spirit. The Spirit of God dwells on the inside of me. in Jesus' name.

❖ The blood of Jesus Christ is a covering and hiding place for me from all my enemies, including satan, in Jesus' name.

❖ The angels of God hear and obey the word of God because it is God speaking to them. As I speak the word of God out of my mouth, it goes forth to execute the purpose for which I send it, in Jesus' name.

❖ I receive the ammunition of angelic guidance and operations in my life right now, in Jesus' name.

❖ The angels have been ordered by God to take charge of me in all my ways, and I receive them, in Jesus' name. They go ahead of me wherever I go and in whatever I do. They go forth and make all the crooked ways straight, in Jesus' name.

❖ The angels of God watch over me in the day time and at night. They make sure that no evil whatsoever befalls me, in Jesus' name.

❖ Right now, I send the angels to pursue all my enemies and make them like chaff in the wind. I also send a grievous whirlwind to hit the enemies, destroy them and cast them into the bottomless pit, in Jesus' name.

❖ In the name of Jesus Christ, the mighty hand of God is

rise up against me, in Jesus' name.

- ❖ Jesus Christ has made His grace available to me. I ask for the grace and receive it by faith, in Jesus' name.

- ❖ When I call upon the name of the Lord He shall stretch forth His mighty hand and lift me up above all my enemies and deliver me from all of them, in Jesus' name.

- ❖ I am inscribed in the palm of God's mighty hand. I am neatly tucked away and hidden from all the evils and troubles of this present world, in Jesus' name.

- ❖ No one whosoever, be it the principalities, powers, dominions, powers of darkness and even Satan himself, can pluck me out of the mighty hand of God, for my God is stronger than all of them, in Jesus' name.

- ❖ I am armed with the gospel of the Lord Jesus Christ which is the power of God, and use it to trample on all the powers of darkness. I tread on all snakes and scorpions and I destroy them, in Jesus' name.

- ❖ My feet are like hinds feet, my appearance is as the appearance of horses. So, I run like horses and chariots and I go forth conquering all my enemies. I am more than a conqueror through Christ Jesus, in Jesus' name.

- ❖ I move faster than the speed of light, in Jesus' name.

- ❖ I pursue my enemies, overtake them and destroy them, in Jesus' name.

- ❖ The Lord has lifted me up and I am seated with him in heavenly placed in Christ Jesus, far above principalities, powers and dominion. And the Lord has put all things under my feet, and I use my feet to bruise and destroy all my enemies, even satan, in Jesus' name.

- ❖ Anywhere the soles of my feet shall tread upon, the Lord has given it unto me, in Jesus' name.

- ❖ I tread upon and destroy completely all strongholds, walls, foundations and barriers of the enemy against me, in Jesus' name.

- ❖ I tread on my enemies with the shoes of the gospel of the

Lord Jesus Christ. I make an utter ruin of them all and an utter end of all their possessions, kingdoms, thrones, dominions, palaces and their kingdom and everything in it, in Jesus' name.

❖ I erase them all and make them complete desolate, in Jesus' name.

❖ My strength is in the Lord Jesus Christ. He is my strength, , in Jesus' name.

❖ There is no weakness in me for I have received the might of God. I am strong and can do all things through Christ who strengthens me. I walk and do not faint, I run and I am not weary, in Jesus' name.

❖ The Spirit of Christ that dwells inside me strengthens my physical body, in Jesus' name.

❖ I have prayer power, in Jesus' name.

❖ I pray without ceasing, I am fortified with strength to pray, in Jesus' name.

❖ Jesus Christ has given me His peace and I receive it, in Jesus' name.

❖ I have the peace of God that surpasses all understanding. It keeps my heart and my mind through Christ Jesus, in Jesus' name.

❖ My mind is renewed by the word of God day by day, in Jesus' name .

❖ My mind is stayed on Christ Jesus. I control my thoughts from thinking evil, in Jesus' name. I cast down every imagination and every high thing that exalts itself against the word of God in my life. I command my thoughts and mind to be in obedience to Christ, in Jesus' name.

❖ I am full of faith in God. I do not doubt and I do not operate in unbelief. I believe and trust God as my helper and I do not fear anything, for God has not given me the spirit of fear. I have the spirit of power and I have a sound mind through Christ, in Jesus' name.

❖ My body is healed by the stripes of Jesus Christ, in Jesus' name.

❖ Sickness and disease of any kind have no place in my body, in Jesus' name, Jesus has taken all my sicknesses and pains on the cross of Calvary, in Jesus' name.

❖ If I ear or drink any deadly or harmful thing it cannot hurt me, in Jesus' name.

❖ Right now, I curse every sickness and disease that have attacked or intend to attack my body, in the name of Jesus. I command them to die and disappear from my body right now, in the name of Jesus Christ.

❖ The Spirit of God is a guide for me, in Jesus' name.

❖ I am led by the Spirit of God, for those who are led by Him are the sons of God: Because I acknowledge God as my Father, He will order my footsteps and will direct my path, in Jesus' name.

❖ I am not lazy and I am not slack to follow the leadings of the Spirit of God in my life. I am energetic at all times, always yielding and ready to be in obedience to God, in Jesus' name.

❖ Right now, I reject, denounce and I bind every voice or leading of the devil, in Jesus' name.

❖ The voice of a stranger I will not hear and his leading I will not follow. The Lord is my Shepherd and it is Him I will hear, and it is Him I will follow forever, for Jesus is my Anchor, in Jesus' name.

❖ Right now, as I conclude this confession, I cancel all negative confessions I have made at anytime in my life, in Jesus' name. I agree with the will of God for my life and I come against all negative confessions spoken by me or by anyone against me. As I speak, I send the power in the word of God to change every negative confession to positive, in Jesus' name.

*Against my health: - I am healed, in Jesus' name.

* Against my finances: - I am rich, I shall lack nothing, i n Jesus' name.

    ★ Against my marriage: - My marriage is stable, I have peace in my marriage, in Jesus' name.

    ★ Against my Children: - My children shall prosper in every area and have peace, in Jesus' name.

    ★ Against my calling: - What God has purposed in my life must be accomplished, in Jesus' name.

    ★ Against my safety: - No accident or evil shall befall me. I do not fear anything, in Jesus' name.

    ★ Against my life: - God has satisfied me with long life, in Jesus' name.

❖ I erase all negative spoken words, all evil statements, all doubtful statements and unbelief and all statements that glorify the devil. I wipe them all away in the blood of Jesus Christ, in Jesus' name.

❖ I have control over my speech, in Jesus' name.

❖ I ask the Lord to help me set a guard over my lips, in Jesus' name.

❖ Right now, as I enter into prayer warfare, I submit myself to God completely, in Jesus' name.

❖ I cast out the devil, rebuke him and I command him to flee from me right now, in the name of Jesus Christ.

❖ I bind the devil from stealing, killing or destroying anything belonging to me, be it life or possession, in Jesus' name.

❖ As I enter into warfare prayer, I bind the devil and his followers from being a hindrance to my prayers, in Jesus' name.

❖ I bind the enemy from throwing any arrow or weapon against me as I pray along, in Jesus' name.

❖ I bind all the enemies' armies and ammunitions against, me in Jesus' name.

❖ The worse things happen in the battle field, but nothing whatsoever, absolutely nothing, will happen to me, in Jesus' name.

❖ Lord, I ask that all these confessions I have made be operational and be as covering and a defence upon me, in my spirit, in my soul, in my body and all these confessions to go forth as a destruction to the devil and all my enemies, in Jesus' name.

❖ As I enter into warfare I send the word of God to damage, destroy and uproot the devil and all his followers, in the name of Jesus Christ.

Praise Worship

1. My Father, I thank You for it is You that exercise control and dominion over the affairs of men.
2. I thank You Father, for You are the King of kings and Lord of lords.
3. Thank You Father, for Your purpose for my life in this election.
4. Oh God, arise and set aside and juxtapose mankind's schemes and ideas over my contest in this election, in the name of Jesus.
5. Father, the heart of the people is in Your hand, let the mind of the electorate be closed to the devil and let their minds be opened to Your will and purpose in this election, in the name of Jesus.
6. I decree that all evil counsels against my contest in this election shall fail and be brought to nothing, in the name of Jesus.
7. I command the tokens of liars on my contest in the election to be frustrated, in the name of Jesus.
8. I command the sorcery and enchantment of diviners on my contest in this election to be frustrated, in the name of Jesus.
9. Let evil diviners assigned against my contest in this election be paralysed, in the name of Jesus.
10. For this election, I apply the blood of Jesus over the mind of the people, election coordinators, the police and the judiciary, in the name of Jesus.
11. Every conspiracy against the will of God for my life on this

election, scatter, in the name of Jesus.

12. Let the craftiness of the wicked against me in this election be disappointed, in the name of Jesus.

13. Every evil enterprise put in place to rig the election against my favour, be disappointed, in the name of Jesus.

14. Let the east wind of God carry away all evil plans against my life in this election, in the name of Jesus.

15. All the counsels of election manipulators shall not stand on my contest in the election, in the name of Jesus.

16. Any evil word being spoken against me in this election, die, in the name of Jesus.

17. Oh God, arise and let the purpose of Your kingdom take its place in this election, in the name of Jesus.

18. All satanic candidates in this election, be judged and overthrown, in the name of Jesus.

19. Any wicked personality sponsoring evil candidates, be exposed and disgraced, in the name of Jesus.

20. Oh God, arise and let evil candidates be rooted out of this election, in the name of Jesus.

21. Oh Lord, work on me and make me a good candidate of Your choice in this election, in the name of Jesus.

22. Any attempt to rig or thwart this election, be frustrated, in the name of Jesus.

23. Let the gate and door of this land be opened unto me in this election, in the name of Jesus.

24. Father, make all my proposals to find favour in the sight of my divine helpers, in the name of Jesus.

25. Let all the demonic obstacles that have been established in the heart of my divine helpers against my prosperity be destroyed, in the name of Jesus.

26. I bind and put to flight all the spirits of fear, anxiety and discouragement, in the name of Jesus.

27. Lord, let divine wisdom fall upon all who are supporting me in these matters.

28. I break the backbone of any spirits of conspiracy and treachery, in the name of Jesus.

29. Lord, hammer my matter into the minds of those who will assist me so that they do not suffer from demonic loss of memory.

30. I paralyse the handiwork of household enemies and envious agents in this matter, in the name of Jesus.

31. Let all evil competitors stumble and fall, in the name of Jesus.

32. Let all my adversaries make mistakes that will advance my cause, in the name of Jesus.

33. Let all the adversaries of my breakthroughs be put to shame, in the name of Jesus.

34. I claim the power to overcome and to excel amongst all competitors, in the name of Jesus.

35. Let any decision by any panel be favourable unto me, in the name of Jesus.

36. Every negative word and pronouncement against my success, be completely nullified, in Jesus' name.

37. All competitors with me in this issue will find my defeat unattainable, in the name of Jesus.

38. I claim supernatural wisdom to answer all questions in a way that will advance my cause, in Jesus' name.

39. I confess my sins of exhibiting occasional doubts.

40. I bind every spirit manipulating my beneficiaries against me, in the name of Jesus.

41. I remove my name from the book of seers of goodness without appropriation, in the name of Jesus.

42. Let the cloud blocking the sunlight of my glory and breakthrough be dispersed, in the name of Jesus.

43. Lord, let wonderful changes begin to be my lot from this week.

44. I reject every spirit of the tail in all areas of my life, in the name of Jesus.

45. Oh Lord, bring me into favour with all those that will decide on my advancement.

46. Oh Lord, cause a divine substitution to happen if this is what will move me ahead.

47. I reject the spirit of the tail and I claim the spirit of the head, in the name of Jesus.

48. I command all evil records planted by the devil in anyone's mind against my advancement to be shattered to pieces, in the name of Jesus.

49. Oh Lord, transfer, remove or change all human agents that are bent on stopping my advancement.

50. Oh Lord, smoothen my path to the top by the hand of fire.

51. I receive the anointing to excel above my contemporaries, in the name of Jesus.

52. Lord, catapult me into greatness as You did for Daniel in the land of Babylon.

53. Lord, help me to identify and deal with any weaknesses in me that can hinder my progress.

54. I bind every strongman delegated to hinder my progress, in the name of Jesus.

55. Oh Lord, despatch Your angels to roll away every stumbling block to my promotion, advancement and elevation.

56. Let power change hands in my place of work to the hands of the Holy Spirit.

57. Let the fire of God consume any rock tiying me down to the same spot, in the name of Jesus.

58. All demonic chains preventing my advancement, be broken, in the name of Jesus.

59. All human agents delaying/denying my advancement, I bind the evil spirits controlling your minds, in the name of Jesus.

60. Holy Spirit, direct the decisions of any panel in my favour, in the name of Jesus.

61. I refuse to fail at the edge of my miracle, in the name of Jesus.

62. O Lord, release Your angels to fight my battle.

63. Let warrior angels be released to fight my battles in the heavenlies, in the name of Jesus.

64. I bind every deception and manipulation targeted against my life, in the name of Jesus.

65. O Lord, let the rain of . . . *(pick from the following)* fall upon my life in abundance.
    - love- power- sound mind- knowledge- understanding- revelation
    - wisdom- freedom- deliverance- boldness
    - zealousness- purity- holiness- excellence
    - praise- joy- peace
    - longsuffering- gentleness- goodness- faith
    - word of wisdom- word of knowledge
    - faith- healing- working of miracles
    - prophecy- discerning of spirits
    - divers kinds of tongues
    - interpretation of tongues- grace- mercy
    - life - health - healing- restoration- well-being
    -counsel- might- strength
66. Thank You Lord, for setting the machinery for my advancement in motion, in the name of Jesus.

VITAMINS FOR EXPLOSIVE MANIFESTATIONS

CHAPTER ONE

DELIVERY VITAMINS

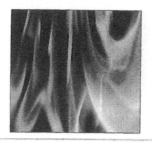

DELIVERY VITAMINS

(1)

If there is any time women need divine intervention, it is at the hour of delivery. When the burden of pregnancy is carried for nine months, there is great anticipation for safe and miraculous delivery. Knowing that the hour of delivery is fraught with danger, anxiety and several mishaps, the devil has chosen that hour as the hour of wicked attacks. God knows the importance and the role of delivery that He has given us what I have termed as delivery vitamins. These vitamins, when used properly, will turn delivery to a time of celebration. When you make use of delivery vitamins, you will be likened to the Hebrew women who were delivered of their babies with ease and miraculously. When you make use of these vitamins, you will succeed at frustrating the agenda of witchcraft and demonic powers. Delivery vitamins will make the process of chil-bearing safe and without unnecessary pains and attack. The moment of delivery will also be made easy by the power of the Almighty.

Delivery vitamins cover the whole range of conception, pregnancy and safe delivery. If you make use of these vitamins, your husband's seed will produce glorious fruits. As a woman, you will be able to get pregnant with ease, carry the pregnancy full term and experience divine presence during the time of delivery. Many have not known how to make use of the delivery vitamins, hence, there are stories of miscarriages, inability to conceive and tragedies at the time of delivery. These vitamins will perform wonders. You need to make use of it if

1. There is any problem in the area of conception
2. If your husband's semen has not been able to get you pregnant
3. If you every experience turbulence during the period of pregnancy
4. If there are problems at the time of delivery in your lineage
5. When you sense spiritual attacks in your womb.
6. These prayers would be effective when you use it to counter every wicked arrow targeted against your pregnancy and safe delivery.
7. You need these vitamins if you have discovered that there is childlessness in your ancestral line
8. You need to make use of these vitamins as a weapon for winning any battle raised against your having children
9. You need these vitamins if you have experienced miscarriages or still-births
10. You need this prayer vitamins to become a joyful mother of children.

For quick manifestation and effectiveness, you must take these prayer points aggressively. Couples can jointly pray them. You can prayer them at midnight hour. Do not allow tiredness or laziness to make you observe this prayer programme half way. Gather your strength together and prayer aggressively. Let your faith be strong and your spiritual strength be at the highest point possible. Every prayer vitamin will work wonders. The delivery vitamins will give birth to testimonies and celebration.

PRAYER SECTION

Confessions: Psalm 113:9: *He maketh the barren woman to keep house, and to be a joyful mother of children. Praise ye the Lord.* **Isaah 65:20:** *There shall be no more thence an infant of days, nor an old man that hath not filled his days: for the child shall die an hundred years old; but the sinner being an hundred years old shall be accursed.* **Deuteronomy 7:14:** *When thou art come unto the land which the Lord thy God giveth thee, and shalt possess it, and shalt dwell therein, and shalt say, I will set a king over me, like as all the nations that are about me.*

Aggressive praise worship

1. Thank the Lord for His power that knows no impossibility.
2. Confess any known sins in your life and ask for forgiveness by the blood of Jesus.
3. Any covenant between my mother and marine powers related to my conception, break by the blood of Jesus.
4. Every known and unknown relationship with spirit husband/wife, I renounce you by the blood of Jesus.
5. I drink the blood of Jesus to purge out of my system any evil food given to me in my dreams, in the name of Jesus.
6. Any hidden property of the queen of the coast in my body, catch fire, in the name of Jesus.
7. Every evil deposit of marine spirits in my womb, catch fire, in the name of Jesus.
8. Every serpent in my reproductive organ feeding on my conception, catch fire, in the name of Jesus.
9. Any evil rope tying my husband's reproductive organs, catch fire, in the name of Jesus.
10. Anything from the waters hindering erection, be roasted, in the name of Jesus.
11. Any marine object storing my husband's sperms, catch fire, in the name of Jesus.
12. Every power using sickness to attack me each time I make love with my spouse, fall down and die, in the name of Jesus.

13. Every marine coven keeping my womb, catch fire, in the name of Jesus.
14. Any power offering evil sacrifice to marine powers against my conception, fall down and die, in the name of Jesus.
15. Every witchcraft bird assigned against my home, crash land, in the name of Jesus.
16. Every witchcraft coven cooking my organs, catch fire, in the name of Jesus.
17. I recover my womb and reproductive organs from witchcraft covens, in the name of Jesus.
18. Every connection between marine witchcraft, marine spirits and land witchcraft against my conception, scatter, in the name of Jesus.
19. Every ancestral power hindering my conception, be arrested, in the name of Jesus.
20. Every evil ancestral dedication affecting my conception, die, in the name of Jesus.
21. Any hidden covenant for me to worship idols of my father's house, die, in the name of Jesus.
22. Every environmental witchcraft, working against my conception, scatter, in the name of Jesus.
23. Every territorial witchcraft of my father's house working against my conception, scatter, int the name of Jesus.
24. Anything in the house where I live that is working against my conception, catch fire, in the name of Jesus.
25. Every household witchcraft working against my conception, scatter, in the name of Jesus.
26. Every power drinking the blood of my unborn children, fall down and die, in the name of Jesus.
27. Any evil shrine having my wedding pictures, catch fire, in the name of Jesus.
28. Any of my clothes being bewitched against my conception, catch fire, in the name of Jesus.
29. Every evil rope tying my babies in the womb, cut to pieces, in the name of Jesus.

30. Every arrow of death fired at my life, go back to your senders, in the name of Jesus.
31. Anywhere any of my sanitary materials are being used against my conception, catch fire, in the name of Jesus.
32. Let irregular menstrual period return to normal, in the name of Jesus.
33. Every evil growth in my womb (fibroid) hindering conception, be uprooted by fire, in the name of Jesus.
34. Every power that makes my husband uninterested in me during my ovulation period, fall down and die, in the name of Jesus.
35. Every spirit of impatience, die, in the name of Jesus.
36. Any third party that is not happy with my home, scatter, in the name of Jesus.
37. Every spirit of miscarriage, be cast out of my womb, in the name of Jesus.
38. Every spirit of still-birth, be cast out of my womb, in the name of Jesus.
39. Any evil hand assigned to touch my pregnancy for evil, wither, in the name of Jesus.
40. I shall not die, but live to nurse my children, in the name of Jesus.

CHAPTER TWO

BRINGING FORTH VITAMINS

BRINGING FORTH VITAMINS

2

It is crystal clear that the spiritual determines the physical. When something happens in the physical realm, it has been programmed in the spiritual realm. Conception does not begin the day a woman actually gets pregnant. It begins in the spiritual realm when the journey into pregnancy and delivery is activated spiritually. This is the most important prayer programme every married couple must observe. Since it is the joy of marital union that the home be blessed with glorious children, couples should raise up a prayer altar to enable them to bring forth victoriously. God has given every couple vitamins for bringing forth. When the Bible says, "Be fruitful and multiply", it shows that the divine intention is that every home should be blessed with children. Therefore, you need a full dose of bringing forth vitamins to experience this divine miracle. These vitamins will activate the process of bringing forth good fruits. The vitamins will work in your body spiritually and ensure that there are biological reactions that will give you the fruit of the womb. Every anti-conception will go back to the sender. Problems that are associated with pregnancy will not be your lot. Evil eyes monitoring your pregnancy will suddenly become blind. The yoke of barrenness will break. Whatever has been done in the kingdom of darkness to make you weep in the area of conception will be subjected to a divine summersault. Spirit husbands or spirit children will swallow these vitamins and leave you alone or die.

This prayer programme is meant for:

1. Husbands who are burden for their wives.
2. Women who want to bring forth without any problem.
3. Couple who have been given negative clinical prophesies.
4. Couples who are struggling with infertility or impotency.
5. Couples who have a history of low sperm count.
6. Couples who are being mocked by the enemy.
7. Women who face the threat of eviction from the families of their husbands.
8. Wombs that have not carried any child.
9. Pregnant women who experience dream attacks.
10. Women who know that they belong to the spirit world and hence are not able to get pregnant.
11. Those who sense that they are under the yoke of barrenness.
12. Women who have experienced multiple miscarriages.
13. Women who are disappointed as they suddenly experience blood flow when they thought they were pregnant.
14. Those who have been threatened in their dreams that they would not give birth to children.

You need to take this prayer programme aggressively. Your story must change. Your mockers must be disgraced. Your enemies must bow. Wicked drinkers of blood and eaters of flesh must drink their own blood and eat their own flesh. You must tell evil powers that your pregnancy is not for sale.

PRAYER SECTIONS

Confession: Psalm 128:2-3: *For thou shalt eat the labour of thine hands: happy shalt thou be, and it shall be well with thee. Thy wife shall be as a fruitful vine by the sides of thine house: thy children like olive plants round about thy table.*

Aggressive praise worship

1. Lord, let the precious blood of Jesus cleanse my life from the evil effects of past immorality life, in the name of Jesus.
2. I renounce every anti-marriage habits in my life, in the name of Jesus.
3. Heavenly surgeons, do all necessary surgical operation in my life for my pregnancy to stay till delivery, in the name of Jesus.
4. Wherever my children are being tied, thunder fire of God, loose them now, in the name of Jesus.
5. Where is the Lord God of Elijah? Arise and enlarge my coast by fire, in the name of Jesus.
6. Every spirit of delay and barrenness, I cast you out of my life, in the name of Jesus.
7. Every hidden ancestral and blood covenant, hindering my conception, break, in the name of Jesus.
8. Every demonic monitoring gadget assigned against my conception, scatter, in the name of Jesus.
9. Every evil monitoring eye, monitoring my conception for destruction, catch fire, in the name of Jesus.
10. Arise, O God, and let the enemies of my conception be scattered, in the name of Jesus.
11. Every yoke of barrenness, be broken by the blood of Jesus.
12. My womb, hear the word of the Lord: your time of weeping has expired, conceive by fire, in the name of Jesus.
13. Every marine spirit assigned against my conception, scatter, in the name of Jesus
14. Every serpentine spirit assigned against my conception, scatter, in the name of Jesus.

15. Every night caterer assigned against my conception, scatter, in the name of Jesus.

16. You eaters of flesh and drinkers of blood feeding on my conception, die, in the name of Jesus.

17. Every demonic child hindering my conception, fall down and die, in the name of Jesus.

18. Every power presenting red objects to me in my dreams, fall down and die, in the name of Jesus.

19. Any material from my body being used against my conception, catch fire, in the name of Jesus.

20. I cancel and nullify premature and still-birth, in the name of Jesus.

21. I release my reproductive organs from any witchcraft cage, in the name of Jesus.

22. I release my reproductive organs from any evil padlock, in the name of Jesus.

23. I release my reproductive organs from any evil chain, in the name of Jesus.

24. Let every tree planted over my umbilical cord and foreskin catch fire, in the name of Jesus.

25. Thou power of impotence and low sperm count in my life, break, in the name of Jesus.

26. Spirits of impotence and low sperm count, loose your hold upon my life, in the name of Jesus.

27. Every high sugar content in my body, be neutralised by the blood of Jesus.

28. Let my nervous and muscular systems receive strength, in the name of Jesus.

29. I fire back every arrow of deadness, in the name of Jesus.

30. Every blood covenant speaking against my reproductive organs, break, in the name of Jesus.

31. O Lord, if my reproductive organs are not functioning well, correct them with the blood of Jesus Christ , in the name of Jesus.

32. I withdraw every power in charge of barrenness in my life, in the name of Jesus.

33. Every spirit of impotent in my life, be destroyed, in the name of Jesus.
34. Every spirit of infertility in my life, be destroyed and be replaced with the spirit of fertility, in the name of Jesus.
35. Every spirit of barrenness, be destroyed and be replaced with the spirit of fruitfulness, in the name of Jesus.
36. Every power that desires to put me to shame, be destroyed by the blood of Jesus.
37. I destroy any power in charge of destroying any good thing coming my way, in Jesus' name
38. Every spirit of unfruitfulness in my marriage, be destroyed by the blood of Jesus.

CHAPTER THREE

LET MY BONES RECEIVE STRENGTH

LET MY BONES RECEIVE STRENGTH

③

More than ever before, we need fire in our bones. We need to take in a great deal of spiritual vitamins in our bones. What you consume is what your body will make use of. A lot of people complain of weakness, tiredness, spiritual attacks and general poor health. It is because such people have not known how to make use of vitamins that will set their entire system on fire. The spiritual aspect of life must not be neglected. When you allow internal weakness, you will experience weakness physically.

This is a prayer programme that must be done regularly. People who go abroad for medical check up will experience better results in their health condition if only they can take this particular prayer programme. What you need to do is to virtually lock yourself up and take these spiritual vitamins like a wounded lion. You need to attack spiritual bacteria, demonic viruses, wicked arrows shot from the kingdom of darkness against your health and every satanic weakness attached to your bones. You must command your bones to receive strength. You must fire prayer arrows against health problems hiding at the foundation of your life and command healing virtues in the blood of Jesus to flow through your entire system, until you experience soundness of health. This prayer programme will be very effective when you make use of it for the following conditions:

1. Weak limbs.
2. Symptoms of paralysis.
3. Weak body organs.
4. Contaminated blood.
5. Attacks by the spirit of death and hell.
6. Satanic sores.
7. Afflictions in the bone marrow.
8. Hearing impairment.
9. Satanically induced ear, nose and throat problems.
10. Spinal cord related ailments.
11. Unexplainable migraine.
12. Attacks on the brain.
13. Weak nervous system.
14. Strange pain in the stomach.
15. Growth in the body.
16. Fibroid.
17. Cancer.
18. Airborne diseases.
19. Pains in the waistline.
20. Ulcer.
21. Partial blindness.
22. Stammering.
23. Lameness in the body.
24. Afflictions that keep people on the bed for weeks and months.
25. Gastrointestinal problems.
26. Speech impairments.
27. Ailments attached to old age.
28. Diseases that women struggle with.

29. Sicknesses that hospitals cannot diagnose.
30. Unexplainable mouth odour.
31. Malignant body rashes.

These and other problems require serious handling. You must make use of these prayer vitamins to tackle known or unknown ailments. When you succeed in tackling them, your body will no longer harbour any health problems. From the sickbed, you will bounce back and you will testify to the power that resides in the blood of Jesus.

PRAYER SECTIONS

Confession: **Isaiah 53:5-6**: *But he was wounded for our transgressions, he was bruised for our iniquities: the chastisement of our peace was upon him; and with his stripes we are healed. All we like sheep have gone astray; we have turned every one to his own way; and the Lord hath laid on him the iniquity of us all.* **Psalm 27:1-2:** *The Lord is my light and my salvation; whom shall I fear? the Lord is the strength of my life; of whom shall I be afraid? When the wicked, even mine enemies and my foes, came upon me to eat up my flesh, they stumbled and fell.* **Isaiah 49:24-26**: *Shall the prey be taken from the mighty, or the lawful captive delivered? But thus saith the Lord, Even the captives of the mighty shall be taken away, and the prey of the terrible shall be delivered: for I will contend with him that contendeth with thee, and I will save thy children. And I will feed them that oppress thee with their own flesh; and they shall be drunken with their own blood, as with sweet wine: and all flesh shall know that I the Lord am thy Saviour and thy Redeemer, the mighty One of Jacob.* **Deuteronomy 7:15:** *And the Lord will take away from thee all sickness, and will put none of the evil diseases of Egypt, which thou knowest, upon thee; but will lay them upon all them that hate thee.* **1 Samuel 2:4** *The bows of the mighty men are broken, and they that stumbled are girded with strength. Thy vows are upon me, O God: I will render praises unto thee.* **Psalm 56:13:** *For thou hast delivered my soul from death: wilt not thou deliver my feet from falling, that I may walk before God in the light of the living?* **Psalm 116:8-10:** *For thou hast* *delivered my soul from death, mine eyes from tears, and my feet from falling. I will walk before the LORD in the land of the living. I believed, therefore have I spoken: I was greatly afflicted.* **Psalm 138:7:** *Though I walk in the midst of trouble, thou wilt revive me: thou shalt stretch forth thine hand against the wrath of mine enemies, and thy right hand shall save me.* **Psalm 145:14:** *The LORD upholdeth all that fall, and raiseth up all those that be bowed down.* **Genesis 1:1-3:** *In the beginning God created the heaven and the earth. And the earth was without form, and void; and darkness was upon the face of the deep. And the Spirit of God moved upon the face of the waters. And God said, Let there be light: and there was light.* **John 1:1-3:** *In the beginning was the Word, and the Word was with God, and the Word was God. The same was in the beginning with God. All things were made by him; and without him was not any thing made that was made.* **Ezekiel 37:1-10:** *The hand of the LORD was upon me, and carried me out in the spirit of the LORD, and set me down in the midst of the valley which was full of bones, And caused me to pass by them round about: and, behold, there were very many in the open valley; and, lo, they were very dry. And he said unto me, Son of man, can these bones live? And I answered, O Lord GOD, thou knowest. Again he said unto me, Prophesy upon these bones, and say unto them, O ye dry bones, hear the word of the LORD. Thus saith the Lord GOD unto these bones; Behold, I will cause breath to enter into you, and ye shall live: And I will lay sinews upon you, and will bring up flesh upon you, and cover you with skin, and put breath in you, and ye shall live; and ye shall know that I am the LORD. So I prophesied as I was commanded: and as I prophesied, there was a noise, and behold a shaking, and the bones came together, bone to his bone. And when I beheld, lo, the sinews and the flesh came up upon them, and the skin covered them above: but there was no breath in them. Then said he unto me, Prophesy unto the wind, prophesy, son of man, and say to the wind, Thus saith the Lord GOD; Come from the four winds, O breath, and breathe upon these slain, that they may live. So I prophesied as he commanded me, and the breath came into them, and they lived, and stood up upon their feet, an exceeding great army.*

Aggressive Praise and Worship

Songs

The Great Physician now is here, Hear the footsteps of Jesus

He has broken all the fetters, He touched me

 # PRAYER POINTS

1. Every arrow fired into my limbs, get out now, in the name of Jesus.
2. Let the creative power of God recreate any organ that has been destroyed in my body, in the name of Jesus.
7. By the power in the blood of Jesus, let every agenda of paralysis for my life be cancelled, in the name of Jesus.
8. Holy Ghost fire, shake paralysis out of my body, in the name of Jesus.
9. My Father, touch my life and make me whole, in the name of Jesus.
10. Every arrow fired into my body to paralyse my destiny, go back to your sender, in the name of Jesus.
11. Blood of Jesus, revive every dead portion of my body, in the name of Jesus.
12. Every agenda of the wicked, to stop my destiny by stopping my movements, I paralyse you now, in the name of Jesus.
13. Every yoke in my life, be shaken off, in the name of Jesus.
14. Holy Ghost fire, revive my body, soul and spirit, in the name of Jesus.
15. Power of wicked oppressors, loose your hold upon my life, in the name of Jesus.
16. Anointing that breaks the yokes, break up every yoke of darkness upon my life, in the name of Jesus.
17. Every satanic command that my body is listening to, I cancel it now, in the name of Jesus.
18. Blood of Jesus, flow into my body, soul and spirit, in the name of Jesus.

19. Fire of God, mobilise heaven to help me, in the name of Jesus.
20. Any area in which the enemy has been tormenting my life, I pull them down, in the name of Jesus.
21. My Father, incubate my life with Your resurrection power, in the name of Jesus.
22. Every chain slowing me down, break to pieces, in the name of Jesus.
23. Holy Ghost fire, incubate my brain, in the name of Jesus.
24. Thou creative power of God, fall upon my brain now, in the name of Jesus.
25. Anything stolen from my brain when I was a child, I repossess you now, in the name of Jesus.
26. Arrows of darkness fired into my brain, die, in the name of Jesus.
27. My brain, wake up by fire, in the name of Jesus.
28. Any power calling my head for evil, scatter, in the name of Jesus.
29. I fire back every arrow of witchcraft in my head, in the name of Jesus.
30. Every evil hand laid upon my head when I was a little child, die, in the name of Jesus.
31. Power of household wickedness upon my brain, die, in the name of Jesus.
32. Every destruction in my nervous system and in my spinal cord, receive the healing touch of Jesus, in the name of Jesus.
33. Every power afflicting my spinal cord, I shake you off, in the name of Jesus.
34. Every yoke of satan troubling my nervous system, be scattered to pieces, in the name of Jesus.
35. My Father, revive every dead part of my nervous system, in the name of Jesus.
36. By the power of resurrection, I command my nervous system to receive life, in the name of Jesus.

37. Organs of my body, hear the word of the Lord: reject the voice of the grave, in the name of Jesus.

38. Thou cleansing power in the blood of Jesus, sanitise my body, in the name of Jesus.

39. Thou Great Physician, send surgeons from heaven to work on me now, in the name of Jesus.

40. Agenda of infirmity for my life, die, in the name of Jesus.

41. Operating theatre of God, arise, admit me and work on me now, in the name of Jesus.

42. Damage done to my body by infirmities, be repaired by fire, in the name of Jesus.

43. Divine antibiotics, divine medication, bombard my body by fire, in the name of Jesus.

44. I withdraw every conscious and unconscious co-operation with any internal disorder, in the name of Jesus.

45. Any power stealing my healing virtues, come out and die, in the name of Jesus.

46. Anointing that breaks the yoke, break every internal yoke and chain, in the name of Jesus.

47. Healing virtues from the King of kings and the Lord of lords, saturate my body now, in the name of Jesus.

48. O Lord, save me and I shall be saved. Heal me and I shall be healed, in the name of Jesus.

49. O God of possibilities, make me whole, in the name of Jesus.

50. Let my body be electrified with the healing power of God, in the name of Jesus.

51. My Father, shake me loose from every grip of sickness, in the name of Jesus.

52. I shall not die but live to declare the works of God, in the name of Jesus.

53. Thou creative power of God, mobilize Your resources into my life, in the name of Jesus.

54. Rain of healing waters from above, soak every organ in my body, in the name of Jesus.

55. Spirit of Goliath, spirit of Herod, spirit of Pharaoh, release my body, in the name of Jesus.

56. Physical and spiritual poisons, come out of my body now, in the name of Jesus.

57. I cough our and vomit any plantation of darkness in my body, in the name of Jesus.

58. Every internal affliction and oppression in my body, die, in the name of Jesus.

59. Agents of disruption in my body, come out and die, in the name of Jesus.

60. My Father, let Your angelic surgeons visit every part of my life, in the name of Jesus.

61. Yoke Breaker, Jesus Christ, break my yoke now, in the name of Jesus.

62. My body, hear the word of the Lord: receive divine repair, in the name of Jesus.

63. I arrest any serpent of infirmity troubling my body, in the name of Jesus.

64. Destructive infirmities, hear the word of the Lord: die, in the name of Jesus.

65. I cut off the tentacles of internal disease spreading in my body, in the name of Jesus.

66. Power base of infirmity, dry up and die, in the name of Jesus.

67. Health arresters, be arrested by fire, in the name of Jesus.

68. Holy Ghost fire, melt away every infirmity in my body organs, in the name of Jesus.

69. I fire back every arrow of affliction tormenting my body, in the name of Jesus.

70. I kill every killer disease by the power in the blood of Jesus.

71. The battle of the terrible and the mighty against my health, expire, in the name of Jesus.

72. Thou Great Physician, Jesus Christ, heal me now, in the name of Jesus.

73. Yokes of infirmity, break to pieces, in the name of Jesus.

74. Authority of infirmity scorpions over my life, terminate, in the name of Jesus.
75. Every cell in my body, hear the word of the Lord: reject evil commands, in the name of Jesus.
76. Let my bodily organs become too hot for any disease to handle, in the name of Jesus.
77. I charge my body with the fire of the Holy Ghost, in the name of Jesus.
78. Blood of Jesus, sanitise my body and make me whole, in the name of Jesus.
79. Eaters of flesh assigned against me, fall down and die, in the name of Jesus.
80. My flesh and my blood, reject the voice of death, in the name of Jesus.
81. Any power feeding on my flesh, come out and die, in the name of Jesus.
82. Agents of killer infirmities, I kill you now, in the name of Jesus.
83. My blood, hear the word of the Lord: reject visible and invisible agents of infirmity, in the name of Jesus.
84. Any power assigned to eat me up, die, in the name of Jesus.
85. Every demon termite eating my body, die by fire, in the name of Jesus.
86. Every witchcraft poison in my body, dry up and die, in the name of Jesus.
87. Every curse of consumption afflicting my life, break, in the name of Jesus.
88. Every clearing pestilence, scatter, in the name of Jesus.
89. Blood of Jesus, pump out any stranger in my body, in the name of Jesus.
90. My body organs, reject the voice of early death, in the name of Jesus.
91. Strangers from the grave, clear out of my body, in the name of Jesus.
92. My life, reject the strangers that smite unto death, in the name of Jesus.

93. I break the yoke of the invisible destroyers, in the name of Jesus.

94. Every venom of the serpent and scorpion eating up my flesh, dry up now, in the name of Jesus.

95. I drink the blood of Jesus. *(Say this for 21 times)*

96. Let God arise and let my infirmity be scattered, in the name of Jesus.

97. I bind and cast out every agent of weakness, in the name of Jesus.

98. Parasites, viruses, bacteria of infirmity, my body is not your candidate, die, in the name of Jesus.

99. Bewitchment of my flesh, blood and bones, terminate, in the name of Jesus.

100. Wasting powers, depart from my life, in the name of Jesus.

101. O God, arise and make me whole, in the name of Jesus.

102. My Father, arise in Your power and have mercy on me, in the name of Jesus.

103. O wind of resurrection, blow upon every organ of my body, in the name of Jesus.

104. Every dead organ in my body, come alive, in the name of Jesus.

105. I fire back every arrow of clinical prophecy, in the name of Jesus.

106. Blood of Jesus, electrify power into my ...., in the name of Jesus.

107. Holy Ghost fire, incubate my ...., in the name of Jesus.

108. Where is the Lord God of Elijah? Arise in Your resurrection power, in the name of Jesus.

109. Every arrow fired from the waters into my ...., backfire, in the name of Jesus.

110. Every strongman assigned to the gate of my ...., receive the fire of God and die, in the name of Jesus.

111. Angels of divine surgery, visit my........., in the name of Jesus.

112. Every oppression assigned to make my .... fail, I crush you, in the name of Jesus.

113. O God, arise and let my _ _ _ experience Your resurrection power, in the name of Jesus.

114. I decree life into my dead parts, in the name of Jesus.

115. I soak every organ of my body in the wonder working power of the blood of Jesus.

116. Power of God that breaketh every yoke, break every yoke upon my _ _ _, in the name of Jesus.

117. Every serpent and scorpion assigned against my _ _ _, receive the fire of God and die, in the name of Jesus.

118. Every witchcraft arrow fired against my _ _ _, backfire, in the name of Jesus.

119. My _ _ _ shall not die but live to declare the works of God, in the name of Jesus.

120. I bind and cast out every spirit of Cain afflicting my _ _ organ, in the name of Jesus.

121. I bind and cast out every spirit of Goliath afflicting my _ _ _ organ, in the name of Jesus.

122. I bind and cast out every spirit of Pharaoh afflicting my _ _ _ organ, in the name of Jesus.

123. I bind and cast out every spirit of Herod afflicting my _ _ _ organ, in the name of Jesus.

124. I bind and cast out every spirit of Hamman afflicting my _ _ _ organ, in the name of Jesus.

125. Insects of death bitting my _ _ _, die, in the name of Jesus.

126. Inherited serpent transferred into my _ _ _, die, in the name of Jesus.

127. Holy Ghost fire, burn to ashes every satanic deposit in my _ _ _, in the name of Jesus.

128. Every satanic rope tied around my _ _ _, catch fire, in the name of Jesus.

129. I breathe in the fire of the Holy Ghost and I breathe out every plantation of darkness, in the name of Jesus.

130. Every evil tree, planted to render my _ _ _ powerless, be uprooted, in the name of Jesus.

131. Every curse issued against my _ _ _, be broken by the power in the blood of Jesus.

132. Every arrow of mockery, shame and reproach, fired against my ___, die, in the name of Jesus.
133. I drink the resurrection water from the Lord and I receive the resurrection power into my system, in the name of Jesus.

CHAPTER FOUR

BREAKTHROUGH TABLETS

BREAKTHROUGH TABLETS

(4)

Vitamins and tablets are not only used to secure bodily healing and wholesomeness, they are also required for activating breakthroughs. There are tablets you can make use of to flag off a season of divine intervention. Breakthrough tablets describe a prayer programme that must be carried out when you need divine breakthrough. This programme was vomited by the Holy Spirit to make your breakthroughs come into manifestation without any hindrance. If you ever experience breakthrough famine and you are desperate for a change, this is the prayer programme you need. Breakthrough tablets when swallowed spiritually will send breakthroughs from heaven and make you to give your testimonies here on earth. This is a comprehensive prayer programme meant to disgrace the powers that try to hijack your miracles and blessings. It is a unique prayer programme that will always work wonders when carried out aggressively. When you swallow breakthrough tablets by taking these prayer points with all the strength you can muster, heaven releases heavy bombshells in the camp of the enemy and you will begin to possess your possessions. This prayer points have been carefully divided into seven sections. Each day, you handle 10 prayer points that will push you to your breakthrough point. By the time you are through with the seventh segment you will be ready for your breakthroughs. You cannot handle this prayer points and not experience breakthrough that would announce the awesome power of the Almighty. Every power trying to hinder your breakthroughs will announce their obituary. No power will escape your prayer arrows. If you can just devote seven days to this prayer programme, everyone around you and beyond your community will testify that indeed you serve a God who answereth by fire. This is one of the greatest prayer programmes that you can carry out. It is result-Oriented, powerful and thorough. Every section addresses a unique area of life and the entire programme is circular. It is like undertaking a prayer chain aimed at locating every area of your need. Breakthrough tablets will make you an overcomer. They will give you victory over stubborn enemies. They will enable you to sing your song and dance your dance and your heart with overflow with joy. Your mouth will sing praises of the God of heaven and earth. You shall rejoice.

DAY 1

Confession: **Psalm 3:3**: *But thou, O Lord, art a shield for me; my glory, and the lifter up of mine head.*

Aggressive Praise and Worship

1. O God, arise and confound my enemies, in the name of Jesus.
2. O God of Elijah, arise and cancel all my afflictions, in the name of Jesus.
3. O God, arise by the thunder of Your power and let my story change, in the name of Jesus.

4. O God, arise in Your yoke-breaking power and break my yoke this day, in Jesus' name.

5. O God of Abraham, arise and mesmerise my enemies, in the name of Jesus.

6. O God of Isaac, arise and multiply my laughter, in the name of Jesus.

7. O God of Israel, arise and promote me by fire, in the name of Jesus.

8. By Your binding powers, O God, arise and bind my tormentors, in the name of Jesus.

9. By Your power of possibilities, O God, arise and manifest in my life, in the name of Jesus.

10. My Father, my Father, my Father, arise and let the world know that You are my God, in the name of Jesus.

DAY 2

Confession: **Psalm 3:3:** *But thou, O Lord, art a shield for me; my glory, and the lifter up of mine head.*

Aggressive Praise and Worship

11. Every storm in my life, become calm by fire, in the name of Jesus.

12. *(Mention your name),* hear the word of the Lord: be still and know that God is God, in the name of Jesus.

13. O God, arise and show me great mercy today, in the name of Jesus.

14. My Father, contend with whatever is contending with my peace, in the name of Jesus.

15. Every power assigned to make God a liar in my life, die, in the name of Jesus.

16. O dragon power assigned against me, I bury you now, in the name of Jesus.

17. Every evil mark stamped on me, dry up, in the name of Jesus.

18. Those that hate me shall be put to all-round shame, in the name of Jesus.
19. My light, hear the word of the Lord: shine brighter and brighter, in the name of Jesus.
20. I decree poverty upon my stubborn enemies, in the name of Jesus.

DAY 3

Confession: **Psalm 3:3:** *But thou, O Lord, art a shield for me; my glory, and the lifter up of mine head.*

Aggressive Praise and Worship

21. Every occultic pregnancy concerning my life this month, I abort you by fire, in Jesus' name.
22. Oh heavens, declare your glory over my life, in the name of Jesus.
23. Every waster and emptier assigned to swallow me up, die, in the name of Jesus.
24. Sickness and infirmity shall not waste my life, in the name of Jesus.
25. Every arrangement to frustrate my breakthroughs, catch fire, in Jesus' name.
26. Every priest of darkness divining against me, die, in the grave of fire, in the name of Jesus.
27. Every wicked mouth opened to swallow my breakthroughs this month, dry up, in the name of Jesus.
28. Oh God, arise and empower the eagle of my breakthroughs to fly this month, in the name of Jesus.
29. Lord elevate me this month by fire, in the name of Jesus. Do something in my life, O Lord, that will make men to celebrate me, in the name of Jesus.
30. I shall sing my song and dance my dance this year, in the name of Jesus.

DAY 4

Confession: Psalm 3:3: *But thou, O Lord, art a shield for me; my glory, and the lifter up of mine head.*

Aggressive Praise and Worship

31. Any power assigned to make me take foolish risks, die, in the name of Jesus.
32. Father, give me a new beginning, in the name of Jesus.
33. My Father, cause this year to be my year of jubilee and rejoicing, in the name of Jesus.
34. Every curse of stagnation, break, in the name of Jesus.
35. O God, arise and fill my mouth with laughter, in the name of Jesus.
36. O God, arise and let my tears expire, in the name of Jesus.
37. O God, arise and let my shame expire, in the name of Jesus.
38. O God, arise and turn my captors to my captives, in the name of Jesus. Miracle, that surpasses explanation, manifest in my life now, in the name of Jesus.
39. O God, arise today, and let my situation change, in the name of Jesus.
40. Today, I position myself by fire for divine intervention, in the name of Jesus.

DAY 5

Confession: Psalm 3:3: But thou, O Lord, art a shield for me; my glory, and the lifter up of mine head.

Aggressive Praise and Worship

41. O God, my Father, burst forth in my life by signs and wonders, in the name of Jesus.
42. Resources of heaven, arise by fire and promote me, in the

name of Jesus.

43. Any power that wants me to die, die, in the name of Jesus.
44. My Father, arise and let the root of hardship in my life die now, in the name of Jesus.
45. O Red Sea of blockage, I cry against you. Divide by fire, in the name of Jesus.
46. Every power holding tight to my instrument of advancement, die, in the name of Jesus.
47. I recover 10-fold all my wasted years, in the name of Jesus.Any satanic threat to my existence, be uprooted, in the name of Jesus.
48. My portion shall not be given to another, in the name of Jesus.
49. Sudden destruction will not be my lot, in the name of Jesus.
50. Every enchantment assigned for my downfall, die, in the name of Jesus.

DAY 6

Confession: Psalm 3:3: But thou, O Lord, art a shield for me; my glory, and the lifter up of mine head.

Aggressive Praise and Worship

51. Any personality carrying the seed of wickedness against me, be exposed and disgraced, in the name of Jesus.
52. The enemy that came while I slept, be disgraced, in the name of Jesus.
53. You ladder of oppression, catch fire, in the name of Jesus.
54. You ladder of affliction, catch fire, in the name of Jesus.
55. You ladder of infirmity, catch fire, in the name of Jesus.
56. You ladder of failure at the edge of breakthroughs, catch fire, in the name of Jesus.
57. Vampire power, drinking the blood of my virtues, die, in the name of Jesus.

58. Every location assigned to dislocate my life, clear away, in the name of Jesus.
59. Every Goliath boasting against my breakthroughs, die, in the name of Jesus.
60. My destiny, hear the word of the Lord: move to Your next level, in the name of Jesus.

DAY  7

Confession: Psalm 3:3: But thou, O Lord, art a shield for me; my glory, and the lifter up of mine head.

Aggressive Praise and Worship

61. Serpents and scorpions assigned to put me to shame, die, in the name of Jesus.
62. Any witchdoctor assigned to terminate my life, die, in the name of Jesus.
63. Evil progress, hear the word of the Lord: die, in the name of Jesus.
64. Birds of darkness assigned to trouble my star, die, in the name of Jesus.
65. Thou power of limitation, you are a liar. Die, in the name of Jesus.
66. My glory, arise from the graveyard of backwardness, shine, in the name of Jesus.
67. Every arrow of confusion, be disgraced, in the name of Jesus.
68. Every assembly of affliction, scatter, in the name of Jesus.
69. Blood of Jesus, cause confusion in the blood bank of witchcraft, in the name of Jesus.
70. I decree against serpents and scorpions. Let their poison die, in the name of Jesus.

CHAPTER FIVE

RAPID MANIFESTATIONS

RAPID MANIFESTATIONS

(5)

This is a strange prayer programme. It runs for 11days. If you carry it out, you are on a high risk. You risk fresh testimonies, amazing miracles, signs and wonders and witnessing the burial of your problems and the powers behind them. There is a time for addressing serious problems, a time when you must declare enough is enough. There is a time when you must refuse to let the status quo remain as it is, a time when you must pray until God shakes the heavens and the earth for your sake, a time when you must carry the battle to the gate of your enemy, a time when you must take charge of your situation through aggressive prayers, a time when you must demand total restitution from the enemy and a time when you must possess what belongs to you and arise to fulfil your destiny. This is an uncommon prayer section to observe. It is for serious students in the school of spiritual warfare. Do not start this prayer programme unless you are serious and you are bent on having God's will fulfilled in your life. It is not for men and women who are lazy when they approach the prayer altar.

You need these prayers when:

1. You are tired of what the enemy is doing.
2. You no longer want to be tossed back and forth by the enemy.
3. You are no longer ready to remain history when you are still alive.
4. You want to see and experience the power of God that saves to the uttermost.
5. You want your testimonies to be loud and clear.
6. You want to become a candidate of supernatural surprises.
7. You want your glory to appear by fire.

I plead with you to give this prayer programme all the attention it deserves. Take each prayer points with holy aggression.

The prayer point are to be said very early in the morning and late at night for eleven 11 consecutive days. There should also be three days of thanksgiving.

DAY 1

A. Make this powerful confessions. Personalise them.

Ps 31:2; Ps 143:7; Isa 58:8; Luke 18:8; Ps 102:2; Jer 1:12; Jer 29:11;

B. Praise Worship: Sing at least seven songs of praise to the Lord. Praise Him from the bottom of your heart for answered prayers.

 **PRAYER POINTS**

1. I dismiss and disband from my heart every thought, image or picture of failure in these matters, in the name of Jesus.

2. I reject every spirit of doubt, fear and discouragement in the name of Jesus.

3. I cancel all ungodly delays to the manifestations of my miracles, in the name of Jesus.

4. Let the angels of the living God roll away every stone of hindrance to the manifestation of my breakthroughs, in the name of Jesus.

5. O Lord, hasten Your word to perform it in every department of my life, in the name of Jesus.

6. O Lord, avenge me of my adversaries speedily, in the name of Jesus.

7. I refuse to agree with the enemies of mt progress, in the mighty name of Jesus.

DAY 2

A. **Make this powerful confessions. Personalise them.**

Ps 31:2; Ps 143:7; Isa 58:8; Luke 18:8; Ps 102:2; Jer 1:12; Jer 29:11;

B. **Praise Worship. Sing at least seven (7) songs of praise to the Lord. Praise Him from the bottom of your heart for answered prayers.**

 PRAYER POINTS

8. O Lord, I desire breakthroughs concerning . . . today, in the name of Jesus.

9. O Lord, I desire breakthroughs concerning . . . this week, in the name of Jesus.

10. O Lord, I desire breakthroughs concerning . . . this month, in the name of Jesus.

11. O Lord, I desire breakthroughs concerning . . . this year, in the name of Jesus.

12. Let there be turbulence, re-arrangement, revision, re-organisation and re-routing of situations and circumstances to give path to my miracles, in the name of Jesus.
13. Let every hole present in the container of my life be blocked, in the name of Jesus.
14. I bind, plunder and render to nothing every anti-testimony, anti-miracle and anti-prosperity forces, in the name of Jesus.

DAY 3

A. Make this powerful confessions. Personalise the confessions.

Ps 31:2; Ps 143:7; Isa 58:8; Luke 18:8; Ps 102:2; Jer 1:12; Jer 29:11;

B. Praise Worship: Sing at least seven songs of praise to the Lord. Praise Him from the bottom of your heart for answered prayers.

 ## PRAYER POINTS

15. The God who answered by fire and the God of Elijah, answer me by fire, in the name of Jesus.
16. The God who answered Moses speedily at the Red Sea, answer me by fire, in the name of Jesus.
17. The God who changed the lot of Jabez, answer me by fire, in the name of Jesus.
18. The God which quickeneth and calleth those things that be not as if they were, answer me by fire, in the name of Jesus.
19. The God of all comfort and joy, answer me by fire, in the name of Jesus.
20. At the name of Jesus, let every foreign knee preventing the manifestation of my miracles in the heaven, on earth and

under-neath the earth bow, in the name of Jesus.

21. I receive my victory over all the forces of wickedness, in the name of Jesus.

DAY 4

A. Make this powerful confessions. Personalise the confessions.

Ps 31:2; Ps 143:7; Isa 58:8; Luke 18:8; Ps 102:2; Jer 1:12; Jer 29:11;

B. Praise Worship. Sing at least seven (7) songs of praise to the Lord. Praise Him from the bottom of your heart for answered prayers.

 PRAYER POINTS

22. Let every evil force gathered against my breakthrough be completely scattered in the name of Jesus.

23. I reject the spirit of the tail and I claim the spirit of the head in the name of Jesus.

24. I command all evil records planted by the devil in anyone's mind against my desire miracles to be shattered to pieces in the name of Jesus.

25. Let my path be smoothened to the top by the hand of fire, in the name of Jesus.

26. Lord, catapult me into greatness as You did for Daniel in the land of Babylon, in Jesus' name.

27. Lord, help me to identify and deal with any weaknesses in me that can hinder the manifestation of my miracles, in the name of Jesus.

28. I bind every strongman delegated to hinder the manifestations of my miracles, in the name of Jesus.

DAY 5

A. **Make this powerful confessions. Personalise them.**

Ps 31:2; Ps 143:7; Isa 58:8; Luke 18:8; Ps 102:2; Jer 1:12; Jer 29:11;

B. **Praise Worship**: **Sing at least seven songs of praise to the Lord. Praise Him from the bottom of your heart for answered prayers.**

 PRAYER POINTS

29. Let power change hands in every area of my life to the hands of the Holy Spirit, in the name of Jesus.
30. I shall laugh my enemies to scorn after the order of Elijah, in the name of Jesus.
31. This year, I shall sing my song and dance my dance, in the name of Jesus.
32. O God, arise and give me a turn-around miracle, in the name of Jesus.
33. Do something in my life, O Lord, that will make me to celebrate, in the name of Jesus.
34. O God, arise and open Your treasures unto me, in the name of Jesus.
35. O God, arise and give me open heavens, in the name of Jesus.

DAY 6

A. **Make this powerful confessions. Personalise them.**

Ps 31:2; Ps 143:7; Isa 58:8; Luke 18:8; Ps 102:2; Jer 1:12; Jer 29:11;

B. **Praise Worship. Sing at least seven (7) songs of praise to the Lord. Praise Him from the bottom of your heart for answered prayers.**

 PRAYER POINTS

36. O Lord, make me a candidate of supernatural surprises, in the name of Jesus.
37. By fire, by force, O God, launch me into my next level, in the name of Jesus.
38. O God arise and restore my past losses, in the name of Jesus.
39. Thou power of God, disgrace my detractors, in the name of Jesus.
40. Lord, contend with them that contend with me, in the name of Jesus.
41. Lord, let my generation celebrate me, in the name of Jesus.
42. Every arrow of mourning and sorrow, backfire, in the name of Jesus.

DAY  **7**

43. Lord, convert any pain in my life to gain, in the name of Jesus.
44. Give me my personal pentecost. Give me fire to fight, O Lord, in the name of Jesus.
45. Lord, make me a blessing to my generations, in the name of Jesus.
46. I cancel tears. I cancel premature death, in the name of Jesus.
47. My Father, my Father, my Father, let people know that I serve a living God, in the name of Jesus.
48. This year, I must not fail, in the name of Jesus.
49. My Father, deliver me from strange battles, in the name of Jesus.

DAY 8

A.   Make this powerful confessions. Personalise them.

Ps 31:2; Ps 143:7; Isa 58:8; Luke 18:8; Ps 102:2; Jer 1:12; Jer 29:11;

B.   Praise Worship: Sing at least seven songs of praise to the Lord. Praise Him from the bottom of your heart for answered prayers.

 ## PRAYER POINTS

50. My Father, cause this year to be my year of jubilee and rejoicing, in the name of Jesus.
51. O God, arise and fill my mouth with laughter, in the name of Jesus.
52. O God, arise and let my tears expire, in the name of Jesus.
53. O God, arise and let my shame expire, in the name of Jesus.
54. I receive uncommon wisdom to excel, in the name of Jesus.
55. My Father, accelerate my speed and close the gap between where I am now in life and where I should be, in the name of Jesus.
56. Every power assigned to put off my light, receive confusion, in the name of Jesus.

DAY 9

A.   Make this powerful confessions. Personalise them.

Ps 31:2; Ps 143:7; Isa 58:8; Luke 18:8; Ps 102:2; Jer 1:12; Jer 29:11;

B.   Praise Worship: Sing at least seven songs of praise to

the Lord. Praise Him from the bottom of your heart for answered prayers.

 **PRAYER POINTS**

57. Let the rainbow of glory appear in my situation, in the name of Jesus.
58. Conspiracy against my life, lift away into the sea, in the name of Jesus.
59. Captivity, arise and trouble my captivity, in the name of Jesus.
60. I recover all my known and unknown opportunities, in the name of Jesus.
61. I put on my dancing shoes, my sorrows are over, in the name of Jesus.
62. Open Your abundance unto me, O Lord, in the name of Jesus.
63. Sword of God, cast off every satanic attachment from my life, in the name of Jesus.

DAY 10

A. **Make this powerful confessions. Personalise the confessions.**

Ps 31:2; Ps 143:7; Isa 58:8; Luke 18:8; Ps 102:2; Jer 1:12; Jer 29:11;

B. **Praise Worship: Sing at least seven songs of praise to the Lord. Praise Him from the bottom of your heart for answered prayers.**

 **PRAYER POINTS**

64. Darkness, break away from my life, in the name of Jesus.

65. Any mouth cursing me, be eaten by poison, in the name of Jesus.

66. O God of 24-hour miracle, where are You,? Appear, in the name of Jesus.

67. Where is the Lord God of Elijah? Divide my Jordan by fire, in the name of Jesus.

68. Pharaoh of my father's house, let me go, in the name of Jesus.

69. O God of the suddenly, arise in the thunder of Your power and appear, in the name of Jesus.

70. Jehovah, the Story Changer, arise and let my story change, in the name of Jesus.

DAY 11

A. Make this powerful confessions. Personalise them.

Ps 31:2; Ps 143:7; Isa 58:8; Luke 18:8; Ps 102:2; Jer 1:12; Jer 29:11;

B. Praise Worship: Sing at least seven songs of praise to the Lord. Praise Him from the bottom of your heart for answered prayers.

 PRAYER POINTS

71. O God of 24- hour miracle, arise and locate me by fire, in the name of Jesus.

72. By the power in the blood of Jesus, O God, arise and disappoint my enemies, in the name of Jesus.

73. Satanic barriers to my breakthroughs, catch fire, in the name of Jesus.

74. Uncommon and extraordinary testimonies, locate me, in the name of Jesus.

75. My Father, do what will make me to forget my past years of

pain, in the name of Jesus.

76. Miracles that will wipe out my past ridicules, manifest, in the name of Jesus.

77. Every power behind my stagnation, die, in the name of Jesus.

Pray these aggressive prayers of the Psalmist with thanksgiving:

78. Every evil power using my glory to shine, die, in the name of Jesus.

79. My Father, arise and let my way open, in the name of Jesus.

80. My Father, empower my angels of blessings to break through now, in the name of Jesus.

81. My past labours, arise and become testimonies, in the name of Jesus.

82. I move from glory to glory, from strength to strength, from grace to grace and from favour to favour, by fire, in the name of Jesus.

83. O God, arise and laugh my enemies to scorn, in Jesus' name.

84. O God, arise and speak unto my enemies in Your wrath, in the name of Jesus.

85. O God, vex my stubborn oppressors in Your sore displeasure, in the name of Jesus.

86. O Lord, break my enemies with Your rod of iron, in Jesus' name.

87. O God, dash the power of stubborn pursuers in pieces like a potter's vessel, in the name of Jesus.

88. O God, arise with all Your weapons of war and fight my battle for me, in the name of Jesus.

89. O God, be my glory and the lifter of my head, in Jesus' name.

90. My Father, be a shield for me in every situation, in Jesus' name.

91. Arise, O Lord, and lift up Thine arm in war, in the name of Jesus.
92. Break Thou the arm of the wicked and the evil man, O Lord, in the name of Jesus.
93. Upon the wicked, O Lord, rain snares, fire, brimstone and a horrible tempest, in the name of Jesus.
94. My enemies shall not rejoice over me, in the name of Jesus.
95. Keep me as the apple of Thy eye, O Lord, and hide me under the shadow of Thy wings, in the name of Jesus.
96. O Lord, barricade me from the wicked that oppress me and from my deadly enemies who compass me about, in the name of Jesus.
97. Arise, O Lord, disappoint my oppressors and cast them down, in the name of Jesus.
98. O Lord, with Thy sword, deliver my soul from the wicked, in the name of Jesus.
99. I will call upon the Lord, who is worthy to be praised, so shall I be saved from mine enemies, in Jesus' name.
100. O God, send out Your arrows to scatter the oppressors, in the name of Jesus.
101. O God, shoot out Your lightening and discomfit the oppressors, in the name of Jesus.
102. Let the smoke go out of Your nostrils and fire out of Your mouth to devour all plantations of darkness in my life, in Jesus' name
103. O God, thunder from heaven against all my oppressors, in the name of Jesus.
104. O Lord, at the blast of Your nostrils, disgrace every foundational bondage, in the name of Jesus.
105. O God, deliver me from my strong enemy which hated me for they are too strong for me, in Jesus' name.
106. O God, bring down every high look downgrading my potentials, in the name of Jesus.
107. I receive power to run through satanic troop, in Jesus' name.

CHAPTER SIX

DELIVERANCE OF THE BRAIN

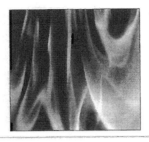

DELIVERANCE OF THE BRAIN

The head is the symbol of life. The brain represents your endowments. When the brain is attacked, destiny is affected. To safeguard your destiny, you need deliverance of the brain. You must ask God to visit your brain by fire and give quit notice to every stranger that is busy converting your brain to a free accommodation.

You need this prayer programme when:

1. Your brain is under attack.
2. Your creative ability has been stolen.
3. You feel strange presence around your brain.
4. Your head has been bewitched.
5. Your mind is under attack.
6. Your intellectual gifts are being stolen.
7. There are terrible battles in your thoughts.
8. You find it hard to succeed in your academics.
9. You suddenly experience a barrage of attacks in your mental realm.

10. You discover that arrows of discouragement are fired at you.
11. There are traces of arrows of insanity in your foundation.
12. There are satanic robbers battling with your destiny.
13. You find it difficult to think straight.
14. Productive thinking has become a battle.
15. You experience strange hotness in your brain.

Your brain must experience total healing and deliverance. Even if you sense no battle at all, this is a prayer programme you still must carry out. Prevention, they say, is better than cure. Make your brain a no-go area for wicked agents of darkness. Let the fire of the Holy Ghost circulate in your brain.

 PRAYER SECTION

Confession: **Psalm 23:5:** *Thou preparest a table before me in the presence of mine enemies: thou anointest my head with oil; my cup runneth over.*

Praise Worship

 PRAYER POINTS

1. Arrows of darkness fired into my brain, die, in the name of Jesus.
2. Power of household wickedness upon my brain, die, in the name of Jesus.
3. My head, reject every bewitchment, in the name of Jesus.
4. My brain, wake up by fire, in the name of Jesus.
5. Any power calling my head for evil, scatter, in the name of Jesus.
6. I fire back every arrow of witchcraft in my head, in the name of Jesus.
7. Every evil hand laid upon my head when I was a little child, die, in the name of Jesus.
8. Ask the Lord to forgive you, all evil thoughts you have ever

entertained.

9. Strongholds in my life battling my destiny, I pull you down, in the name of Jesus.

10. Every power using my thoughts against me, bow, in the name of Jesus.

11. Anointing for productive thinking, come upon my life, in the name of Jesus.

12. Confusion, hear the word of the Lord,: bow, in the name of Jesus.

13. Anointing for uncommon success, fall upon my life, in the name of Jesus.

14. Every power assigned to hinder my breakthroughs, rush into the Red Sea and die, in the name of Jesus.

15. I pronounce blessings and good things upon my life, in the name of Jesus.

16. Holy Ghost fire, incubate my brain, in the name of Jesus.

17. Thou creative power of God, fall upon my brain now, in the name of Jesus.

18. Anything stolen from my brain when I was a child, I repossess you now, in the name of Jesus.

19. Creative power of God, arise and move me forward, in the name of Jesus.

20. Anointing to excel, incubate my life now, in the name of Jesus.

21. Anything planted in my life to pull me down, die, in the name of Jesus.

22. Creative power of God, here I am, locate me, in the name of Jesus.

23. O God, arise and connect me to Your creative power, in the name of Jesus.

24. Creative power of God, arise and manifest in my life, in the name of Jesus.

25. My destroyed virtues, receive the creative power of God, in the name of Jesus.

26. Hardened enemies of my destiny, hear the word of the Lord,: Scatter, in the name of Jesus.

27. Every power assigned to make me cry, you are a liar, die, in the name of Jesus.

28. Every power assigned to lock me up, receive angelic slap, in the name of Jesus.

29. Uncommon breakthroughs, uncommon favour and uncommon success, locate me by fire, in the name of Jesus.

30. Oh God, arise and make a way for me where there is no way, in the name of Jesus.

31. Holy Ghost bulldozer, clear my obstacles by fire, in the name of Jesus.

32. God of Elijah, arise and kill my obstacles by fire, in the name of Jesus.

33. Any power declaring that I will not make it, you are a liar, in the name of Jesus.

34. Any power circulating my name to native doctors, die, in the name of Jesus.

35. Any power assigned to disgrace me, die, in the name of Jesus.

36. My Father, catapult me to the next level of my breakthroughs, in the name of Jesus.

37. Bad feet that have walked into my life, clear away, in the name of Jesus.

38. My life, hear the word of God: Tragedy shall not locate you, in the name of Jesus.

39. Every hidden enemy assigned against me, die, in the name of Jesus

40. Every evil eye monitoring me for evil, be destroyed by fire, in the name of Jesus.

CHAPTER SEVEN

FIRE PRAYERS

FIRE
PRAYERS

The devil detests fire. In fact, fire threatens dark agents. The more you take fire prayers, the more you experience and enjoy spiritual immunity. Fire prayers vomited by the Holy Ghost to set your life on fire. Fire begets victory. It gives birth to testimonies and makes you untouchable. It makes you a threat to the kingdom of darkness. Fire prayers will keep you safe when people around you are being attacked. They will make you to be victorious when those who are around you are defeated. You need to challenge the foundation of your life with the fire of the Holy Ghost. This prayer programme is a revival programme. It will take you to the mountain of victory. Every lukewarmness and laziness would jump out of your life. Your vision shall be clear. Your strength shall be unique, Your victory shall be unchallengeable. This is a programme you need to remain at the mountain top of victory. It is a spiritual programme that would catapult you to greatness and change your destiny.

Use this prayer programme when:

1. You need a revival.
2. You need divine visitation.
3. You need spiritual alertness.
4. You need your prayer life to be set on fire.
5. You need your spirit to be alert.
6. You need spiritual gifts.
7. You want to send evil strangers packing.
8. You want God to take your roots deeper.
9. You want to become a spiritual firebrand.
10. You want to make your election sure.
11. You want to experience complete deliverance.
12. You need fresh fire and anointing.
13. You want to experience God's glory.
14. You want to possess your possessions.
15. You want to experience victory over petty sins.
16. You need spiritual purging.
17. You want to wake up from slumber.
18. You want to receive the mantle of fire.
19. You want to arise and shine.
20. You want to wear the overcomer's crown.

Beloved, do not joke with this prayer programme. When you observe it, it will give you far reaching consequences.

PRAYER SECTION

Confession: Habbakkuk 3:2; John 12:24; 2 Cor. 6; 1 Cor. 9:16; Deut. 28:13; Rom. 8:35-39.

Aggressive Praise and Worship

1. Lord, forgive my sins of spiritual carelessness, in the name of Jesus.
2. Lord, I confess my sins of grieving and wounding the Holy Spirit. Have mercy on me, in the name of Jesus.

3. Father, forgive me the sin of lukewarmness in spiritual activities, in the name of Jesus.
4. Father, give me a thirst and hunger for Your presence, in the name of Jesus.
5. Father, let my soul have satisfaction only in You and not in anything else, in the name of Jesus.
6. I rebuke every spirit of prayerlessness in my life, in the name of Jesus.
7. Every satanic altar ministering against my spiritual life, catch fire, in the name of Jesus.
8. Every tiredness and lukewarmness fashioned against my prayer altar, die, in the name of Jesus.
9. You spirits of laziness in prayer, get out of my life, in the name of Jesus.
10. Every satanic deposit blocking my communication line with heaven, melt away by the fire of Holy Ghost, in the name of Jesus.
11. Every addiction to physical things that are causing lukewarmness to prayer, die, in the name of Jesus.
12. Father, help me to always have meaningful time in Your presence, in the name of Jesus.
13. Every embargo, placed on my spiritual life, be lifted away by fire, in the name of Jesus.
14. I release myself from the bondage of food and sleep, in the name of Jesus.
15. My spiritual life will not collapse, in the name of Jesus.
16. Lord, give me thirst and hunger for prayer, in the name of Jesus.
17. I rededicate my life to God the Father, God the Son and God the Holy Spirit, in the name of Jesus.
18. Every spirit of impatience in the presence of God, die, in the name of Jesus.
19. Father, always give me alertness in my spirit when I'm in Your presence, in the name of Jesus.
20. Every spirit of prayer-procrastination, I bind you, in the name of Jesus.

21. Every demonic fire extinguisher assigned against my prayer altar, be arrested, in the name of Jesus.
22. Every demon assigned to see to the pulling down of my prayer life, fall down and die, in the name of Jesus.
23. Every hook and hold of prayerlessness in my life, catch fire, in the name of Jesus.
24. Father, increase Your fire on my prayer altar, in the name of Jesus.
25. Father, light my candle and enlighten my spiritual darkness, in the name of Jesus.
26. Father, make me a prayer addict, in the name of Jesus.
27. Father, make me Your orator, in the name of Jesus.
28. Father, give me hearing ears like Samuel, in the name of Jesus.
29. Father, give me seeing eyes like Elisha, in the name of Jesus.
30. Father, always make me have quick answers to my prayers, in the name of Jesus.
31. Father, make me holy to be like You, in the name of Jesus.
32. Father, help me to be an intercessor, in the name of Jesus.
33. Every wandering spirit in prayer, I bind you out of my life, in the name of Jesus.
34. Father, let the Holy Spirit fill me afresh.
35. Father, let every unbroken area in my life be broken, in the name of Jesus.
36. Father, incubate me with the fire of the Holy Spirit, in Jesus' name.
37. Let every anti-power bondage in my life break, in Jesus' name.
38. Let all strangers flee from my spirit and let the Holy Spirit take control, in the name of Jesus.
39. Lord, catapult my spiritual life to the mountain top.
40. Father, let heavens open and let the glory of God fall upon me, in the name of Jesus.
41. Father, let signs and wonders be my lot, in the name of Jesus.
42. I decree the joy of the oppressors upon my life to be turned

into sorrow, in the name of Jesus.

43. Let all multiple strongmen operating against me be paralysed, in the name of Jesus.

44. Lord, open my eyes and ears to receive wondrous things from You.

45. Lord, grant me victory over temptations and satanic devices. in the name of Jesus.

46. Lord, ignite my spiritual life so that I will stop fishing in unprofitable waters.

47. Lord, release Your tongue of fire upon my life and burn away all spiritual filthiness present within me.

48. Father, make me to hunger and thirst for righteousness, in the name of Jesus.

49. Lord, help me to be ready to do your work without expecting any recognition from others.

50. Lord, give me victory over emphasising the weaknesses and sins of other people while ignoring my own, in the name of Jesus.

51. O Lord, give me depth and root in my faith, in Jesus' name.

52. O Lord, heal every area of backsliding in my spiritual life, in Jesus' name.

53. Lord, help me to be willing to serve others rather than wanting to exercise authority, in Jesus' name.

54. Lord, open my understanding concerning the Scriptures, in the name of Jesus.

55. Lord, help me to live each day recognising that the day will come when You will judge secret lives and innermost thoughts, in the name of Jesus.

56. Lord, let me be willing to be the clay in Your hands, ready to be molded as You desire.

57. Lord, wake me up from any form of spiritual sleep and help me to put on the armour of light.

58. Lord, give me victory over all carnality and help me to be at the centre of Your will, in the name of Jesus.

59. I stand against anything in my life that will cause others to stumble, in the name of Jesus.

60. Lord, help me to put away childish things and put on maturity.

61. Lord, empower me to stand firm against all the schemes and techniques of the devil.

62. Lord, give me a big appetite for the pure milk and solid food in the word.

63. Lord, empower me to stay away from anything or anybody that may take Your place in my heart, in the name of Jesus.

64. I declare that I am called of God; no evil power shall cut me down, in the name of Jesus.

65. O Lord, give me power to be faithful to my calling, in the name of Jesus.

66. I receive the anointing to remain steady, committed and consistent in my ministerial life, in the name of Jesus.

67. I shall not deviate into politics, church rivalry or rebellion, in the name of Jesus.

68. O Lord, give me the wisdom to respect my teachers and seniors who have trained me, in the name of Jesus.

69. O Lord, give me the heart of a servant so that I can experience Your blessings everyday, in the name of Jesus.

70. I receive power to rise up with wings as eagles, in the name of Jesus.

71. The enemy will not waste my calling, in the name of Jesus.

72. The devil will not swallow my ministerial destiny, in the name of Jesus.

73. Power for effective development in my calling; come upon me now. in the name of Jesus.

74. I declare war against spiritual ignorance, in the name of Jesus.

75. I bind and cast out every unteachable spirit, in the name of Jesus.

76. I receive the anointing for success in ministry, in the name of Jesus.

77. I shall not be an enemy of integrity, in the name of Jesus.

78. I shall not steal God's money, in the name of Jesus.

79. I shall not disgrace the call of God upon my life, in the name of Jesus.
80. I shall work in holiness everyday, in the name of Jesus.
81. I bind the spirit of sexual immorality, in the name of Jesus.
82. I receive the culture of loyalty in my ministry, in the name of Jesus.
83. I shall not become an old king that is resistant to advice, in the name of Jesus.
84. I shall not live a wasteful and extravagant life, in the name of Jesus.
85. I shall not serve my wonderful Saviour for filthy financial gain, in the name of Jesus.
86. I bind every spirit of quarrel and opposition from my wife/husband, in the name of Jesus.
87. My wife/husband shall not scatter my church members, in the name of Jesus.
88. Every Judas in my ministry, fall into your own trap, in the name of Jesus.
89. My ministry will not destroy my marriage, in the name of Jesus.
90. My marriage will not destroy my ministry, in the name of Jesus.
91. My children will not be misfired arrows in my ministry, in the name of Jesus.
92. I claim progress and excellence for my ministry, in the name of Jesus.
93. My church shall experience prosperity, in the name of Jesus.
94. O Lord, let my ministry reach the unreached, in the name of Jesus.
95. Multitude will go to heaven because of my ministry, in the name of Jesus.
96. I kill every attack on my ministry; I shall prevail, in the name of Jesus.
97. I shall not bite the fingers that fed me, in the name of Jesus.
98. I shall not engage in rebellion, in the name of Jesus.

99. Every power of my father's house working against my calling, die, in the name of Jesus.

100. Anointing for excellence, fall upon me, in the name of Jesus.

101. Lord, break me and re-mould me, in the name of Jesus.

102. I will not surrender to the enemy, in the name of Jesus.

103. I shall not die before my time, in the name of Jesus.

104. I shall not capture the prosperity of Naaman, in the name of Jesus.

105. Let God arise and let every enemy of my calling scatter, in the name of Jesus.

106. I receive fresh fire and fresh anointing, in the name of Jesus.

107. I shall not be a misfired arrow in the hands of my Maker, in the name of Jesus.

108. Any foundational power working against my calling, be destroyed, in the name of Jesus.

109. Every yoke working against my spiritual growth, be broken, in the name of Jesus.

110. The enemy will not make me a bad example, in Jesus' name.

111. Every destructive habit designed to waste my calling, die, in the name of Jesus.

112. Every area of incomplete deliverance in my life, receive complete deliverance by fire, in the name of Jesus.

113. Every spiritual cataract, clear away from my vision, in the name of Jesus.

114. Every spirit of slumber, I bury you today, in Jesus' name.

115. The eagle of my calling shall mount up by the power in the blood of Jesus.

116. Every anti-ministry arrow fired into my life, backfire, in the name of Jesus.

117. Holy Ghost fire, destroy all works of darkness in my life, in the name of Jesus.

118. Every door opened to the enemy of my calling, be closed, in the name of Jesus.

119. Let the waters of life flow into every dead area of my spiritual life, in the name of Jesus.

120. Every weapon fashioned against my high calling, be destroyed, in the name of Jesus.
121. Any foundational serpent and scorpion programmed into my life to destroy my calling in future, die, in Jesus' name
122. O God of Elijah, arise and give unto me my mantle of fire, in the name of Jesus.
123. Anything planted within me that has not manifested now but will manifest in future to make me backslide, dry up, in the name of Jesus.
124. Every witchcraft power drinking the blood of my spiritual life, die, in the name of Jesus.
125. Glory of God, overshadow me, in the name of Jesus.
126. Strength of God, empower me, in Jesus' name.
127. Every internal bondage magnetising external bondage, be broken, in the name of Jesus.
128. O glory of my calling, arise and shine, in Jesus' name.
129. I will not mortgage my calling on the lap of Delilah and Jezebel, in the name of Jesus.
130. I refuse to retire, I must refire, in Jesus' name.
131. I receive power to meet the needs of this present generation, in the name of Jesus.
132. All the rough places in my life targeted at my spiritual breakthroughs, be smoothened by the blood of Jesus.
133. Let Your glory, O Lord, overshadow my destiny, in the name of Jesus.
134. I refuse to tarry in the valley of powerlessness, in the name of Jesus.
135. I rise above my roots by the power in the blood of Jesus.
136. I receive the anointing to remain steady, committed and consistent in my ministerial life, in Jesus' name.
137. Power for effective development in my calling; come upon me now, in the name of Jesus.
138. I declare war against spiritual ignorance, in Jesus' name
139. I bind and cast out every unteachable spirit, in the name of Jesus.

140. I receive the anointing for success in ministry, in the name of Jesus.

141. I bind the spirit of sexual immorality, in Jesus' name.

142. I shall not become an old king that is resistant to advice, in the name of Jesus.

143. Let God arise and let every enemy of my calling scatter, in the name of Jesus.

144. My Father, whether I wake or sleep, let Your presence go with me, in the name of Jesus.

145. Oh Lord, deliver me from the natural darkness of my mind, in the name of Jesus.

146. Oh Lord, deliver me from the daily snares that are assigned against me, in the name of Jesus.

147. I declare that I shall not grieve or resist the Holy Spirit, in the name of Jesus.

148. My Father, help me to listen to Your voice everyday, in the name of Jesus.

149. Oh Lord, let me stand for discipline, in the name of Jesus.

150. Oh God, come as power and expel every rebellious lot from my heart, in Jesus' name.

151. Oh God, come as a teacher, and fill me with all understanding, in Jesus' name.

152. Oh God, come as light and illuminate the Scriptures unto me, in Jesus' name.

153. Oh God, let me see my sins as the nails that bind You to the cross, in Jesus' name.

154. Oh Lord, let me see my sins as the swords that pierced Your side, in Jesus' name.

155. Oh God, give me a deeper knowledge of Thyself, in Jesus' name.

156. Oh God, give me deeper power in private prayers, in Jesus' name.

157. Oh God, dig deep unto me and fill me to overflowing with living waters, in the name of Jesus.

158. My Father, purge me from every false desire and unprofitable aspiration, in the name of Jesus.

159. Oh God, arise, kill my envy and command my tongue, in the name of Jesus.
160. Oh God, arise and deliver me from attachments to unclean things, in the name of Jesus.
161. My Father, open to me the spring of divine knowledge, in the name of Jesus.
162. Oh God, while I live, let my life be exemplary, in the name of Jesus.
163. My Father, let me never slumber nor sleep the sleep of spiritual death, in the name of Jesus.
164. Oh God, take me, sanctify me and use every faculty that I have, in the name of Jesus.
165. My Father, focus my mind on You and turn my trials to blessings, in the name of Jesus.
166. Oh God, give me deadness to the world, in the name of Jesus.
167. My Father, let every part of my character and conduct make serious divine impression on others, in the name of Jesus.
168. Every power assigned to injure the prosperity of my soul, die, in the name of Jesus.
169. Every spirit of slumber, I bury you today, in Jesus' name.
170. Every spiritual cataract, clear away from my vision, in the name of Jesus.
171. Every witchcraft power drinking the blood of my spiritual life, die, in the name of Jesus.
172. Strength of God, empower me, in Jesus' name.
173. I refuse to tarry in the valley of powerlessness, in the name of Jesus.
174. Anything planted within me that has not manifested now but will manifest in future to make me backslide, dry up, in the name of Jesus.
175. I shall not be a misfired arrow in the hands of my Maker, in the name of Jesus.
176. Any foundational power working against my calling, be destroyed, in the name of Jesus.
177. Every yoke working against spiritual growth in my life, be

broken, in the name of Jesus.

178. The enemy will not make me a bad example, in Jesus' name.

179. Every destructive habit designed to waste my calling, die, in the name of Jesus.

180. Every area of incomplete deliverance in my life, receive complete deliverance by fire, in the name of Jesus.

181. Every spiritual cataract, clear away from my vision, in the name of Jesus.

182. Every spirit of slumber, I bury you today, in Jesus' name.

183. The eagle of my calling shall mount up by the power in the blood of Jesus, in the name of Jesus.

184. Every anti-ministry arrow fired into my life, backfire, in the name of Jesus.

185. Holy Ghost fire, destroy all works of darkness in my life, in the name of Jesus.

186. Every door opened to the enemy of my calling, be closed, in the name of Jesus.

187. Let the waters of life flow into every dead area of my spiritual life, in the name of Jesus.

188. Every weapon fashioned against my high calling, be destroyed, in the name of Jesus.

189. Any foundational serpent and scorpion programmed into my life to destroy my calling in future, die, in Jesus' name

190. O God of Elijah, arise and give unto me my mantle of fire, in the name of Jesus.

191. Anything planted within me that has not manifested now but will manifest in future to make me backslide, dry up, in the name of Jesus.

192. Every witchcraft power drinking the blood of my spiritual life, die, in the name of Jesus.

193. Glory of God, overshadow me, in the name of Jesus.

194. Strength of God, empower me, in Jesus' name.

195. Every internal bondage magnetising external bondage, be broken, in the name of Jesus.

196. O glory of my calling, arise and shine, in Jesus' name.

197. I will not mortgage my calling on the lap of Delilah and

Jezebel, in the name of Jesus.

198.I refuse to retire, I must refire, in Jesus' name.

199.I receive power to meet the needs of this present generation, in the name of Jesus.

200.All the rough places in my life targeted at my spiritual breakthroughs, be smoothened by the blood of Jesus.

201.Let Your glory, O Lord, overshadow my destiny, in the name of Jesus.

202.I refuse to tarry in the valley of powerlessness, in the name of Jesus.

203.I rise above my roots by the power in the blood of Jesus.

204.I receive the anointing to remain steady, committed and consistent in my ministerial life, in Jesus' name.

205.Power for effective development in my calling; come upon me now, in the name of Jesus.

206.I declare war against spiritual ignorance, in Jesus' name.

207.I bind and cast out every unteachable spirit, in the name of Jesus.

208.I receive the anointing for success in ministry, in the name of Jesus.

209.I bind the spirit of sexual immorality, in Jesus' name.

210.I shall not become an old king that is resistant to advice, in the name of Jesus.

211.Let God arise and let every enemy of my calling scatter, in the name of Jesus.

CHAPTER EIGHT

HOLY PURGING

HOLY
PURGING
8

One of the greatest problems today is that of spiritual contamination. Unknown to many, they have gathered dust and contamination in the course of their journey on earth. To be wholesome, you must submit yourself for holy purging. When the Holy Spirit is at work in your life, satanic deposits would be located and whatever is not of God will be expelled from your system. Holy purging will get to your evil spiritual deposits and cleanse them. It will relieve you of all manner of inherited bondage. When the fire of God enters your system, witchcraft food or drink will be flushed out. This prayer programme will enable you to get rid of the effect of food positioning. Many have consumed meals prepared by dark powers in the dream. Night caterers have fed multitudes in the dreams while they slept. These meals must be vomited by fire. You need a form of spiritual cleansing if you must attain the height that God has destined for you.

You need this prayer points when:

1. You want to get rid of satanic food that you have consumed knowingly and unknowingly.
2. You want to get rid of poison deposits in your blood system.
3. You need to nullify the effects of the food you have mistakenly eaten from the table of the devil.
4. You want to sack demonic caterers.
5. You need powers to sack satanic caterers.
6. You want to put an end to the pollution of anointing of God upon your life.
7. You want to nullify the effect of ancestral pollution.
8. You want to release yourself from satanic ancestral umbrellas.
9. You want to become too hot for the enemy to handle.

These prayer points will take you to the realm of victory and separate you from the powers of your father's house. When you are purged, you will experience the unadulterated glory of God in your life.

PRAYER SECTION

CONFESSIONS: Galatians 3:13-14 : *Christ hath redeemed us from the curse of the law, being made a curse for us: for it is written, Cursed is every one that hangeth on a tree: That the blessing of Abraham might come on the Gentiles through Jesus Christ; that we might receive the promise of the Spirit through faith.* **2 Timothy 4:18:** *And the Lord shall deliver me from every evil work, and will preserve me unto his heavenly kingdom: to whom be glory for ever and ever. Amen.* **Colossians 1:13:** *Who hath delivered us from the power of darkness, and hath translated us into the kingdom of his dear Son:* **Colossians 2:15:** *And having spoiled principalities and powers, he made a shew of them openly, triumphing over them in it.*

Praise worship

 PRAYER POINTS

1. Thank God for HIS mighty power to save to the uttermost and to deliver from any form of bondage., in the name of Jesus.
2. Confess your sins and those of your ancestors, especially those sins linked to evil powers and idolatry.
3. I cover myself with the blood of Jesus.
4. I release myself from any inherited bondage and limitations, in the name of Jesus.
5. O Lord, send Your axe of fire to the foundation of my life and destroy every evil plantation, in the name of Jesus.
6. Holy Ghost fire, neutralise every projected food in my dream that is working against my life, in the name of Jesus.
7. Every witchcraft food or drink I have taken in the dreams, I neutralise and flush it out by the blood of Jesus, in Jesus' name.
8. I paralyse all the night caterers and I forbid their food in my dream, in the name of Jesus.
9. Let all avenues of eating or drinking spiritual poisons in the dream be closed, in the name of Jesus.
10. I drink the blood of Jesus to neutralise every satanic food or drink taken in the dream, in the name of Jesus.
11. Every witchcraft food in the dream, die, in the name of Jesus.
12. Father Lord, let there be a disassociation between my body and the evil food I have eaten, in the name of Jesus.
13. Father Lord, in the name of Jesus, I vomit every evil food I have eaten, in the name of Jesus.
14. Let the blood of Jesus flush out every poison deposited in my blood system as a result of any evil food, in Jesus' name.
15. All that I have lost as a result of eating evil food, Father Lord, let me have them back, in the name of Jesus.
16. I cough out and vomit any food eaten from the table of the

devil, in the name of Jesus. *(Cough them out and vomit them in faith. Prime the expulsion.)*

17. You my mouth, I fortify you with the blood of Jesus to reject any satanic food, in the name of Jesus.

18. Blood of Jesus, purge me of every satanic food I have eaten in the marine kingdom, in the name of Jesus.

19. Every demonic caterer in the dream, receive the fire of God and die, in the name of Jesus.

20. You demonic caterer in the dream, eat your evil food, in the name of Jesus.

21. Every satanic agent serving me evil foods in my dreams, fall down and die, in the name of Jesus.

22. Every satanic hand assigned to be serving me evil foods in my dreams, be cut of by the fire of God, in the name of Jesus.

23. Blood of Jesus, purge my system of demonic foods eaten in the dreams, in the name of Jesus.

24. Every evil contamination introduced into my life through foods in the dream, be dissolved by the blood of Jesus.

25. I receive divine power to always reject demonic 65. L e t the blood of Jesus frustrate every activity of familiar spirits in my dreams, in the name of Jesus.

27. Every satanic agent on evil assignment to poison my life through foods in the dream, fall down and die, in the name of Jesus.

28. Every evil power siting on the seat of my life, be uprooted by fire, in the name of Jesus.

29. Every satanic agent planning to harm my life, destroy your senders and yourself, in the name of Jesus.

30. Every satanic plan to pollute the anointing of God upon my life through demonic foods, be frustrated, in the name of Jesus.

31. Every legal ground for satan to be feeding my life with demonic foods, blood of Jesus, destroy them, in the name of Jesus.

32. I vomit every food with idolatrous influence that I have

eaten, in the name of Jesus.

33. Let the blood of Jesus flush out from my system every inherited satanic deposit, in the name of Jesus.

34. I release myself from the grip of any problem transferred into my life from the womb, in the name of Jesus.

35. Let the blood of Jesus and the fire of the Holy Ghost cleanse every organ in my body, in the name of Jesus.

36. I break and loose myself from every inherited evil covenant, in the name of Jesus.

37. I break and loose myself from every inherited evil curse, in the name of Jesus.

38. I vomit every evil consumption that I have been feed with as a child, in the name of Jesus.

39. I command all foundational strongmen attached to my life to be paralysed, in the name of Jesus.

40. Let any rod of the wicked rising up against my family line be rendered impotence for my sake, in the name of Jesus.

41. I cancel the consequences of any evil local name attached to my person, in the name of Jesus.

42. *Pray aggressively against the following evil foundations.* You *(pick the under listed one by one),* loose your hold over my life and be purged out of my foundation in the name of Jesus.
- Destructive effect of polygamy   - Evil physical design
- Unscriptural manners of conception   - Parental Curses
- Envious rivalry- Demonic blood transfusion
- Evil dedication- Demonic alteration of destiny   - Demonic incisions   - Demonic marriage
- Dream pollution   - Evil laying on of hands
- Demonic sacrifice   - Fellowship with family idols - Fellowship with local idols -   Fellowship with demonic consultants

- Wrong exposure to sex   - Exposure to evil diviner
- Demonic initiations   -   Inherited infirmity

43. You evil foundational plantations, come out of my life with all your roots, in the name of Jesus.

44. I break and loose myself from every form of demonic bewitchment, in the name of Jesus.

45. I release myself from every evil domination and control, in the name of Jesus.

46. Let the blood of Jesus be transfused into my blood vessel, in Jesus' name.

47. Let every gate opened to the enemy by my foundation be closed forever with the blood of Jesus, in Jesus' name.

48. Lord Jesus, walk back into every second of my life and deliver me where I need deliverance, heal me where I need healing, transform me where I need transformation, in Jesus' name.

49. Let the power in the blood of Jesus separate me from the sins of my ancestors, in Jesus' name.

50. Let the blood of Jesus remove any unprogressive label from every aspect of my life, in Jesus' name.

51. O Lord, create in me a clean heart by Your power, in Jesus' name.

52. O Lord, renew a right spirit within me, in Jesus' name.

53. O Lord, teach me to die to self, in Jesus' name.

54. O Lord, ignite my calling with Your fire, in Jesus' name.

55. O Lord, anoint me to pray without ceasing, in Jesus' name.

56. O Lord, establish me as a holy person unto You, in Jesus' name.

57. O Lord, restore my spiritual eyes and ears, in the name of Jesus.

58. O Lord, let the anointing to excel in my spiritual and physical life fall on me, in Jesus' name.

59. O Lord, produce in me the power of self-control and gentleness, in Jesus' name.

60. O Lord, let the anointing of the Holy Spirit break every yoke of backwardness in my life, in Jesus' name.

61. Holy Ghost, breathe on me now, in the name of Jesus.

62. Holy Ghost fire, ignite me to the glory of God, in Jesus' name.

63. Let every rebellion flee from my heart, in the name of Jesus.

64. I command every spiritual contamination in my life to receive cleansing by the blood of Jesus, in Jesus' name.

65. Let the brush of the Lord scrub out every dirtiness in my spiritual pipe, , in Jesus' name.

66. Every rusted spiritual pipe in my life, receive wholeness, in the name of Jesus.

67. I command every power eating up my spiritual pipe to be roasted, in the name of Jesus.

68. I renounce any evil dedication placed upon my life, in the name of Jesus.

69. I break every evil edict and ordination, in the name of Jesus.

70. O Lord, cleanse all the soiled part of my life, in Jesus' name.

71. O Lord, deliver me from every foundational Pharaoh, in the name of Jesus.

72. O Lord, heal every wounded part of my life, in Jesus' name.

73. O Lord, bend every evil rigidity in my life, in Jesus' name.

74. O Lord, re-align every satanic straying in my life, in Jesus' name.

75. O Lord, let the fire of the Holy Spirit warm every satanic freezing in my life, in the nema of Jesus.

76. O Lord, give me life that kills seath, in Jesus' name.

77. O Lord, kindle in me the fire of charity, in the name of Jesus.

78. O Lord, glue me together where I am opposed to myself, in the name of Jesus.

79. O Lord, enrich me with Your gifts, in the name of Jesus.

80. O Lord, quicken me and increase my desire of things of heaven, in Jesus' name.

81. By You rulership, O Lord, let the lust of the flesh in my life die, in the name of Jesus.

82. Lord Jesus, increase daily in my life, in the name of Jesus.

Printed in Poland
by Amazon Fulfillment
Poland Sp. z o.o., Wrocław

74002510R00278